What others are saying about this book:

"If you want wealth and wisdom, buy this book."
–Jeffrey Fox, best-selling author of
How To Make Big Money in Your Own Small Business

"Every business owner or executive can profit from this book's exceptional insights into how to create business and financial leaps forward. For inspiration, for reinforcement, or just for a healthy dose of business wisdom, I highly recommend it."
–Tony Alessandra, Ph.D., author of *The Platinum Rule* and *Charisma*

"*Create the Business Breakthrough You Want: Secrets and Strategies from The World's Greatest Mentors* is filled with excellent, practical, vital advice that's sure to help you achieve success."
–Ric Edelman, best-selling author of
Discover the Wealth Within You

"This book offers a great collection of insight and advice that could be of help to most business executives and business owners."
–Bob Nelson, Ph.D., president of Nelson Motivation Inc.;
best-selling author of *1001 Ways to Reward Employees,*
1001 Ways to Energize Employees, and *Managing for Dummies*

"The most powerful advice in life – and business – is often deceptively simple. This book contains nugget after nugget of wisdom for any leader, in any organization. Keep it handy."
–Patrick Lencioni, author *The Five Dysfunctions of a Team,*
president, The Table Group

"Buy this book! You will get wisdom and encouragement! You will learn to be an effective, serving leader who gets more out of work and life, encourages and empowers employees, while achieving strategic success."
–Ken Jennings, Ph.D., co-author of *The Serving Leader* and Dean of the
School for Executive Leadership at Bethel

"This book is filled with concentrated, practical advice from some of the brilliant successes of our time. Learn from them. You too can succeed, if you apply these principles."
–Marc Allen, co-founder of the New World Library,
author of *Visionary Business* and *The Millionaire Course:*
A Visionary Plan for Creating the Life of Your Dreams

Create the
Business
Breakthrough
You Want

Secrets and Strategies from
the World's Greatest Mentors

The World's Greatest Mentors™ Series

Create the
Business
Breakthrough
You Want

Secrets and Strategies from
the World's Greatest Mentors

Compiled by John Robert Eggen

Las Vegas, Nevada and Palo Alto, California

Disclaimer

This book is sold with the understanding that the authors and publisher are not engaged in rendering legal, accounting, or other professional services and advice. Every effort has been made to make this book as complete and as accurate as possible. However, there may be mistakes, both typographical and in content. Therefore, this book should be used only as a general guide and not as the ultimate source of the information contained herein. Furthermore, this book includes contact information for the authors which has been furnished by them for the book. To the best of the publisher's knowledge, the contact information is accurate as of the printing date of this book. The authors and publisher shall not be liable or responsible to any person or entity with respect to any loss or damage caused, or alleged to have been caused, directly or indirectly, by the information contained in this book.

The World's Greatest Mentors™, The World's Greatest Mentors ™ Seal, and Mission Publishing™ are trademarks of Mission Publishing, a division of The Mission Marketing Mentors, Inc.

04 05 06 07 HH 10 9 8 7 6 5 3 2 1
Printed in the United States of America
ISBN: 0-9749618-0-9
LCCN: 2004101375

Requests for permission to make copies of any part of this work can be made to:

Mission Publishing
101 Convention Center Drive, Suite 700
Las Vegas, NV 89109
1.702.385.5738
publisher@missionpublishing.net
www.missionpublishing.net

For bulk purchases or corporate premium sales, call the office at 1.650.321.1306 or email sales@missionpublishing.net

"Every few hundred years in Western history there occurs a sharp transformation. Within a few short decades, society—its worldview, its basic values, its social and political structures, its arts, its key institutions—rearranges itself. And the people born then cannot even imagine a world in which their grandparents lived and into which their own parents were born. We are currently living through such a transformation."

—Peter Drucker, Post-Capitalist Society

Contents

Section Two – Leadership Development

Section Three – Marketing and Sales

Contents

Section Four – Personal Growth

Section Five – Wealth Building

Introduction

by John Robert Eggen, Publisher

I f you are like most business owners, corporate executives, and professionals, you are facing challenges today that are significantly different than those encountered even a decade ago. Why?

A dramatic paradigm shift of historic proportions is occurring today, and it is influencing the fate of every business on Earth. Characterized by an explosive rate of change, this transformation is the result of huge trends converging.

For instance, in information technology, the power of computer chips doubles about every 18 months, giving us ever-more powerful tools with which to create. In communication technology, computers, telephones, televisions, and satellites are merging into a global communication network, allowing billions of us to communicate with one another. Instantaneous communication worldwide increases the cross-fertilization of ideas, spawning innovations that radically alter how we live and work. These new ideas and practices are disrupting our traditional ways of living and doing business. Emerging, new opportunities look different and have no national boundaries.

As a result, the new millennium economy is a far cry from anything in the past. Intangible assets, such as strategies, systems, relationships, and brands, have become the currency of the realm, supplanting and devaluing the customary role that physical resources and human labor have played in the production of goods and services.

Today's trends demand that companies large and small create value in new ways. If they do not, they will surely perish.

Considering the new reality, it's no surprise that business owners and corporate executives like you are experiencing bewildering new problems. Tried-and-true solutions often no longer work. Fortunately, wise leaders exist who can help you discover appropriate solutions to the 21st century's new wave of dilemmas.

The Mentor's Special Role

At crucial times in history, individuals have always emerged as pathfinders and wayshowers. Mentors always have played a special role. More than just professionals or experts in their field, mentors are a distinctive breed of wise and trusted advisors or teachers. Study the lives of leaders in any field throughout history and you will find that most of them spent some of their formative years as students of one or more mentors.

Today's best business mentors can provide you with shortcuts to business and financial success because they impart transformational ideas as well as time-tested strategies and systems.

Nothing is as powerful as an idea whose time has come, as 19th century thinker Victor Hugo first asserted. In fact, some ideas are so powerful that they are closely guarded secrets only a few know. Look closely, and you can find such secrets in these pages.

Strategies and systems are extremely valuable intangible assets. For instance, a few years ago I had the opportunity to help Mark Victor Hansen and Robert G. Allen develop sections of their # 1 *New York Times* best-selling book, *The One Minute Millionaire*. During our work on the book, Bob shared with me findings from the internationally famous quality guru, Dr. W. Edwards Deming. Deming's research found that 94% of all failures occur when a person is not following a tested system. You will find valuable strategies and systems in these chapters, too.

We published this book to provide you with a compilation of secrets, strategies, and systems from some of the world's greatest business mentors in a single resource that is easy to use and benefit from.

Learn From the Best

The authors in this book all are part of Mission Publishing's The World's Greatest Mentors™ Publishing Program, a highly selective, mission-driven effort that publishes authorities whose expertise can transform their professions, their industries, and the world. This book is the first in a series of books and other information products intended to make a positive difference in the lives and businesses of leaders like you.

 Some of the mentors in these pages are world-renowned, including Brian Tracy, Mark Victor Hansen, Robert G. Allen, and Bob Proctor.

But an emphasis of the book is to feature secrets and strategies from a number of "rising stars," mentors who have been virtually unknown to those outside of their own specialized niches before now. Why? We all know of the elite cadre of internationally recognized business authorities. But too often we miss the wider circle of wise experts whose insights and strategies are significantly transforming people's personal and professional lives, and who are making a positive impact in their communities. The knowledge many of these lesser-known mentors possess is extraordinary. They are genuine experts from all corners of the globe who are helping business owners, professionals, and corporate executives achieve significant goals.

The biggest benefit of a compilation book such as this is that when a series of outstanding business mentors' ideas are presented together, you can dissect, compare, and contrast them. This process can lead to a new synthesis—a genuine breakthrough.

How To Use This Book

To help you create the business breakthrough you want, here are suggestions on how to use this book:

This book contains five sections: Business Strategy, Leadership Development, Marketing and Sales, Personal Growth, and Wealth Building. A celebrity business mentor opens each section of the book. This guru's viewpoint sets the stage for the remaining chapters in that section, all of which are presented alphabetically according to the authors' last names.

In order to trigger the breakthrough you want, be spontaneous in your approach to reading the book. Instead of reading the chapters chronologically, you may want to "skip around" as you read. Let your intuition guide you. The beauty of a compilation is that each chapter stands on its own and needs not be read in any particular order.

Each mentor's chapter has been designed to speak volumes in just a small number of words. This makes it easy to come to the book often for the day-to-day advice you need to grow your business successfully. In addition, feel free to contact these mentors whenever you want more help. Take advantage of the contact information listed at the end of each chapter. Many of these wonderful mentors will provide a free, initial session in which you can get to know more about their work and how it can help you.

Combined, these featured mentors have helped millions of business owners, professionals, and corporate executives create the needed breakthroughs to succeed. Now it's your turn to benefit!

Section One –
Business Strategy

How You Can Create an Unbeatable Business Strategy

by Brian Tracy

When businesses offer a similar product or service, what makes one more successful than the other? Is it product quality? Customer service? Price? No; it's none of those things. More often than not, the one factor that leads to unbeatable business success is the company's business strategy. With a great strategy, a business thrives; without a great strategy, the business suffers.

A business strategy is a process of deciding what you want to accomplish at the end of the road, looking at all the different ways you might get there, picking the very best route to follow, and then making a plan to achieve what you want. Those business professionals who have a strategy know that they are ultimately responsible for every aspect of their work and life, and they persist to make sure their strategy comes to fruition.

Smart professionals also commit their strategy to writing. This is important, because when you write down your strategy, you accomplish ten times more than if you do not. Doubtful? Consider this: A recent *USA Today* report asked people if they set New Year's resolutions. A year later, they went back to those people who said "yes" and asked, "Did you write down your resolutions last year?" Those who had New Year's resolutions but did not write them down only had a 4% success rate. However, those who wrote down their resolutions had a 46% success rate. That's a difference of more than eleven times, and it's all because of committing a plan to writing.

To help you devise your own winning business strategy and use it successfully, consider the following strategy creation and implementation guidelines.

Key One – Use a proven approach

GOSPA is a model of business strategy that many political and business leaders use. It gives people a straightforward and step-by-step approach to strategy success. **GOSPA** stands for:

G – Goals: A goal is a measurable, describable end result. Many people make the mistake of stating goals such as money, success, health, family, etc. But these things are not really goals. They are general categories under which goals appear. A goal is specific, such as to earn $25,000 per month, to increase sales by 30%, or to live in a $500,000

21

home. So to create your strategy, first list the end results you want to achieve for your business and your life. And remember, write it down!

O – Objectives: Objectives are what you need to do to reach your goals. Imagine a ladder. At the top of the ladder is the goal. Your objectives are the rungs of the ladder that you must take, one at a time, to get to the goal. For example, if you want to sell a certain amount of product, you first have to work out the exact cost of the product, devise an advertising campaign, create promotional materials, etc. You have a series of objectives you must complete before you actually sell the product. Identify those steps for each of your goals.

S – Strategy: Your strategy is the different ways you can achieve the individual objectives. For the product sales example, you could hire an outside sales force, do it yourself, advertise on television and radio, mail brochures, etc. You must analyze the pros and cons of each strategy to ensure you pick the best one.

P – Plan: Your plan is like a recipe. You've identified the various ingredients you need to successfully reach your goal, and now you identify the best order to add them to your business mix.

A – Action: With all the elements identified, you must finally take action and work your plan. During WWII, Winston Churchill would manage his time with a sheet of paper. At the very top it said: "Action for this day." He knew the importance of planned actions to reach his goal. Business leaders must do the same to win the fight against the competition.

Key Two – Have a clear focus, but be flexible

Recently, Baptist College interviewed a tract of graduates in their entrepreneurial MBA program. They found that after graduation, 90% of them did nothing they were trained for even though they had to produce a complete business plan to graduate. The 10% that did succeed launched their business according to their business plan even though they had no guarantee for success. The other 90% were still waiting for everything to be just right–for the finances to be right, for the customers to be lined up, and for the economy to be perfect.

The successful 10% had stumbled upon the "corridor principle," which says that when you launch down a corridor towards your goal, you will eventually reach a roadblock. However, at that roadblock, a door will open to the right or left. You choose which way to go. Eventually that new road ends, but another starts. It's what philosopher and inventor Buckminster Fuller called the theory of precession, which means that as you move towards a goal, you get deflected in different directions. But weeks, months, or years later, you will arrive at the original goal. Granted, the path you took was totally different than what you initially planned; however, you never would have gotten there if you hadn't started.

Successful people are flexible and open to the various corridors. They launch with no guarantee of success while failures wait until every moment is right and exactly as they planned. Now, this is not to discount the value of planning, as planning is vital. But you must remember the military principle that says, "No strategy survives the first contact with the enemy." That means you can lay out a beautiful strategy on every single point, but when you actually hit the marketplace, you have to be flexible and adapt. Something will come up that you hadn't expected. But by having a very clear goal and thinking through your resources, manpower, money, etc., you can know what's possible, change your strategy, and be flexible when the time arises.

Key Three – Focus on your three key skills and delegate the rest

As you implement your strategy, think of a marathon runner. The best runner breaks from the pack and distances him or herself from the others. In our society, you break away when you pass the $100,000 mark of income. To get to that point, you must have special talents that enable you to achieve better results. Once you hit this point, however, if you're not careful, you will begin to scatter; you will diffuse your energy. You will focus on so many skills and tasks that you'll lose your momentum.

At this point you must identify the three skills that enabled you to be successful in the first place. Even if you do twenty activities per day, if you look closely, you'll find that three of those activities account for more than 90% of your income. To stay on track with your strategy, double the amount of time you spend on those three activities and delegate, outsource, or eliminate any of the others that you can. Research shows that those who hire an assistant and delegate the little things to that person double their productivity and attain their goals faster. So if you're currently doing all the prospecting, all the follow-up, all the paperwork, etc., but those tasks aren't your core three skills, delegate those activities. By spending your time on what you do best, your strategy will succeed.

Create Your Own Strategy of a Lifetime

Align your strategy with your life and business vision so you can tap into the power of cause and effect, which states that every action you take today has a direct impact on the outcome you experience tomorrow. Those who strategically pursue their goals and plan their success have the greatest chance of reaching the outcomes they desire.

Remember that when you're clear on what you want and put your heart and life toward that endeavor, you discover opportunities you never thought possible that lead you to your goal. While your strategy may change over time, your focus is clear and you have a sense of personal and professional satisfaction. As a result, you earn the respect and esteem of the business community, you earn more money than you ever dreamed, and you have a wonderful life.

About the Author

Brian Tracy is legendary in the areas of human potential, sales, management, and success. He addresses over 450,000 people each year, has produced over 300 audio and video learning programs, and has authored 22 books. His two newest books are *Victory* and *Create Your Own Future*. Brian has a background that includes sales, marketing, investment, real estate development, importation, distribution, and management. His audio program *The Psychology of Achievement* has been a best seller for over a decade. For more information, please visit www.briantracy.com.

Ten Strategies for Running Your Non-Profit Like a For-Profit Business

by Claire Haaga Altman

A corporation organized as a non-profit must operate at least as efficiently and effectively as a for-profit business in order to fulfill its mission. The fact that the organization is a public trust and its "profits" do not directly benefit its leaders does not mean that the organization shouldn't operate as a successful business. Therefore, it makes good business sense to manage your non-profit using the same strategies used by private businesses.

For most of the 20th century, the business world regarded non-profits as charities whose sole purpose was to do good works. The Boards of Directors usually consisted of well-meaning individuals who paid little attention to how the organization actually operated. The result was that sound operating principles were ignored because there was always too much to do, too much financial pressure, and too many needy clients. This management approach didn't work very well in the 20th century, and it is a prescription for failure in the 21st century.

Given the competition for resources and limited public funds, non-profit organizations must excel at corporate governance and operational efficiency if they are to survive. The following principles will help you establish a strong foundation on which to build a successful program and ensure your organization is operating efficiently and ethically.

1) **Define your mission and stick with it.** Your mission is your specialty; it is what you do best. Don't sacrifice your organization's purpose simply to chase money that government or various foundations make available. If you do, you will sap the energy and resources that you could better use to achieve your goals. If you stick with your mission, then you will stay focused on accomplishing those things your organization was created for. Concentrate your efforts on building and refining that expertise.

2) **Build a strong Board of Directors and use them.** The Board of Directors is your greatest ally. Many private sector business leaders are thrilled by the opportunity to "give back" by serving on a non-profit Board. Consult with them to discover their strengths, and then use them as a resource for information and problem solving.

Well-connected community members can also help you make contacts in the private and public sector. Report your progress to them regularly, and thank them for their efforts. Remember, their time is valuable.

3) **Develop strong internal financial management systems.** Hire a knowledgeable Chief Financial Officer to avoid financial headaches. Work with your CFO to establish clear fiscal processes and to develop a system of checks and balances so several people in your organization understand and can oversee the fiscal procedures. You and your CFO will have to agree on which regular reports to produce. At a minimum, you should initiate a monthly cash report by revenue source or project, an income statement, a receivables report, and a payables report. Receivables typically become a huge issue for non-profits, so generate invoices in a timely manner and follow up diligently with those who owe money.

4) **Know the numbers.** Make sure you base your budget on real projections, meaning those contracts or grants that are already approved. If you're providing services or selling retail products, project your revenues conservatively. Allocate extra money for unanticipated expenses, and remember that these can be greater than expected. Keep in mind that revenue sources might not materialize or public funding may be cut. Don't promise raises or benefits until you know you have the finances available.

After you have forecast your budget, review and revise it several times to make sure you have eliminated wishful thinking. When you present the budget to your Finance Committee, ask for their honest input and encourage them to ask tough questions. If the resources are not there to do what you and your Board want, you should delay that particular project or service until a later date. The biggest temptation for Executive Directors of non-profits is trying to rescue everyone in need by stretching the organization's limited resources too thin. If you and your Finance Committee are satisfied that your organization has or will obtain the resources needed to support the budget, then prepare to finalize it for presentation to your Board.

5) **Manage the risks.** First, make sure you have adequate insurance coverage to provide for unexpected events. You can manage risk in many other ways, such as investing in fidelity bonds, directors' and officers' insurance, workers comp., unemployment insurance, and disability insurance. Also, establish a system for paying mandated withholding taxes, and to make sure your organization complies with wage and hour laws.

6) **Hire staff carefully.** Check the qualifications and references of prospective job applicants, and if something in their background raises a flag, check it out thoroughly. To ensure that you hire qualified people, establish a probationary period for new hires, and evaluate them in writing after 90 days of service. Continue to monitor their performance at regular intervals. All employees should have a review at least once a year to measure job performance. Remember that your organization has an important job to perform, so you can't afford to become a caretaker for unprofitable employees. If they can't do the job, don't be a welfare program for staff. Decide how you will measure each person's performance and develop regular reporting on those indicators. This is the only way you have to measure what your organization is accomplishing.

7) **Plan for new business development.** New business development is usually the job of the Executive Director. The Director will need to develop a strategy for "selling" your services or products. This is no different than in the private sector, although your sales pitch will be tailored to your specific customer. So find someone who can help you develop an effective sales pitch. In the private sector, salespeople are accustomed to making 100 sales calls for every sale made. You will have to work just as hard. Target your sales pitch to your audience and be prepared to make dozens of calls before you get a "hit." Make your best pitch, and then *follow-up*. The follow-up is an extremely important part of your sales strategy. If you are too busy to follow up with a potential grant maker, then recruit some of your staff. Fundraising and obtaining contracts doesn't all have to fall on your shoulders.

8) **Build a support network.** Build strong allies in the community. Realize that residents and businesses can be your most valuable supporters. Listen to their needs, and be prepared to demonstrate to them how your community will benefit if your non-profit does a good job. Maintain contact with the community through events, invitations, and fundraisers to keep them involved in your organization.

9) **Be ethical.** Unethical behavior in the non-profit sector is fatal. Non-profit staff is entitled to decent compensation packages, but they should be in line with industry standards and approved by your Board of Directors. Financial record keeping must be pristine, and employee relations must be by the book. Non-profits are held to a higher standard than the private sector and government. A brighter light shines on non-profits because they utilize "good will" donations from the public and the government to fund many of their activities. As such, non-profits are public trusts and must be held to this standard.

10) Stay focused on the finish line. Non-profits are increasingly called upon to do work that was once the exclusive domain of government. This new role often makes good business sense because non-profits can avoid the bureaucratic red tape and can get the job done faster, at less expense. To position your non-profit as a leading provider of public services, make sure that your services are equal to or better in quality, and less costly than anything the private sector could provide.

As you position your organization, do what you need to do, but don't complain. If you need to go to court to remove tenants who obstruct construction, do it. If you need to work with the police department to deal with drug dealers, do it. If you need to go above lower level public officials you are dealing with when they tell you "no," do it. Don't be afraid of critics, as someone will always be waiting to criticize you. Meet with your critics if you can and work with them if possible, but don't compromise on your goals. Always keep your goals in mind.

Create a Plan for Success

When you lead your non-profit according to the above guidelines, you can tackle any challenges that arise with confidence because you have a strong board of directors, staff, and community in your corner. You will be able to sleep at night knowing that the project costs are covered, and that your projects will be successful. When you run an efficient operation, you will have the support from the community and from your financing partners, including the government, the private sector, and the public. By establishing your reputation as an ethical, efficient, effective, and energetic organization, you can become recognized and sought after in your community as the non-profit of choice.

About the Author

Claire Haaga Altman has been leading non-profit organizations in New York City for 25 years. Her innovations include creating and operating a para-transit service for the handicapped and elderly, an ex-offender construction company, a housing development and management company, a residential health facility for persons with AIDS, and an integrative health center. Ms. Haaga Altman earned a Masters Degree in Public Administration from NYU and a JD from Fordham University School of Law. More information about non-profit business strategies is available by contacting Ms. Haaga Altman at clairehaaga@aol.com or by calling 1.212.252.9377.

Creating Governance That Works In Your Organization

How to Establish an Effective Board of Directors

by Ann Atkinson, Ed.D.

In many industries, boards don't work as well as they should. Therefore, we need to make some changes.

Ideally, a board should labor to pursue excellence in the governing process while simultaneously producing results for the organization. Since continual improvement requires stepping out of our comfort zones, all too often, boards give up the chase and settle for the status quo. The solution is for all members to be willing to challenge and motivate each other. Only then will they create lucid values and trusteeship for their stakeholders.

Sometimes, in a business with as few as eighty employees, there are as many as thirty or more board members. By the same token, large organizations with 300-50,000 employees also have thirty or more board members. Realistically, large boards don't work for either group. For a more effective board, you need to limit the number to no more than eleven voting members that rotate off every three years. Additionally, most boards today have committees on everything, from finance to strategic planning to fundraising. The best option is to eliminate standing committees entirely. Operate at the board level through ad-hoc committees designed for a specific purpose within the necessary timeframe. Then eliminate the committee.

All board members must strive for accountability in the boardroom, confident that when quality dwells there, the rest of the organization will take care of itself. However, the sacrifices required of an effective board member are difficult, and often, board governance takes a back seat to other responsibilities, such as family or career. In the end, though, the desired results of any company are in direct proportion to the commitment of each board member.

Remember that the sole reason boards exist is to ensure the organization works. A corporate board exists to speak for the shareholders and to speak for the company's interests.

In most organizations, statements of ethics, conduct, self-governance, vision, and strategic plans are not created in a day, but hammered out in a series of meetings, word-by-word, comma-by-comma, sentence-by-sentence. The values determined in those meetings ultimately guide the organization's initiatives and help evaluate them. The problem with many boards is that intelligent, caring individuals regularly exhibit procedures of governance that are deeply flawed, hence the saying, "Boards tend to be incompetent groups of competent people."

An excellent board seeks quality governance that grows as it does, yet perfection always remains a little beyond its grasp. With that in mind, here are some tips that will ensure better board leadership.

1) **Limit terms of service.** In most boards, members stay on indefinitely. As a result, many boards operate today the way they did twenty years ago. Boards should be inclusive and have a term clause that allows participation by other members of the community, thus guaranteeing a more accurate representation of the shareholders. To accomplish this, establish the following Terms of Service rules:
   - A term is five years and cannot be renewed.
   - For the first year of the term, the member has no voting privileges. He or she undergoes specific training on being an effective board member.
   - For the next three years, the individual is an active voting member.
   - For the fifth year, he or she is once again a non-voting board member; however, the individual helps train those in their first year.
   - If a board member wants to rejoin the board after completing his or her term, the person must wait a minimum of two years. At that point, he or she starts over with training, as after seven years the training will (or should) be vastly different.

2) **Create staff-driven boards.** All boards must be staff-driven. In fact, the staff should develop the strategic plan that the board approves. Ultimately, the staff carries out the plan, which makes their ownership of that plan vital to the organization's success.

3) **Define the president's role**. The board's one employee is the organization's president. When the board defines the breadth and depth of the president's duties and authority, the organization will operate more smoothly. Remember that the board's job is to ensure that the organization is well managed, not to manage the organization itself.

4) **Institute the Board Governance Plan.** The Board Governance Plan is divided into three distinct phases: Training, Governance, and Mentoring.

Phase One – Training

The first year is the training phase, in which the board member will be non-voting and will participate in a series of at least four half-day training sessions during the year. Because a board should *always* speak with "one voice," this first year sets the tone for the board member's term. The training session content varies from board to board, but, in general, should include the following:

Session One:

- Taking the Myers-Briggs Type Indicator test, as it helps members better understand communication styles and organizational aptitude.
- Completing a Position Results Statement (PRS), which defines the board member's responsibilities and expected key results. It also introduces the individual to group authority of the board member(s).
- Outlining the commitment required of a board member: time commitment, attendance expectations, conflict of interest concerns, confidentiality, code of behavior, and communication expectations.
- Evaluating each board member yearly by the membership. Ideally, every three years, an outside, objective, third party should evaluate the board.

Session Two:

- Reviewing the organizational strategic plan, including the organization's purpose, the vision, the mission, the declaration of principles, the three-year strategic plan, management of assumptions, benchmarks, and the evaluation process.
- Reviewing the planning process itself and planning for the future by creating something that does not currently exist.

Session Three:

- Evaluating the president.
- Teaching how to evaluate a position based on whether it achieves desired results.
- Reading financial documents.
- Identifying the steps for resolving internal conflicts within the board.

Session Four:

- Holding focus groups with members for the incoming, voting board members to have data on what members really want.
- Reviewing the by-laws and the board's actions for the past five years as defined by the corporate minutes.

- Establishing corporate protocol.

Phase Two – Governance

Too often board members make decisions about the organization's future based on their *opinions* rather than the *facts*. Make decisions as a board only after you have obtained, reviewed, and documented the facts as accurately as possible.

Remember that the board doesn't speak as individual members, except in achieving the desired results of the strategic plan. The board speaks with one voice or not at all. The "one voice" principle makes it possible to know what the board has said and what it has not said. This is important when the board gives direction to the organization's president. "One voice" does not require unanimous votes, but it does require all board members, even those who lost the vote, to respect the decision that was made.

The board must be very clear about the desired results and how it evaluates those results. Only in this way is everyone clear about what constitutes success and who has which role in achieving it. For example, the board will examine regular financial reports using the criteria of the desired results articulated in the strategic plan. Similarly, the board will use these established rules to approve or disapprove the president's budget. The board does not control everything, but it must control and be accountable for the definition of success.

The board's role then becomes very clear: to demand organizational achievement in a way that empowers the president, allowing him or her the creativity, innovation, and latitude to achieve the desired results. The board hires and fires only one employee: the president. The president is then responsible for hiring and firing the rest of the staff and assigning their individual responsibilities. The board does not get involved in personnel decisions, purchasing decisions, or in service, but only in the outcomes that are articulated in the strategic plan.

Phase Three – Mentoring

Board members help others by sharing all the mistakes previously made so the new board members won't repeat them. Board members can evaluate themselves by asking these two questions: "How do I think I did as a board member?" and "If I had to do it all over again, what would I do differently?" The answers to these questions form the basis of the mentoring model. In sharing their experience, past board members are now in a position to help others achieve greater success.

Effective Board Governance for Tomorrow

Board governance asserts that boards be visionary and provide long-term leadership. This challenge requires tremendous discipline by board members not to seek refuge in rituals, reports, meetings, luncheons, or politics. Board members need to think conceptually over a long period of time and welcome a diversity of opinions from current and future members. They must place organizational accountability above personal gratification. They must place commitment above publicity. They must place ethics above politics. They must place desired outcomes above trivia or ritual. They must be proactive, not reactive.

The board's ultimate responsibility is to be as effective and committed as possible. Remember, organizations never rise above their leadership, so make sure your board is as well led as possible.

About the Author

Ann Akinson has had her own consulting practice for over 30 years, specializing in strategic and organizational planning and design, executive coaching, board of director training, leadership mastery, organizational culture, economic development, and managing change. She currently teaches for eCornell and the US Chamber of Commerce Institute for Organization Management. She helps hospitals, hospitality/tourism, economic development, non-profit, technological and multi-national firms in change management processes, cultural transformations, and strategic initiatives as well as executive coaching and keynote addresses. Previously, Dr. Atkinson has served as Vice President of Management, Leadership and Organizational Development for Days Inns of America, Inc.; Director of Educational Programs for the Georgia Center for Continuing Education at the University of Georgia; Dean of Education and Chief Academic Officer at The Art Institute of Atlanta; and Director, Training & Strategic Planning for Georgia Tech. For more information, please contact Ann Atkinson at: 575 Orme Circle NE, Atlanta, GA 30306. Phone: 1.404.876.2831; Fax: 1.404.872.3279. e-mail: annatkinson@bellsouth.net website: www.annatkinson-associates.com.

The Two-Tier Approach to Business Growth

by Maria Carlton

Shelley, a self-employed graphic designer, shook her head as she thought, "I could be SO successful if I just got better at closing some of the opportunities that come my way. I'm a great graphic designer, but when it comes to sales and marketing, I'm completely useless!"

Like many self employed professionals, Shelley left a great job and good pay because she thought that doing what she's great at for her own company would be easier than working for someone else. What she overlooked is that running a successful company requires more than just technical expertise; it also requires a host of other skill-sets that may be totally unrelated to the business's core activity.

So while you may be a fantastic doctor, lawyer, tradesperson, consultant, or teacher, you may not have excellent administration, sales, marketing, design, customer service, human resources, debt collection, or networking skills. In fact, the chances are high that you will range anywhere from "very bad" to "very good" across each one of these areas. Eventually, most people realize that in order to be successful in their own business, they need to either get a lot better, or find someone who can help them handle some or all of these roles.

Whether you are starting a new business or are an existing small to medium sized business owner who needs to develop new strategies for sustainable growth, then the following strategies will help you succeed.

Learn From Others

Large companies have separate departments that take care of the various needed procedures, and each department is set up to link together and ensure that every aspect of the company's operation knits together. In a very small company or professional practice, it may seem absurd to have such a complex set-up; however, you need to remember that all of the large companies and corporations were once small. The edge they have over you is that they have well-established systems of information flowing in and around to make sure that each critical area optimizes knowledge and expertise.

Whether you have one person working with you or fifty, you need to establish a system for obtaining information and advice from a two-tier group. The following guidelines will help you:

Tier One – Your Family of Business Mentors

The first tier is your <u>Family of Business Mentors, which is a team of</u> <u>three to four professionals who</u>, between them, cover your legal, accounting, finance, sales, marketing, and human resources knowledge base. They may include your:

- Accountant;
- Tax advisor;
- Business attorney;
- Employment specialist;
- Marketing specialist;
- Business/industry mentor.

[handwritten margin note: Legal / Acct / Finance / Sales / Mktg / HR]

This team is your external group of advisors whom you meet with collectively two or three times a year to discuss your progress, opportunities, goals set and achieved, and how you are progressing in relation to your business plan. From within this group of your paid professional advisors, you may find a few people with whom you'd want to form a stronger relationship that goes beyond the services they provide your business. For example, your accountant may have some business management skills, and may be willing to mentor you through your growth on areas not related to accounting. Therefore, you may want to meet with this person individually on a regular or as needed basis to keep your company on track and strong. You can elect to either pay these experts for their time, or simply work out a very firm reciprocal referral system (or a combination of both). Do what you must to create a win/win relationship for both of you.

How to Assemble a Great Family of Business Mentors

You may already know and work with your team, or you may need to search for one or two members to join you. Before you go looking for mentors, consider the following:

1) Identify the key areas in which you need advice on a regular basis. What parts of running a business intimidate or confuse you the most? For example, are you a great people person but lost when it comes to numbers? Are you great at understanding legal documents but awful at creating marketing materials? Delve deep and be honest to pinpoint your areas for improvement.

2) Ask your personal and professional contacts to recommend anyone who may be able to help you. Tell them what you're doing and the caliber of people you're looking for.

3) Approach these referrals with a clear explanation about what you wish to discuss with them. Initially, make it a simple "get to know you" meeting over a cup of coffee or lunch, where you pay the tab. Explain that you have a small or medium sized business, or are starting one up,

and that you have identified a regular need to confer with someone with his or her expertise. Discuss that you are establishing your own "board of directors," and ask if he or she would be open to being involved with such an endeavor.

4) After the meeting, and if you are comfortable with your initial conversation and believe you might be able to form a long-term mentoring relationship with the person, ask him or her the following questions:
   - Have you mentored anyone like me before?
   - How can your advice add value to my business?
   - How often could we meet individually and as team?
   - How would you like to be compensated for your services?

Once you have your Family of Business Mentors established, you need to know what to ask them and when to follow through. Don't feel that just because you have asked for help that you *have* to take it. These people will give you perspective and guidance. You then must trust yourself to assimilate the information in the best way for your business. Realize, however, that if you decide never to take the advice of one of your trusted advisors, then that person will likely leave. No one wants to waste his or her time dispensing advice that never gets used.

Tier Two – Your Extended Family of Experts

The second tier consists of your associates and networking contacts. While these are the people you may regularly call on for advice or information and to share resources or ideas, this group goes way beyond simple networking. Those in your Extended Family of Experts are centers of influence that will tell others about you and your business. If encouraged to do so, they may become strong advocates for you.

From within your extensive group of contacts you may have many people with various specialty services and expertise. Select one or two of those close associates from each area of your business's needs with whom you can form a closer reciprocal working relationship or even a strategic alliance. Doing so means you won't have to look as hard to find someone with whom you can regularly exchange referral opportunities.

How to Work with Your Extended Family of Experts

To make the most of your Extended Family of Experts, consider the following:

1) Think of each member of your Extended Family of Experts as a center of influence who will carry your banner into every meeting they have. Encourage reciprocal referrals with this group on an informal basis, and make it a win/win situation. Remember that in order to make this a reciprocal relationship, you must do the same word of mouth advertising for them. Speak positively about these people at all times and refer

them to others. The power of word of mouth advertising is incredibly strong and cost effective when you harness it and use it wisely.

2) Always thank them for their time and advice, and let them know the outcome of anything you have achieved through your contacts with them. This will help nurture the relationship, as people like hearing the positive results that they helped create.

3) Follow up on any referrals they send to you immediately, and do the absolute best job you can for those referrals. If people suspect that you're taking advantage of referrals or not doing as good a job for them as you do for other clients, they'll send their referrals elsewhere.

4) Let them know of any changes or additions to your business practices, especially if that may affect (either positively or negatively) your ability to provide service to them or their network of possible referrals to you.

5) Make yourself available to them when they call on you for help or advice. Be free and generous with your advice and the knowledge you share with them.

Onward and Upward

Unfortunately, no single handbook exists for a small business or solo practitioner that will tell you everything you need to know, and it may take far longer than your average business lifetime to read all the information available in bookstores and libraries. However, when you assemble a great team of people who are experts in their own chosen fields to help guide your business, you reap the rewards of an expanded knowledge base that propels your business forward. Ultimately, having an on-call team behind you will enable you to do more of what you love so you truly *can* love what you do!

About the Author

Maria Carlton is Managing Director and co-founder of Compass Development Group, a specialist marketing, branding, and coaching group based in New Zealand. She helps small and medium companies and professional practices to identify and realize their potential through a powerful combination of consulting and coaching them to work out their marketing and business planning based on the direction and success they want to achieve. Maria works with clients from all over the world, who all find she is as effective by phone and email, as she is in person. For more information, please call: +64-21-849 948, email: Maria@compassnz.com, or visit: www.compassnz.com.

Rent a Maverick
Tap Into the Energizing Power of Entrepreneurial Youth
by Diane Carroll

"The inner fire is the most important thing mankind possesses."
–Edith Södergran, Scandinavian poet

What happens when the energy and enthusiasm of youth combine with the experience and wisdom of seasoned professionals in a business setting? If blended properly, the result is something akin to the re-discovery of "inner fire." So the next time your business needs a boost or you're thinking about adding another employee to your organization, consider this alternative: hire a young entrepreneur.

Let's say you need someone to help shoulder an ever-increasing workload. Maybe it's time to inject a new idea, system, or technology to make things run better. Perhaps a critical project has been on your to-do list for months and you've accepted that it's time to delegate it. Before you succumb to the standard practice of simply adding another warm body to your staff or investing thousands in the services of a consultant, consider the benefits of handing the assignment over to a young, independent thinker on the entrepreneurial track—a maverick.

At first it may sound risky to hire "a kid." While it's true that many young adults don't fully understand the business world, if you look carefully and in the right places, you can tap into the brilliance of young upstarts who possess something vital to your success: the contagious fire, the fresh outlook and the sharp intellectual assets that can add new life to your organization. Today's generation of young entrepreneurs are ready, willing, and able to join your team, even if briefly. Furthermore, they can be one of the world's greatest untapped resources. Choose them wisely, work with them in the right way, and chances are you'll be astonished at the benefits you see.

How to Spot a Maverick
So who are these unique individuals and how do you spot them? Often, they are still in high school, college, or grad school. You won't be able to miss that rare "fire in the belly" quality. They have goals (often lots of them), are proactive about their lives and careers, exhibit an ethical foundation, and are often involved in community projects. In addition, mavericks are creative and outspoken with their ideas. One of their key assets is that they have developed as "independents" while they were young.

To find these mavericks, look for participants or graduates of some form of entrepreneurial development. Sometimes they have been developed internally in an entrepreneurial family. In some cases, an entrepreneurial boss or mentor trains them. Some are self-taught or emerge from formal or informal independence training. Don't make the assumption that college students automatically have what it takes. Instead, use the following checklist to interview your candidates carefully and ferret out the real mavericks.

Basic Maverick Traits
- Previous work or training with entrepreneurs (e-schooled);
- Business ethics and personal integrity;
- Communication skills–written, oral, and organizational;
- Belief in teamwork and teambuilding;
- Sees the big picture view of the world;
- Thinks independently and creatively;
- Strong work habits and ethics;
- Control of their entrepreneurial spirit;
- Advanced people skills;
- Disciplined and driven;
- Voracious learner;
- Knows how to ask questions and get answers;
- Resourceful and self-reliant;
- Can enter and exit a job or company smoothly and without disruption.

Maverick Advantages

Most businesses don't realize what many of today's young entrepreneurs have to offer. For example, they are comfortable learning and using new technologies and methods. They have fewer insecurities or doubts about trying new ways of thinking regarding business models, marketing strategies, and communications techniques. Additionally, they are outspoken and very much inclined to share their perspective.

Taking time to hire the right maverick for your business (and taking the time to assimilate them carefully with your staff) is the ultimate win-win situation. For the maverick the benefits include gaining real world business experience; opportunities to see and become involved in the inner workings of business organizations; the ability to try out their gifts, talents, and skills (and possibly discover new ones); and the chance to work with and learn from other entrepreneurs. From the business owner's perspective, it's more cost effective than hiring a full-time employee or consultant. It also helps take the blinders off your own thinking and most often that of your current employees. With a maverick on board, even for a short time, you'll get an injection of fresh ideas and new perspectives.

In addition, the right maverick might be a future business partner or someone who you may want to sell your business to when you're ready to leave. Hiring them on contract for a limited engagement or for a special project is an easy way to try them out.

Here are some ideas for how to effectively integrate mavericks into your business:

Create an "InVision" Team

An InVision Team is an idea-generating group that tackles the question, "How do we improve and grow uniquely?" The group's mission is to explore niches, additional products or services, and income streams. An InVision Team accelerates the company by providing ideas that make the most of existing resources. The team's challenge is to look at your company and what you do through innovative, futuristic eyes.

An InVision Team is a mix of young mavericks and seasoned entrepreneurs. They should meet once a month face-to-face or via teleconferences, with six people being the ideal number on the team. The pay or perks will vary but are necessary. Incentives based on success are the best way to sweeten the pot. For example, if the team's idea is implemented then the group should share in any success with the reward tied directly to the outcome. The company would gain new insights, accelerate growth, set itself apart as unique, gain a cross-generational business review, and garner a "what's next?" vision.

Most groups burn out after one year together. At that point the fertile idea generator slows down and it's time to change most of the players.

Hire a Maverick "Analyst"

A Maverick Analyst is someone hired to view your company from fresh entrepreneurial eyes, analyze how things run, and offer improvement suggestions. New eyes often see inefficiencies in systems and customer needs that most long-time employees may have missed. Additionally, mavericks have a passion for the truth. They thrive on taking things apart and finding new ways to get things done. What "can't be done" is not in their vocabulary; instead, they will often show you how it *can* be done.

When hiring a Maverick Analyst, give them parameters and terms of their mission. Allow them the freedom to walk around and ask questions. They will bring back to you a wealth of information. Have the maverick learn the process and document it on paper. You may find your system works differently than you think.

Manage Your Mavericks

The phrase "maverick management" is really an oxymoron because mavericks often do a great job of managing themselves. They have an unconventional work style and an inner fire to succeed. Usually all you need to do is provide them with a written contract that includes some guidelines, objectives, goals, and expectations (be sure to include non-compete and non-performance clauses).

In addition, spend time with them to share what you know and listen to their thoughts. Good communication is mutually beneficial. However, do not make the mistake of micro-managing mavericks with too many rules and methods. Remember, they are independents who thrive in an entrepreneurial environment.

Hire a Maverick for Maximum Benefit

The world benefits from bridging knowledge across age and cultural borders. For example, a Chinese company interested in expanding their products to North America would hire a group of Canadian and American mavericks. The company would bring the mavericks to China for the duration of the project. In addition to the development benefits, the company would gain many intangible benefits as they studied how young North American entrepreneurs think and how they create. From the mavericks' perspective, the immersion in the Chinese company, the people, and the culture provides a rich learning experience. In addition, language is more easily adopted, lifelong connections are forged, and communications are bridged.

Young minds have the creativity and open thinking needed to find out-of-the-box solutions that can help both profit and non-profit organizations survive and thrive. At the same time, experienced professionals offer stability and knowledge tested by time. All this information can combine to create mutual power and diversity. As a result, organizations run better, which ultimately means less waste and fewer failures.

The assumption that entrepreneurs are born and, therefore, do not require business and entrepreneurial development has cost the world a fortune. Entrepreneurs of all ages need to team up to flatten out the learning curve of business, stay current with technology, and maneuver successfully and efficiently in the business world. When the creative minds of youth combine with the wisdom of seasoned business leaders, it accelerates this process, and the outcome will positively affect the individual, the organization, the economy, and our global society.

About the Author
Diane Carroll is the founder of Maverick Center, located in Austin, Texas. From preparing high school and college students for future career independence to supporting entrepreneurs as they discover or design their first (or next) business, Maverick Center provides customized programs and consulting specifically developed (and led) by entrepreneurs. In addi-

tion, Maverick Center provides accelerated development programs tailored for "mom and dad" entrepreneurs and alternative independent lifestyles. It also provides unique youth and adult independence career counseling. Diane Carroll is most noted for her knowledge and understanding of the inner workings of entrepreneurs and the powerful development of independent youth. For more details, please contact the Maverick Center at 1.512.345.7178 or visit: www.maverickcenter.com.

Strategic Planning – A Small Business Necessity

by Jacquelyn Gernaey

> **Alice:** Which way should I go?
> **Cheshire Cat:** That depends on where you are going.
> **Alice:** I don't know where I am going!
> **Cheshire Cat:** Then it doesn't matter which way you go!
> –Lewis Carroll, *Through the Looking-Glass*
> *and What Alice Found There*, 1871

In a recent survey of 2,500 small business owners across the United States, only 4% had a strategic plan. Most small business owners think strategic plans are only for large public companies. Their reasons for not planning include, "I have my plan in my head," and "I don't have time to develop a strategic plan." But the fact is, small business owners can reap big rewards when they develop a strategic plan and put it in writing.

Strategic Planning Benefits

We are in an age of rapid change and economic uncertainty where every organization needs a roadmap. A strategic plan helps you:

- Gain more control over your company's future;
- Respond successfully to internal or external threats;
- Take advantage of an opportunity or introduce a new product or service while defining and controlling your risks;
- Expand your marketplace or market share;
- Measure and track your progress.

Putting these challenges into perspective through a well thought out plan allows your business to modify its environment and gain control of its future by developing a total solution. Since strategic planning culminates in goal setting, when done correctly it can help a business operate better and therefore dramatically increase the chances of its long-term success. Without a strategy, a business has no direction and therefore little chance of achieving its goals. Strategy tells you where to go and how to get there.

Strategic planning for the small business is a simple four-step process.

Step One – Organization

Once you make a commitment to begin the strategic planning process, you need to decide who belongs on the planning team. The team

43

should be a combination of "visionaries" (individuals who recognize the potential of the company) and "actionaries" (those who are cautiously optimistic about the company's resources yet are also objective about the reality of the projected goals and tasks).

The team should include individuals with varying levels of power, while not making the group too large—a few key employees will suffice. Once you select the participants, appoint a facilitator to be in charge of organizing the planning meetings, developing timelines, and creating probing questions in order to begin the planning process. If you need help, a professional facilitator can help you complete your plan and lend objectivity.

Step Two – Company and Environmental Audit

The next step is to complete a performance audit of your organization. Using the team, identify the company's current internal strengths and weaknesses, along with its current and future external opportunities and threats.

When addressing the organization's internal strengths and weaknesses, the facilitator should develop thought-provoking questions in some or all of these categories:

- History and reputation of the company and its products and services;
- Financial status;
- Human resources and compensation programs;
- Facilities and location;
- Current products and services;
- Risk aversion or tolerance;
- Current and past strategies.

By defining an organization's strengths and weaknesses, you answer the question, "What is the true nature of the organization and what can it accomplish?" For a mature organization, addressing the internal strengths and weaknesses is usually the easy part. When addressing the organization's outside environment in the form of opportunities and threats, "facts" may be more difficult to obtain, trust, analyze, and incorporate into a strategic plan. To help, the facilitator should again formulate questions to address the following categories:

- Economy;
- Competitors;
- Government regulations;
- Products, market share, geographic market, and product positioning within the market;
- Clients/Customers and distribution channels;
- Suppliers and strategic alliances.

Defining the opportunities and threats an organization faces answers the question "What is the possible future environment in which the organization will operate and what actions can it take to be successful?"

Step Three – Selecting Long and Short-Term Goals

From the **SWOT** (Strengths, Weaknesses, Opportunities, and Threats) analysis, the team can create a specific number of goals to serve as positive action-oriented responses to the opportunities and threats identified. Each goal, whether it's a short-term goal (one year or less) or a long-term goal (two to five years), needs to be challenged by the company's vision and mission statements. Goal development ties strategic planning with implementation, which is the action necessary to produce change; therefore, each of the goals needs to have established measures.

For example, if your year-one goal is to differentiate your company as a regionally focused, low-cost manufacturer, you need to establish efficiency measures and customer analysis measures supporting the strategic position. You also need to specify exact levels of the performance desired for each measure. To ensure each of your goals meet these requirements, challenge them to ensure they are considered **SMART**: Specific, **M**easurable, **A**ction **O**riented, **R**ealistic, and **T**ime Constrained.

Some examples of year-one goals would be:
- Increase gross profit from 21% to 23%.
- Reduce delivery costs by 10%.
- Reduce bad debt percentage from 3% to 2%.

Some examples of long-term goals would be:
- Add twenty new clients for a $250,000 increase in annual sales by year two.
- Open second location in a neighboring city by year four.

Application of Strategies

How you define your strategic goals is a direct function of the goal complexity, the status of goals being considered, the financial benefit of completing the goal, and the company's strategy for change. Some examples of strategies for an organization are:
- Concentrated growth of a single product or service.
- Increased sales by adding new customers, expanding geographic market, entering new market segments, or developing new products or services.
- Horizontal integration by acquiring or merging with similar organizations; concentric integration by acquiring or merging with organizations that produce compatible products or services; or

vertical integration by adding everything needed to develop a product from raw materials to finished products.

- Joint ventures or strategic alliances.
- Increased efficiency and retrenchment to reverse negative trends.
- Divestiture of a poorly performing portion of an organization or liquidation of the entire organization.

Developing Focused Actions

To further define how you will achieve each goal, define each task required to reach the goal. These actions are the essence and the culmination of the whole planning process. Each action must have a start and completion date, identify the responsible person(s), and estimate the cost of the completion. By defining actions this way, managers can ensure each task is easily implemented.

Step Four – The Implementation Process

Implementation is the final phase of strategic planning wherein the specific tasks or actions are completed, resulting in the achievement of the company goals. The role of the facilitator is to work with each planning team member to ensure each department integrates and internalizes each action the planning team identified. The facilitator also needs to track the progress of each of the actions and goals and report the status to the business owner and the management team.

All Businesses Need a Strategic Plan

Many small business owners resist the concept of strategic planning, but all businesses, even successful ones, benefit from a carefully constructed strategic plan. Strategic planning serves as a tool to analyze and collate the massive amount of information associated with any challenge or opportunity your business faces. It allows you to synthesize and prioritize a wide range of possible tasks for implementation.

Until you commit a plan to paper, you may never know the missing vital issues that may pose a serious threat to your business's success. With a good plan, management stays focused. Periodic assessments to re-examine employee roles and responsibilities help focus efforts, leverage resources, reduce organizational redundancy, and ensure accountability within a business.

An effective strategic plan is a "living" document that, with ongoing monitoring and revision, serves as a compass to guide the business through inevitable change. It charts a business's direction, shapes its future, and secures its growth and prosperity. No privately owned business should be without one.

About the Author

Jacquelyn Gernaey, an independent owner of The Alternative Board TAB®, Suffolk County, Long Island, and President of HyTech Consulting, has more than twenty-five years experience leading both entrepreneurial and large corporations. She now focuses on helping CEOs, presidents, owners, and partners create, execute, and exceed their personal and business success goals. She has extensive experience facilitating the development of strategic plans for small businesses and is a Certified Strategic Business Leadership® Coach. She has developed a web-based product to help small business owners in the development and tracking of their plans called PlanTracker™. More information on this topic is available on her websites www.tabny.com, www.hytechny.com, www.plantracker.com or by calling her office 1.631.474.4310.

Do More With Less
Five Rules to Maximize Your Team's Performance
by Kay Graham-Gilbert

The business environment is changing more rapidly than ever before. Customers update their requirements by the hour. Businesses strive to leap ahead of one another in the competition for clients. Global markets expand at an unforeseen pace. eCommerce provides new opportunities, while also adding new risks. If only we could concentrate on one or two critical objectives, our jobs would be easier, but that is simply not possible today. We have multiple demands and have to respond quickly in order to thrive and prosper. It's a daunting challenge.

In today's competitive marketplace, your people are your greatest asset to help you reach your company's objectives. As a business owner or leader, you make an enormous investment in your people–everything from hiring and training to providing career development opportunities. Once you have invested in your employees, you must provide the right environment in order to maximize their productivity and performance. In essence, you need to get the absolute most from the fewest number of people to enhance the bottom line.

When implemented, the following rules will help managers, executives, and business owners get the best from their most important resource: their employees. With good employees, you can rise above the competition, and the energy generated within your organization will amaze you.

Rule One – Get a Good Fit

Many employees fall into their jobs by chance, not necessarily by inclination, aptitude, or vocation. Very often, circumstance limits a person's job choice, and employees may accept a position because it was the only one available, it was close to home, or their friend could get them hired. The problem with this shotgun approach to employment is that people's true talents and abilities may be miscast in jobs that limit their true potential. The result is that the employer has great resources of skill and talent that are not being used effectively. If employers could find a way to optimize these human resources, everyone would benefit.

People truly are much more productive and effective when they are doing what comes naturally and what they enjoy. The best way to identify talent is to give your employees a chance to work in a wide variety of areas within your organization. When you take a chance and trust their ability, they will often perform beyond your expectations. Allow employees the freedom to explore the organizational processes as well as the different disciplines that interest them. Encourage them to increase their knowledge areas and learn new skills. Everyone needs challenge, even those who seem comfortable with what they already know.

Train supervisory and management staff to identify natural talents and interests so that you can discover employees' natural abilities and find the right "fit" between employees and their job roles. People will respond positively to the attention and interest you express, and you will see performance levels improve when people are working at something they are good at and enjoy.

Rule Two – Refine, Refine, Refine

To make the most efficient use of your employee resources, thoroughly understand the business processes and why they exist. Once you are well versed in the "why" of the processes, you can begin to ask questions that may lead to improving these processes, such as "Is there a way to reduce the number of steps in the process?" and "Is someone else better equipped to handle this task?" By using a question and answer format, you will identify ways to increase productivity and can begin to allocate responsibility for processes to those who exhibit the greatest ability in a specific area of need. Ensuring that your company actually benefits from your existing processes and then combining the right people with the right processes allows you to respond more quickly to your customers and to market forces.

This exercise requires a systematic approach, with attention to detail and follow-through. You will need to coordinate your efforts with all department heads, managers, and supervisors. Everyone within your organization has specialized knowledge that will contribute to the overall picture, so use them as valuable resources to dig beneath the surface, map the cause and effect from beginning to end, evaluate the integrity of data, realize technology benefits, and integrate solutions throughout the organization. These steps are but a few of the many essential elements to a successful refinement campaign. Do not give short shrift to this exercise, thinking that it has already been done, because chances are that it was not performed with the depth and breadth that will ensure maximum effectiveness.

Rule Three – Set High Standards

When you set high standards, your employees will rise to the occasion. Be attentive to quality issues in particular. For example, if your employees routinely miss a customer deadline by one day, that practice can easily become a benchmark. Therefore, be careful about what develops into an acceptable practice. Expect the best from yourself and from those around you, and the results will be astounding. Do not be afraid to set high standards. You'll be amazed at what people achieve, particularly when you show confidence in their abilities, simply by clearly defining your expectations.

Never make excuses for people who fail to perform as expected. When you begin to rationalize poor work performance, with excuses such as "Bob can't give good customer service because he was not trained to do it," you do a disservice to your employee and your business. If a learning curve is associated with the task, give the employee the tools and support to gain the required knowledge, and then expect him or her to perform the job well. This may seem like a simple concept, but to consistently demonstrate high quality work is not easy. Superiors, customers, and even subordinates will often pressure you to cut corners and deliver inferior quality. Do not give in. You will take heat at the beginning, when the monthly numbers are down because a delivery was held due to a quality control issue. But in a short time the rewards to you and to the organization will far outweigh the struggle. Setting high standards and standing behind them takes strength. The benefit is that high standards create high quality, which leads to more effective operations and greater profits.

Rule Four – You Are What You Attract

We all have a significant influence on others, and both positive and negative attitudes are contagious. Have you ever noticed how one department can be very productive and upbeat, and another unit is always complaining and pointing fingers? In most cases, attitude–whether good or bad–is a learned behavior. The good news is that you can change a negative behavior, whether in an individual or within an entire department. Just as positive attitudes affect how we perform, so does working beside talented and skillful people. With the right role models, positive attitudes breed optimism, learning increases the desire to learn more, and interest leads to accomplishment. A "can-do" mindset becomes addictive.

You have the ability to nurture the "best" within your employees. When you hear someone make a negative comment, shift the focus to what the team has accomplished or how you can do it better next time. Let complainers know that you do not agree with their comments by explaining the true situation and the potential inherent therein. Help your employees have a vision filled with possibilities. Create opportunities for your team to share their talents with others. You will soon see them shift their focus from bad to good and from complacency to action. Change takes time, but each small improvement will have an impact and soon will spread to others.

Rule Five – Experiment!

Trying something new with your employees can be scary, since there's always a chance of failure. To overcome your hesitation, concentrate on the wealth of learning opportunity and potential "big" win when you experiment with a new tactic, perspective, or method.

Don't worry about potential problems. We learn from each new experiment, and all trials have redeeming qualities. When trying to improve efficiency and performance, do not hold back or wait until the idea is a trend or commonplace; rather, be the first to step up and make it happen. True breakthroughs come from exploration. Although by nature we are averse to change, when change becomes commonplace we accept it more easily. In time, you'll find that the rewards can be tremendous.

Treasure Your Resources

The wealth of information you possess about your people, internal systems, and corporate culture is the key to finding the strengths that lie dormant within your organization. Use what you have as well as what you know and build from there to maximize the effectiveness of your existing people resources.

Implementing some of the rules above will be easier than others. Elicit help when necessary and have patience. Some results will be immediate; others will take time. Change does not come easily, so stay focused. Treasure your resources and use them wisely. Your company and your entire team will both benefit from this approach.

About the Author

Kay Graham-Gilbert of Interactive Consulting helps organizations increase their speed and flexibility to become more competitive. Her years of business knowledge have guided her from corporate executive to respected business advisor. She has leveraged her diverse industry and operational experience to help organizations achieve higher performance, increased income, improved effectiveness, and business practice insight. Particularly skilled in quickly understanding business practices and their interrelationship, Kay excels in providing solutions that complement the organization as a whole and provides the framework for continual improvement. She earned her MBA from the Florida Institute of Technology and is a Certified Management Consultant (CMC) awarded through the Institute of Management Consultants. More information can be found at Interatctive Consulting's website www.interactiveconsultingusa.com or by calling 1.830.864.4267.

Grow or Die!

Ramp Up Your Revenues and Your Career With a Strategic Growth System

by Bill Howe

W all Street's infatuation with short-term quarterly profits is summed up by the phrase ... *"Show me the money!"* This demand by public and private shareholders has contributed to an epidemic of executives guilty of *over-managing* the bottom-line. They raise their gaze just enough to zero in on costs as the culprit. Over the past few years, this phenomenon has spawned a frenzy of cutbacks, both in budgets and in headcount.

In the short-term, these Draconian measures appear to work. Costs go down and profits rise, but trouble is on the horizon. After all the "right-sizing" of people and budget slashes, the survivors must face the ugly reality that fewer people must achieve far more with far less. Is it any wonder that managers are burned out? They live in a world of "permanent whitewater," careening from one crisis to the next, with little control over the companies they are paid to manage.

Misguided Mastery ... Failing on the Fundamentals

In many situations, cost cutting is prudent. However, this approach has become a crutch for many executives who see cutbacks as their *first course of action, rather than the last resort.*

Management must go upstream to the true headwaters of the cash flow that sustains every company: top-line revenue. Revenue growth is the true measure of business vitality. It reflects a company's competency to acquire, satisfy, and grow its customer base. Management Guru, Tom Peters' directive on this issue is clear. *"You can't save your way to prosperity."*

Management teams that focus too much on cost-containment and not enough on revenue growth often suffer from the following symptoms:

- Static or declining revenues;
- Loss in market share;
- Personal feelings of lost control, constantly reacting to market-place... "permanent whitewater;"
- Disappointing results from new "big bet" growth initiatives (i.e. a new product launch);
- Employees who are confused about the strategy.

If any of these symptoms sound like your organization, you're not alone.

Reality Check – Corporate America's Planning Process is Broken

The real problem is this: Many executives do not know how to create an effective plan, mobilize their team, and make revenue growth a reality.

Planning of any kind is hard work, whether it's the annual business plan or the long-range strategic plan. The most elemental job of management, *"to Plan the Work and Work the Plan,"* really is not so elemental. Because planning is typically done once year, most executives aren't proficient and it always feels above and beyond one's normal job.

It is easy to understand why planning of any kind is a major source of stress for executives. No one has ever taught them how to do it…it is just something they are expected to do. But a business can only be as good as its growth strategy. Most experienced managers would also agree that "bad systems beat good people every time," yet the fact is their planning system is failing and beating them.

Classic planning failures include:

- **Budgets on Steroids** – The plan is little more than an explosion of budget details and financials with virtually no thought given to the actual strategy required to achieve the numbers.
- **"Inside-out" Management** – Management's preoccupation with internal operational matters results in little or no focus on the outside marketplace, including competitors, intermediary customers, and the end-consumer.
- **Quick and Dirty "Outside-in" Analysis** – A rudimentary list, or SWOT Analysis (strengths, weaknesses, opportunities, and threats), is performed by listing problems without defining an action plan.
- **Confidential "For Our Eyes Only"**– The sensitive nature of the plan causes management to overreact by keeping *"where we are going and how we will get there"* a top-level secret. Mid-level managers and employees, those who perform the work, haven't a clue.
- **3 Inch Thick Shelf-ware** – These plans are both exhaustive in scope and exhausting to read with too much data and not enough insight and usable information. Their bulk discourages use and defies comprehension, thus the plan becomes dusty shelf-ware.

Contrast these all-too-common failure modes with the very reason for creating a plan in the first place. The unspoken hope is that time and effort will spark insights leading to significant competitive advantage and business growth. The pivotal word here is *insight*, and this can be thought of as *seeing* things differently, of envisioning potential opportunity where others (competitors) do not. This brings us to an exciting revelation.

A Nobel Prize-Winning Discovery Points to a Better Way

Neuroscientist Roger Sperry won a Nobel Prize in 1981 for discovering the human brain has two hemispheres that operate separately and with distinctly different capacities. The logical, linear left-brain is the *Verbal* brain; it has the ability to construct meaning from words and numbers. The emotional, creative right brain is the *Visual* brain; it has the unique ability to comprehend pictures, discern patterns and to conceptualize.

While awareness of the existence of two specialized brains in human beings is common knowledge today, surprisingly few people attempt to leverage these findings. Considerable research since 1981 suggests the visual brain can process pictures much faster, perhaps hundreds of times faster, than the verbal brain can process words. Although the expression "a picture is worth a thousand words" is commonplace, the potential application of this insight, if properly directed, is enormous.

The irony is that corporate America focuses on traditional planning processes that are almost entirely left (Verbal) brain in nature. Generating vast quantities of words and numbers makes the effort a non-starter for effective knowledge transfer. Rather than perpetuating a process that doesn't work, it's time to stretch our thinking and try a new approach. As Albert Einstein noted, *"The current problems we face cannot be solved at the same level of thinking with which they were created."*

Success Formula – Putting Leadership and Vision Back In Planning

Executives have a significant opportunity to boost performance in management's most important job…create a plan that builds the business by growing revenues. Over the past few years alone, thousands of companies and millions of careers have lost the struggle to "grow or die."

Today's executives will certainly recognize the inherent challenge to suddenly "*think* differently." If any real change is to happen, executives must first be encouraged to "*see* differently." The pictures that follow provide a template to guide the strategy-setting process and should in turn be used to facilitate understanding throughout the organization. Each graphic addresses a specific problem that management teams face in today's planning process:

    1) Complex problems constantly bombard management teams and require their entire focus. Meeting each day's new challenges makes it almost impossible to step back and see The Big Picture.

The *Strategic Line-of-Sight™* Growth System provides the necessary perspective to proactively lead the organization against four key components.

2) Executives struggle to find a way to effectively communicate their position in the market, with whom they compete, and where they hope to take the business. *The Market Map* is a powerful tool that captures how your customers actually perceive competing brands.

3) Managers want an edge over their competitors, but few have clarity on how to get it. This issue fundamentally boils down to differentiation, and there are only *3 Competitive Advantage Strategies* to achieve it. They must focus everything they have on mastering one strategy and avoid the common trap of trying to straddle two or more.

4) Many companies perform rudimentary SWOT Analyses (strengths, weaknesses, opportunities, and threats) resulting in lengthy *laundry lists* with *no accountability.* The crucial question is, "So What?" A Smarter SWOT is to first prioritize the findings, and then assign one person to *Own and Resolve* each.

5) Executives recognize the imperative to build revenues, but most are only aware of one way–growing the number of Customers. This simplistic view steals important focus from three other equally viable alternatives. *The Revenue-Customer Purchase Model* highlights all four components.

The following methodology addresses five deceptively simple questions that are equally applicable in both B2B and B2C industries. In stark contrast, many companies are unable to answer these today, even *after* a protracted planning process. By illustrating the progression from target market segments to top-line revenues, you create a picture of success that you can broadly communicate throughout the organization.

Strategic Line-of-Sight™ Growth System

Five Fundamental Questions

The graphics (pictures) below would be used in the Plan to illustrate the answers.

1) Where – *Where* are you currently positioned in the marketplace and what space do you seek to control at the end of the planning horizon? (1/3/5 years)

A. Label the market segments you are targeting.

B. Locate your current and desired Brand position.

C. Plot location (proximity) and relative size of direct Competitors.

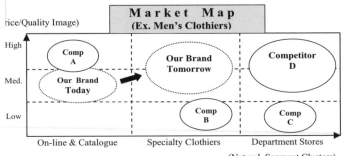

Market Map
(Ex. Men's Clothiers)

(Natural Segment Clusters)

2) How – *How* will you attack the market? Business strategy boils down to *Difference*. Which of the three fundamental (differentiation) strategies for Competitive Advantage will you pursue?

A. Low Cost: There can only be one!

B. Differentiation: Possibilities depend on market.

C. Customer Loyalty: Whatever it takes to please the customer; not tied to our standard offering.

---

3 Competitive Advantage Strategies

Low Rd.
(Low Cost)
1

Different Rd.
(Differentiation)
2

High Rd.
(Customer Loyalty)
3

---

3) and 4) What and Who – W*hat* are the top three priorities for each environmental assessment quadrant? The focus is on proactively managing today's realities and anticipating tomorrow's possibilities. *Who* will be responsible for:

A. Leveraging Strengths?

B. Improving Weaknesses?

C. Capturing Opportunities?

D. Mitigating Threats?

A *Smarter* S-W-O-T Analysis

Strengths:		Opportunities:	
Priority	Owner	Priority	Owner
1.		1.	
2.		2.	
3.		3.	
Weaknesses:		Threats:	
Priority	Owner	Priority	Owner
1.		1.	
2.		2.	
3.		3.	
Today's Realities		Tomorrow's Possibilities	

5) Which – *Which* of the four fundamental Revenue components are you targeting for growth? Specify objectives and strategies for each:
   A. Customers – Traditional focus; but difficult.
   B. Frequency – Purchase cycle time interval.
   C. Transaction – # of units Purchased at a time.
   D. Price – Opportunity to increase or up-sell/cross-sell.

R E V E N U E			
Customer Purchase Model			
C x	**F** x	**T** x	**P**
Customers	Frequency	Transaction	Price

See Your Future Success

True leaders readily embrace the critical insight that business success is about the ability to help the rest of the organization see the desired *destination* and the bold *path forward*. The *Strategic Line-of-Sight™ Growth System* delivers a guided discovery of the necessary steps to achieve revenue growth.

Rather than remaining stuck in the "work harder" trap of managing today's sub-optimal planning process, executives must step-up to the *leadership* challenge of discovering a better way. One of the qualities ascribed to leaders is *Vision*…literally the ability to see and comprehend what others (followers) do not. In this context, it is clear that "working smarter" means leveraging the extraordinary power of the visual brain to rapidly communicate complex information by illustrating four high-leverage planning tools integral to a strategic growth system.

About the Author

Bill Howe is President of Strategic Marketing Group, a management consulting firm specializing in "Go-to-Market" Strategy. This methodology integrates total business strategy with marketing, sales, and brand strategy. Clients range from corporate giants in the U.S. and Europe to small businesses in a variety of industries. Bill's unique experience spans both ends of the business spectrum from V.P. Marketing in Fortune 100 corporations, such as the Pillsbury Company and Bell Atlantic (now Verizon), to President/CEO of small and mid-size companies. The new businesses he has launched and the failing ones that were turned have gone on to collectively generate over $2 billion in annual revenues.
Email: info@growthguru.com or Phone: 1.703.629.1452

Deliver That Plan!
How Leaders Convert Their Strategic Plans into Winning Results
by Meredith Kimbell

One of a leader's most painful moments comes when a strategic plan fails. Fortunately, you can avoid this setback. Your plan can deliver the strategic results you want.

Realize that your plan is not likely the source of your disappointment; rather, your plan implementation is the probable culprit. Why? Because the skills you use to define strategy are different than the skills you use to implement it. Strategic plans are rational. They depend on data. Implementation is not rational. It depends on people. Most strategic plans collapse because "real world" demands divert attention from priorities. Markets shift, customer needs change, and functional leaders compete instead of cooperate.

Implementation falters when people lose their focus, urgency, or optimism. As a business owner or senior level executive, you can use the following keys to create the clarity, accountability, coordination, speed, and consistency you need to transform your ideas into results.

Key One – Create Individual and Joint Ownership
Your strategy has goals and success metrics, but those aren't enough. Someone must say, "It's my job!" Without one person accountable for "owning" delivery of each goal, no one will drive the organization's focus, performance, and collaboration to achieve the result.

Goal owners build plans and budgets, negotiate cross-functional agreements, drive resolution of issues, and deliver monthly milestones. In addition to appropriate technical competence, check that each owner has these three traits:

- Enthusiasm to enroll others, spark creativity, and sustain momentum through tough times. If no one has passion for a particular goal, reconsider its value. Proceeding without passion is a prescription for mediocrity.

- Control of sufficient resources (budget, people, access to information) to achieve results. Wrestle the issue of "sufficient" to the ground as a team to reduce this common source of breakdown.

- Influence to protect fledgling projects, enroll support, secure resources, and keep the goal a top priority on everyone's agenda.

You face constant trade-off decisions during implementation, so expect owners to wear two hats: one for their individual goal, and another for the whole plan. Have them guarantee that they will collaborate, rather than compete, by asking all to sign off on their commitment to deliver the entire plan together. Expect the team to deal with the tension of achieving every goal and it will deliver the whole plan.

Finally, as a leadership team, review and approve each goal owner's plan, metrics for success, resource requests, and cross-functional agreements. Realistic preparation encourages staff to implement goals with optimism and ambition, not eye-rolling skepticism.

Checkpoints:
- Does your plan have one enthusiastic owner for each goal?
- Does each goal owner have the resources to deliver your targets?
- Has each team member committed to collaboratively deliver every goal in the plan?

Key Two – Monitor and Publicize Goal Metrics Monthly

Every hospital emergency room routinely checks "vital signs." Similarly, your leadership team must monitor your company's vital signs so it responds quickly if they reveal deteriorating strategic health. When you manage by gut feel rather than data you risk veering off course and delaying recovery.

At least once a month, discuss your company's "vital signs" and progress on each strategic goal. A scorecard will keep everyone focused on your most important priorities, build momentum, catch surprises, and help address obstacles. Initially, public reviews can be stressful, but they will improve consistency and velocity if you emphasize positive progress and resolve problems collaboratively.

Publish results to the whole organization each month, both successes and shortfalls. Engage hearts and strengthen the culture by showing how each step of progress advances the company's mission, vision, and values. Create urgency by highlighting how each shortfall threatens them.

Remember that strategy should provide laser focus, not a fireworks display of diverse goals vying for attention. Cut complexity and choose a critical few milestone goals for the coming months. Chances are slim that a team or organization will recall, much less implement, more than ten key priorities successfully. Keep it simple. Expect every function to define and monitor goals and metrics for each priority they support. Aligning the whole organization's targets in this way puts everyone's oars in the water and synchronizes the work that produces success.

Checkpoints:
- Is your team monitoring and publishing the organization's vital signs and strategic progress every month?
- Do you prioritize only the "critical few" milestone goals each month to keep everyone's focus clear?
- Do you cascade goal setting and monitoring to ensure everyone is achieving your most important priorities?

Key Three – Learn from Successes and Mistakes

Mistakes are both inevitable and necessary if you stay on the leading edge. Winners make mistakes, but they also catch them and correct them faster than others.

Use your monthly meetings as an opportunity to identify and explore issues openly as peers collaborating to discover success. Accelerate learning by creating a culture of high-participation, curiosity, dialogue, support for risk taking, and clear decision-making as you implement strategy. The following practices will help:

- Publicize best practices. Follow reports of progress with, "How did you do that?" Sharing practices that work builds not only new competence across the organization, but new excitement and confidence as well.

- Say "Thanks!" to those who surface problems quickly. Breakdowns are a terrific source of learning and the first step toward new success, so appreciate those who speak up.

- Move past frustration and disappointment. Explore the cause of setbacks and resolve questions in a safe environment for learning.

- Require everyone to suggest solutions rather than decry the problems. "What would you suggest we do to move forward on this issue?" is a powerful question that keeps everyone advancing towards success.

- Define new agreements and publicize these to all contributors. As you adjust the plan, bring all players on board the new train of thought and action.

While the practices above will help every team learn effectively, the senior leadership team has two unique tools for accelerating progress: 1) Use systematic employee, customer, and vendor feedback to give you quick insight to trends and problems. The faster you identify issues, the faster your organization can resolve them. 2) Be ready to change infrastructure and core processes, re-allocate resources, and re-design performance systems to accelerate strategic success throughout implementation. Little frustrates and de-motivates employees more than distraction and interference from these core systems.

Executives who master use of these learning tools build a clear source of competitive advantage. When they model and coach these practices across the organization they help create the agile, resilient, "learning organization" needed for market leadership.

Checkpoints:

- Is your executive team confronting issues, exploring solutions, and adapting quickly?
- Are you publicizing and driving adoption of best practices across your organization?
- Are you designing policies and processes to encourage the behavior and results you want?

Key Four – Sustain Enthusiasm

Enthusiasm is the magic ingredient for greatness. Those who love their work are creative, tenacious, and resilient. They produce outstanding results. You can fuel enthusiasm six ways:

- Assure the goals you set are truly meaningful to those who implement them. Show people how their efforts create meaningful value for customers and not just financial gain for stockholders.

- Tell employees about the strengths of your people and organization. Tell stories of going the extra mile for a customer, of collaborating across functions to create a breakthrough innovation, and of contributing to a community project. These accounts fuel the sense of belonging, pride, and courage needed to persevere day in and day out.

- Be honest about setbacks (everyone probably knows about them already) and plans to correct them. Your people will respond with rededicated effort when you handle problems publicly, fairly, and quickly.

- Invest in success. Assure teams have the resources, training, and political access they need to succeed. Major change is hard. When people feel equipped, they rise to the challenge.

- Challenge everyone to answer the "how" questions. "How can we accomplish this goal? How can we overcome this obstacle?" What people create, they identify with and will help improve. Engaging people in innovation, project teams, cross-functional experiments, or direct customer contact builds their competence and commitment.

- Address non-performers, fast. Whether moving them into a new role or out of the organization, you will improve everyone's performance when they know they are part of a top-flight team.

Captivating attention and igniting enthusiasm with powerful goals, stories of outstanding performance, and a positive work environment mobilize learning, innovation, and productivity. With both head and heart engaged, your people will distinguish your organization with style, service, and quality that is exceptional in your marketplace.

Checkpoints:

- Do you create optimism and strengthen ambition in your interactions with others?
- Are you personally enthusiastic about your strategic agenda?
- Do you address poor performers quickly?

Deliver Your Strategic Goals

Implementation is about people, not plans. Give people a meaningful challenge, show them the organization's performance monthly, help them learn, and unleash their enthusiasm. Unless your markets change substantially, hold firm to your goals to provoke creativity and change. Breakthroughs happen during tension. When your leadership team holds high expectations, you leverage everyone's learning, creativity, collaboration, and success.

Converting a strategic plan into results is an adventure filled with turns, surprises, and dangers. Unlock success today by using these four keys. Also remember to ask for the support of experts who can help you acquire new finesse, navigate the course, and reach the finish line. Enjoy the victory celebration.

About the Author

Meredith Kimbell is President and founder of Corporate Adventure, located in Reston, VA. As an organization performance consultant and leadership coach for mid-sized businesses nationally and internationally, she has helped clients in diverse industry segments achieve new levels of productivity, fulfillment, and profitability. As a licensed Psychologist (VT-Master), she brings a unique combination of business and people insight and solutions to senior leaders. Ms. Kimbell can be reached at mkimbell@corporateadventure.com and 1.703.471.7745.

Design Your Business as a System

How to Manage Through Processes, Not People

by Erik S. Olson

According to the Small Business Administration, 80% of new businesses fail within the first five years. Most *franchises,* however, survive, with only a 20% failure rate within those same five years. Why the big disparity? Most "regular" businesses are people driven, inclusive of all the inconsistencies people possess. Most franchise businesses, however, are systems-driven. Franchises go beyond the people running it and develop the needed standardization in order to achieve success.

Before delving into the crucial differences between a franchise and a "regular" business, let's first answer the question, "What is a business?" *A business is an entity designed to consistently deliver a specific type of result to a specific type of consumer, and to endlessly improve itself over time.* We can break each part of this statement into four concepts that can benefit your company.

1) **A business is an entity** – An entity is, "The existence of something considered apart from its properties." This means your business is something apart from you, apart from your employees, and apart from your current customer list. Your business has its own life.

2) **Designed to consistently produce a specific type of result** – For all businesses, lack of consistency is the number one customer complaint. Customers prefer predictability to occasional brilliance. Businesses get into trouble when they lose focus on their core deliverable. If you own a dry-cleaning business, for example, don't branch out into unrelated fields, like cable installation. Focus on cleaning clothes and do it right every time. After you have mastered that skill, then and only then, think about adding related services, such as tailoring.

3) **To a specific group of consumers** – Don't ever say your target market is "everybody!" Unless you're selling air to people on the moon, your product can't possibly appeal to "everybody." Design your business to attract and serve a specific type of consumer. Stamp collectors, retired military personnel, manufacturers with revenues between five and fifteen million dollars per year . . . you get the picture. Be specific.

63

4) Endlessly improve itself over time – Nothing is static. The universal law of nature is, "If you're not growing, you're dying." Whether we're referring to people, plants, or businesses, that law is a universal constant. You must plan for competition getting tougher and customers becoming more demanding.

How Your Business Can Get These Benefits

No matter what business you're in, you can break your business down into a series of processes. Each process consists of a series of steps that produce your consistent result. For example, making a pizza starts with rolling out the dough. Then you spread out the sauce. Next you add cheese, and then finally the toppings. If you spoon the sauce onto the counter first, then add cheese, you have a mess, not a pizza. You must complete each step in the correct order to end up with a quality finished product.

An entrepreneur who is very skilled at a particular trade, like plumbing, advertising, welding, or graphic design, starts most "regular" businesses. The entrepreneur typically starts his or her business to capitalize on those skills, paying little attention to market demand. Because the entrepreneur is so skilled, the business depends upon the entrepreneur to satisfy the customers' needs. Without the entrepreneur, the business does not exist. In short, the *business* owns the entrepreneur.

Most franchise-type businesses, however, are started to satisfy a verified market need independent of the owner's skills, talents, or abilities. For example, if you own a McDonald's franchise, it doesn't matter how skilled a cook you are. In fact, your technical skills have nothing to do with delivering the product to the consumer. Such "franchise-type" businesses are systematized to produce and deliver consistently acceptable products for a specific market segment, regardless of who owns it or who works there.

How do "franchise-type" businesses achieve that independence? They do it by mapping out the processes of each business segment and integrating each of those processes into a seamless whole–a systems-driven business.

In order to own a successful "franchise-type," systems-driven business, balance the following four key processes in your "regular" business.

1. Finance Processes

Control the money or the money will control you. We can sum the systemization of Finance into three words: Planning, Budgeting, and Tracking.

- **Planning** is looking forward and predicting what will happen in the future. Planning is an on-going process, not a "one-time" task. Most entrepreneurs do very little planning, which hurts them terribly. Not planning is like driving by only looking in your rear-view mirror. Planning allows you to influence the future. The better your planning, the more influence you have.

- **Budgeting** is the end product of your planning. Budget your expenses. More important, budget your revenues. By budgeting income for the next twelve months you predict exactly how much money will come into your business, how much money will flow out of your business, and how much profit your business will earn for you. If you don't plan for profit, chances are, like most other business owners in America, you won't have any.

- **Tracking** reality against budgets and planning completes the circle. Tracking allows you to adjust budgets to reflect reality. Track performance, compare to budgets, and review your plan. This feedback loop is critical to successfully designing a "franchise-type" business.

2. Marketing Processes

By developing a marketing process, you won't need to question what your sales will be a year from now. The two keys of a marketing process are **Lead Generation** and **Lead Conversion**.

- **Lead Generation** is consistently getting your message in front of new, specific potential clients with a series of compelling reasons ("offers") for them to call, write, e-mail, come into the store, or otherwise contact your business. Design a series of "offers" that will easily allow you to measure their effectiveness. You can measure the offer by simply questioning, "How much money did we spend to get 20 (or some other number) new clients?" Now you have feedback as to which offers were the most profitable. Keep the winners, cut the losers, and keep experimenting to see which work best.

- **Lead Conversion** creates actual clients from possible clients. The definition of a client is someone who gives you money for your product or service. Lead Conversion is commonly thought of as "Sales."

Train your staff with a methodical sales system and you will increase your overall conversion rate, control the client experience, and make sure each and every client receives consistent, respectful, professional treatment, regardless of which salesperson he or she speaks to.

With your Marketing Budget, you can map out how many offers you will advertise and when you will offer them. And because you have tracked the profitability of each offer, you can now plan your revenues with certainty. One of the best uses of a Marketing Budget is to systematically increase sales during seasonal slumps. By doing so, you boost annual profits, smooth cash flows, and avoid "feast/famine" headaches.

3. Management Processes

To satisfy the goal of creating a "franchise-type" model, your business cannot depend on any one "key" individual (especially you!). Management processes document exactly how each employee will act, talk, dress, interact with customers and fellow employees, and so on.

Far beyond mere dress codes, you are designing the business so that if your manuals were shipped to another country, someone who has never met you could duplicate your entire enterprise. And if you, the founder, walked into such a place, you would instantly understand everything that was going on.

Map out exactly what each position in your company entails, including the duties involved, work schedule, compensation plan, etc. Now you are managing positions instead of people. When you do this, you will find that your employees are happier because they know precisely what you expect of them, how they will be held accountable, what resources are available to them, and how much authority they have. In short, creating Management Processes takes the guesswork out of working for your company.

4. Operations Processes

The purpose of Operations is Client Fulfillment, which means satisfying each and every client to expectation (and beyond). To predictably achieve Client Fulfillment, you need to control every step of creating your deliverable.

Start by creating a flowchart that includes each step in the deliverable chain. Involve your Operators (employees directly involved in client fulfillment). These people know how to improve your processes, make changes that improve productivity, improve consistency, and make everyone's lives happier.

Be warned that your employees may be skeptical at first. You must follow through with any commitments, otherwise you will sabotage the program. You and your team will also need to review the process chart periodically to streamline it again and again.

Make the Processes Work for You

Map out each of your four main processes (Finance, Marketing, Management, Operations). Then map out each sub-function (Lead Generation, Lead Conversion, and Client Fulfillment.) Combining each set of processes gives you a "franchise-type" or systems-driven business.

Creating systems in your business will enable your business to more independent, your customers more satisfied, and your employees to feel more job stability and security. Most important, systems are your key to freedom. You can now truly own your business instead of it owning you.

About the Author

Erik Olson is founder and president of Entrepreneurial Success, LLC, a management consulting firm based in St. Cloud, MN that is revolutionizing the way businesses are run. Erik has created the *Jumpstart! Your Business – An Entrepreneur's Guide to Getting Going* program, designed to help new entrepreneurs start their business successfully, and the *6 Months To Success – Increase Your Bottom Line by a Minimum of 20% in 6 Months, Guaranteed!* program. Erik has authored over 150 articles dealing with business ownership, profitability, marketing, customer service, and entrepreneurial thinking.

For more information about Entrepreneurial Success, LLC, please call 1.320.257.7770, e-mail: InfoStCloud@EntrepreneurialSuccess.com, or please visit Erik's website: www.EntrepreneurialSuccess.com.

Providing Customer Service to the Customer Service Team

by Sat Singh Panesar

One of the biggest challenges senior level executives face is getting frontline employees to consistently deliver on the company's promise. Since these are the employees who interact with customers on a daily basis and represent the company to the public, it is crucial, and somewhat obvious, that frontline workers have the tools, resources, and support to do their jobs effectively. Unfortunately, this is not always the case. As a result, frontline employees in most companies are frustrated and not performing to their full potential. They feel under-appreciated, irrelevant and, thanks to the psychological structure of the corporate hierarchy, dispirited with carrying the burden of a variety of managers and supervisors bearing down on them at every moment. Even though most are willing and perfectly capable of performing to company expectations, they choose to not step-up above and beyond the bare minimum.

Why do they feel this way? In many companies today, leaders invest thousands of dollars in marketing and advertising to promote their promise of a better product or service. They then spend thousands of dollars more on customer surveys and guest satisfaction reports in order to find out how well the company delivered their promises, what they can do to improve things, and what exactly their customers want. Then they implement new processes and procedures based on the data they collect, circumventing the very people who often know the customers' needs most intimately—the frontline worker. The simple task of company leaders listening to their frontline employees and asking for their input on customer matters could result in the company saving thousands of dollars on costly surveys and boosting morale in the process.

Turn Things Around

The secret to getting valuable feedback from frontline workers and saving the company money is to symbolically turn the organizational chart upside down. In a typical organization, the organizational chart is a triangle, with the CEO at the top. From there it branches off to the various department managers and supervisors and then down to the sub-departments and employees, who form the triangle's base. The mentality is that those on the lower levels report to those on the upper levels.

When you turn the organizational chart upside down, you change the mindset from "the lower level reports to the upper level" to "the upper level supports the lower level." The shift is simple, yet profound, and it's more than mere semantics.

Unfortunately, when most senior level executives hear this statement, they panic and get defensive. They immediately think: "Does this mean I'm losing my office?" "Am I losing my authority?" "Do I give up my assistant?" In reality, when companies turn the organizational chart upside down, they lose nothing yet gain plenty. They gain focus on the company's goals; they gain happier employees; they gain more satisfied customers; and they gain higher profits. It's a win-win situation on all sides.

In order to create such a mindset shift in your own organization, follow the guidelines below.

1. Gain senior level buy-in.

In order for any new directive to take hold, you need the buy-in of everyone involved. And regardless of the directive, whether it involves how you organize a report to how you view the organizational chart, you will encounter resistance. The key is to show the senior level executives how this new mindset will save them time and money and achieve company goals in the long run.

In most companies, executives spend about 34% of their time handling frontline customer service challenges. To win back this third of their day and have more time to handle other tasks, executives need to constantly ask themselves, "What do I need to do to make the frontline jobs easier?" When this question guides every decision they make, they automatically begin acting like a supporter rather than a reporter (someone who watches from the sidelines and does nothing). They begin thinking beyond current challenges and "flavors of the day" and start seeing more clearly the full impact their decisions have on every employee.

Now, this does not mean that they ignore their usual job duties in order to assist the frontline employees. It means that they address and take care of the obstacles and hurdles that prevent the frontline from performing their one and only job—that of delivering on the company promise. This proactive support results in less interruption between the frontline and management day in and day out.

Fifty percent of your executive team will embrace the shift right away; for the remainder, a series of get-togethers or short retreats will solidify the buy-in.

2. Gain frontline employee buy-in.

With the support of the senior team, it's time to gain buy-in from the frontline workers. Schedule a team briefing with all your employees. Call it a Town Hall, a Huddle or whatever you'd like, just be careful not to call it a meeting. When most employees hear there'll be a meeting, they automatically think, "Uh-oh. Now what?" Strive to keep the mood light and conversational. Having food, music, and giveaways during the team briefing helps keep everyone upbeat.

Once everyone is gathered, encourage an open dialog between the senior level members present and the frontline workers. Ask the frontline employees for their feedback on the following questions:

- What do you need to make your job easier?
- What do you hear from customers?
- Where are your frustrations?
- Where are your successes?
- Where are your challenges?

As they give you feedback, write their answers on a flipchart so everyone can see them. Now is not the time to defend or justify management positions; just listen and write. Once you have all the answers you need, explain that you will be analyzing the answers and conducting another team briefing in exactly one week.

At the next team briefing, recap the information you gathered. For most companies, they'll find that 30% of what their frontline employees do works well for both customer and employee and does not need adjustment. Another 30% of their tasks are actually holding them back and could do with delegation or flat-out elimination, and the rest need only slight refinements. Then, introduce your team to the new mindset shift (upside down chart) and detail how it will help eliminate some of the barriers that hold them back.

Explain that part of this mindset shift is that their supervisor is there to provide support and to supervise only through guidance and reminders of the company's policies. The interactions between employee and supervisor are no longer, "I'm doing what you want me to do." Rather, they become: "This is what I need from you to deliver on this promise to our customer." The supervisor will then support the team with this mission.

Empower the frontline workers to do whatever they must to make the customer happy, including matching prices, buying meals, and upgrading products or services, without having to get a supervisor's approval each time. This helps the employees realize that they have the ability to listen to the customers and make immediate and appropriate decisions. Simple appeasement charts, listing which acceptable actions to take to appease customers in various situations, may help.

If you get resistance at the frontline level, paint the picture of "how the dollar travels." Many companies often neglect to share the big picture with employees. During the hiring/training process, they focus on the specific job duties only. They fail to spell out how relevant that job is to the entire company. So during this team briefing, detail how the dollar travels from the customer, up through the ranks in accounting, through profit margins, and ultimately to the stockholder. This will help solidify the frontline mentality that their jobs are absolutely relevant and important. They'll see that they are the touch-point where the dollar transfers from the customer to the entire company.

3. Create an environment of sharing

Every week, allow all employees to come together to share best practices. What did they do to wow a customer or turnaround a challenging situation? Also ask employees for their suggestions on what needs to be done to improve customer relations or the company in general. Write down what you hear, and be sure to implement at least one suggestion each week. If you always ask for feedback but never act on it, eventually people will stop offering their ideas.

Additionally, keep employees up-to-date on their progress in terms of customer satisfaction. Keep a chart in their work area, in the break room, or at the employee entrance that lists each time an employee's name is mentioned on a customer survey card, every time a customer writes a complimentary letter about an employee, and any other positive feedback that would boost morale. Update these charts on a daily basis. Get teams together, give them team names, provide prizes monthly, and make it fun.

A New Mindset for a New Business Environment

After this mindset shift takes hold in the company, conduct employee and customer satisfaction surveys every three months. Each time you do, you'll see the satisfaction ratings in both areas improve. Within a year, you'll notice a marked increase in profits as well.

The fact is that your customers can get similar products and services as yours from a variety of sources. The only thing that sets you apart is your customer service and your genuine appreciation of their business. When your frontline workers know they have the support of the entire executive team, they're more apt to deliver the quality service that keep customers coming back.

About the Author

Sat Singh Panesar is a veteran of the Hospitality/Restaurant and Retail industry. He has trained thousands of frontline employees in the art and science of delivering the company promise for nationally recognized companies such as Starwood Hotels and Resorts, Morton's of Chicago Steakhouses, Palomino Restaurants and Weider Health & Fitness Europe. He is President of Sat Panesar & Associates, a Business Development and Management firm located in Palm Desert, California. Trained in London, England he currently lives in Rancho Mirage, California with his wife and son. Contact him at 1.760.774.1516 or e-mail: satpanesar@hotmail.com.

Partnering in the New Economy for Increased Market Share

by Charles Stubbs

The combination of telecommunications and information technology creates a growing opportunity for businesses to access new markets and deliver products and services to a wider range of end customers. Universality, a rapidly burgeoning and increasingly sophisticated customer demand, and a complex and interrelated supply chain characterize this new Information and Communications Technology (ICT) economy.

For success in this economy, you and your business need to adapt to take advantage of new market opportunities. You also need to focus on what you do best and what distinguishes you from the competition–your key competences. Finally, you need to learn how to outsource some activities currently performed in-house, such as product manufacture or managing your corporate network, and you need to become less risk-averse.

Most important, all businesses in the ICT economy need to learn how to partner with other organizations in ways they haven't done before, and with far less certainty about the outcome. Businesses will experience less certainty because partnerships will be established on the basis of a loosely defined market opportunity, rather than for a specific project. However, for those that do succeed, the rewards will be substantial. The ICT economy will be a "winner takes all" game in which a few, well-organized and coordinated consortia of collaborating companies will take control of the markets they choose to play in.

Your first steps towards getting your business prepared for new economy markets are:
- Understand the partnering issues that will arise;
- Incorporate these issues into your strategy development process.

The New Competitive Model for Business

The role of information has a profound effect on the way products and services are delivered. Alongside the physical delivery channel, suppliers must ensure they have effective, interactive electronic channels for delivering information. This takes companies outside their areas of key competence and forces them to gain access to new skills and new distribution channels. So rather than being able to "go it alone," every company will need to find partners who can deliver those ingredients of the product and services mix that they either are unable to or choose not to provide themselves.

Market forces (the "economics of information") combined with growing technological capability result in a new "partnering imperative." For most ICT companies, it is a simple choice: either collaborate or die. Only a few large organizations will attempt to do everything, through organic growth and/or acquisition. So you must:

- Analyze how your products and services will be delivered in the new economy;
- Identify which elements of the overall value proposition are important for you to keep or develop.

The Orchestrator

A small proportion of commercial operations will develop the key competence to organize collaborations of companies and market the capabilities of the consortia to the end customer. This type of business has been termed an "orchestrator." The competence it develops to make these collaborations successful and sustain them can be thought of as "corporate glue." This is a type of organizational capital–a unique and distinctive knowledge that enables the company to orchestrate product and service portfolios and develop successful, sustainable strategic linkages between partner companies.

Orchestrators build "value webs," which are groups of companies brought together to serve a particular market or market niche. Some companies in the value web have products, technology, intellectual property, skills, or some other attribute unique and crucial to sustain value in the target market. These are kept close to the orchestrator through recognized partnerships. Others in the web have contributions to make, but their lack of uniqueness or peripheral importance means the orchestrator's relationships with them are more transactional (i.e. similar to many outsourcing deals today). The result is a set of commercial arrangements much like a spider's web, with the orchestrator at the center of this web, guarding its own set of key competences; a small number of partners within an "inner circle," each contributing a vital component of the overall; and a larger number of remote suppliers–all held together by the orchestrator's "corporate glue." Ultimately, success of a value web depends on how well the orchestrator co-ordinates the activities of the companies involved to deliver what the market wants.

Every new economy player must strive to be part of one or more successful value webs. The question is: Where do you want to play? As a supplier, a partner, or an orchestrator?

Therefore:

- Decide in which market segments of the new economy your business fits;
- Identify which companies are likely to become orchestrators in those segments;
- For each market segment decide where you want to play: as a supplier, a partner, or orchestrator.

Don't think you must be a large company to be a successful orchestrator. What is more important is that you have a strong presence and brand in your target market segment. Within specific niche or geographically local markets (for example, providing information services to a metropolitan area), it is quite feasible for smaller businesses to develop the core competences, "corporate glue," and brand awareness necessary to be an orchestrator. Of course, it is also possible for your business to be an orchestrator in one market segment, and a partner or supplier in others. For example, you might have the knowledge, contacts, and brand recognition in your home market to be an orchestrator for your industry, but overseas you would seek to ally yourself with other companies positioning themselves to be orchestrators.

Partnering Issues

Unless you do everything yourself, or act as an orchestrator, there will arise some fundamental issues. In the composite value chain (the "value web"), how do companies articulate value to the end user? Traditionally, the power drifts downstream to those few companies close to the customer. Players in the new ICT economy must avoid becoming just a commodity supplier by finding new things to do. The customer base is becoming more of a spectrum than a set of discrete market segments. The organizations in direct contact with end users, with the flexibility to react quickly, will win.

All these changes will affect players' negotiating power with partners. You must work hard to make yourself attractive, either with protected and unique technology, excellent cost/quality, or other product/ service features, or by creating end user demand through branding (like "Intel inside"). One thing is for sure: The traditional way of setting up partnerships for collaborative work will change. Those organizations that anticipate and prepare for this change will be successful. Those that don't will be left out of the value webs.

- Work out what you can or need to offer to other companies in value webs;
- Analyze what preparations you must make to work this way.

Larger companies currently positioning themselves to take advantage of the opportunities the new economy brings are building loose confederations or associations, usually with smaller companies that have unique technology or some other distinctive advantage that "might be useful one day." In these cases, the developing partnership agreements cannot refer to specific projects, opportunities, or even market segments. They are more like an agreement to work together when a market opportunity arises. If your company is too risk-averse or otherwise unprepared to collaborate in this way, then you are already missing out on this growing trend. So the question is, "If an orchestrator knocked on your door tomorrow, would your business know how to respond?"

Partnering in the New ICT Economy

As a player in the new economy, you will have to make partnering simpler. You need to:

- Make your offerings easy to understand;
- Make your products/tools/support simple;
- Share information to raise your partners' awareness of what you can do.

Your legal/commercial advisors need to draw up guidelines for partnering, rather than creating bespoke contracts for every opportunity. They should check the activities of business development managers rather than drive the partnering process; otherwise it will take far too long.

Your company should also make itself "partnership ready." Ensure it has the right cultures, people, and systems in place to quickly negotiate and "bolt on" partnerships. You need to learn how to measure the performance of partnerships cost-effectively and manage them indirectly. This means you must set mutually agreed goals with your partners and develop automated processes to feed the results of partnering into your day-to-day corporate management systems. Specifically, you must ensure there are people in your organization who are targeted on making the partnerships successful and are rewarded appropriately.

Be Partnership Ready

For success in the new ICT economy, you and your business must understand that things are going to be different. Educate senior managers about the dynamics and structure, and then debate where your company wants to play in the value webs. Identify what competences the company will build and which ones it will outsource.

To prepare, every ICT business must identify suitable partners and learn how to collaborate on activities, knowledge, and competences, rather than on specific projects. Your company must be "partnership ready" and able to respond quickly to opportunities. Internally, you should set targets and manage the relationships that are already in place. Externally, you need to communicate value to partners and customers.

The bottom line is that you must build the right partnerships within value webs to support your company's goals and objectives. Only then will your company prosper in the new ICT economy.

About the Author

Charles Stubbs is a Partnerships and Channels Consultant based in Warwick, England. He advises companies how to develop business partnerships and make them successful and how to maximize sales channel effectiveness. You can contact Charles on +44 7753 600481, or sign up for his free monthly ezine at www.istaris.com/articlespage.html.

Power Partnerships™
Your Key to Exponential Growth
by Denise Trifiletti and Donald Treinen

A re you struggling to wear all the hats, juggle all the balls, and balance your personal and professional roles? Do you feel like you have too little time to do it all? Is it difficult to decide where to focus your efforts for maximum effectiveness?

Power Partnerships™ can provide the answer to these common difficulties and enhance your personal and professional growth. Your business and personal life both depend on effective partnerships, as these relationships *are* your competitive edge. They can help you create more referrals, higher sales revenues, greater sales margins, and product or service differentiation–all of which add up to more profits and exponential growth.

Power Partnerships are easy to build, once you know how. Let's first define what we mean by partnerships. The two fundamental types of partnerships that relate to your business are:

Partnerships internal to your business –
those between your:
- Organization and its leadership;
- Leadership and management;
- Managers and employees;
- Employees.

Partnerships external to your business –
those between you and:
- Your clients;
- Your prospects;
- Your networking associates;
- Your vendor and supplier network.

Both internal and external partnerships are important to the growth and well being of your company. In order to implement these partnerships effectively, you first need to evaluate your company by asking a few incisive questions developed to assist you in defining your areas of need.

Does your business...
- Struggle to find high quality, consistent leads?
- Spend too much time doing 'shotgun' networking to secure these leads?

- Want to convert more prospects to partners, raving fans, revenues, and referrals?
- Want to spend less time struggling and more time growing–exponentially?
- Want more referrals and testimonials from your clients?
- Need employees who are more satisfied, committed, and productive?

After you assess the answers to these questions, determine which ones apply to your company. This will tell you where you lack the necessary tools or information. You can then move on to the solution and building your partnerships.

Developing effective partnerships requires "**ASK**" (**Attitude**, **Skills** and **Knowledge**) with:

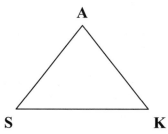

- Attitude at the top of the ASK triangle;
- "Asking" as the primary **Skill**; and
- **Knowledge** of a proven-effective partnership building model – **GROW**.

(A) Attitude

Your attitude shapes everything you think, say, and do, and your actions in turn shape how the world sees you and your business. Therefore, your attitude toward your business relationships should be supported by your business strategy, and should also agree with the attitudes of your business partners. If you believe your company is a "value-added" *solution provider*, and that you will win when you solve the problems of others, then you have already developed a winning attitude.

Next, you must decide how to go about solving your clients' problems. The best way to do this is to find as many Power Partners as you can to meet the needs of your prospects and clients. People and partnerships are your competitive edge and your primary strategy to grow exponentially. That means you will build internal and external partnerships at *every* opportunity. When businesses are linked through partnerships, everybody can win. Once you adopt this "abundance" mentality, you realize that business does not have to be a zero-sum game; that in fact, there is enough success to go around for everyone.

With this new attitude, you will be able to solve problems rather than just sell your product. You will also gain a competitive edge through differentiation, increased client satisfaction, referrals, and the increased revenues that are sure to follow. Your reputation for success in the marketplace will grow, and others will begin to emulate you.

It may help to remember the words of Charles Swindoll, the renowned minister, who said "We cannot change our past. We cannot change the fact that people will act a certain way. The only thing we can do is play on the one string we have, and that is our attitude. Life is 10% what happens to me, and 90% how I react to it. And so it is with you. We are *in charge of our attitudes*."

(S) Skill

The most important skill in life is to know how to successfully relate to others. In business–as in life–this means learning how to be a good partner. We learn a skill only by practicing, and practicing often.

To relate well, we must first seek to understand. To gain understanding, we ask questions…the more we ask, the greater our understanding, and the more powerful our partnerships. Thus, we have to practice "ASKing" to become skillful at developing partnerships. A good partnership can be formed only through learned skills.

Do you know how to ask in-depth questions that will uncover what the prospect believes is the value of your product or service? You need to know what your prospect sees as the value in your product so that you can use "value-based" pricing instead of "price war" pricing–and increase your margins.

If you and your team become competent in the skill of "ASKing," you will experience exponential growth. Hire a coach if you must, but commit to continuously improving this essential skill. Make this skill your competitive edge so you never lose a sale to the competition. You may win by a margin, but you win and so do your margins. Be like all the greatest athletes. Continuously hone your skills.

Make a list of the skills you and your team possess, as well as those you need but do not have. Then seek out those who can provide the needed skills, and build Power Partnerships with them.

(K) Knowledge

Knowledge means knowing where you are, where you want to go, and how to get there. This is the key to building effective business partnerships.

Knowledge is what you *know*–it's different than what you can do. Start by defining what you know, such as your company's vision and purpose. If you don't have a clear plan in writing, make one. It should contain every required aspect of your business. You can then integrate the plan into every professional partnership you create.

Next let's explore the knowledge you need to build Power Partnerships. This is the essential information necessary to grow your business. It encompasses all your knowledge about your business, your competition, your current markets, and your potential markets

Who can help you gain such knowledge? The answer is that your Power Partners can be your greatest source of information. Power Partners include individuals and companies who:

- Have the same target market but offer complimentary products and services.
- Offer the same products and services, but are in different target markets or in markets you wish to enter but have a different niche.
- Provide products and services you need in your business in order to grow.
- Need what you provide.

Create a written list of your potential Power Partners so that you have an easy list of resources for reference. After creating your list, begin to approach those partners with your model for exponential growth—for both you and your partner. In other words, make them an offer they can't resist!

Time to GROW

The following **GROW** model will allow you and your partners to grow together, and to grow exponentially. This model is useful for any professional partnership you wish to build.

- **G** – Goals
- **R** – Roles
- **O** – Operating
- **W** – Winning

GROW consists of:

- **Goals** – What are your goals? Do they include finances, marketing, client satisfaction, and ROI? Do they include a healthy relationship between your business and its partners? What do you need to grow your business?
- **Roles, responsibilities and resources** – What are your core competencies, strengths, and interests? What skills do you have? What resources can you and your people bring to others, and they to you?
- **Operating principles, expectations, and rules of engagement** These are the rules you will follow no matter what the situation.

They are your "Holy Book," what you will not compromise. They are your expectations and rules of engagement for doing business.

- **Winning, and how you know you've won** – Winning does **not mean** someone else must lose. On the contrary, it means 2 + 2 equals far greater than 4! It means abundance, mutual benefit and "gains for all."

For each rule, you need knowledge about your own company, as well as those of your partners. Once again, the best way to understand is to "**ASK**." The more you "**ASK**," the more you will build on your skills and knowledge base. So ask in-depth questions related to each area of the model to truly understand goals, roles, and operating principles. Remember:

- **A** – Have an "all-win" and "value-added" **Attitude!**
- **S** – Practice the **Skill** of asking in-depth questions related to each aspect of the GROW model to understand as much as possible.
- **K** – Use your **Knowledge** of the GROW model to clearly understand yourself and your partners.

Use **ASK** to build your Power Partner relationships. You can then apply these principles to Sales and Marketing, Client Satisfaction, and Employee Productivity and Retention. Any way you look at it, "**ASK**" is the key to Power Partnerships so that your company can **GROW** exponentially!

About the Authors

Denise, an ambitious graduate, entered corporate America, making her way to the top of Control Data as National Sales Training Manager, discovering her passion–the development of others. At subsequent and numerous sales positions she held top honors, and more important, developed a different view of sales. She became consciously competent in "value-based" solution selling through partnership building. Her mission is to help people achieve breakthroughs and exponential gains in their lives, through Power Partnerships.

Donald has over 37 years of experience, most in the corporate arena. He currently serves as the co-leader of three firms. His greatest achievement is being a mentor and change leader for individuals and groups committed to success through strategic partnerships. Don has extensive experience in developing and sustaining labor-management partnerships based on mutual gain, working with some of the largest firms and labor unions.

Denise and Don have been interviewed and published internationally. They speak, lead workshops, and consult one-on-one. They become change agents and partners within their client organizations. Dynamic Destiny Partnerships, LLC, a Maryland, USA-based firm, is about bottom-line results based on Power Partnerships!

Email: denise@d2partners.com or don@d2partners.com for a complimentary consultation or assessment of your partnership potential. And, visit our website at www.d2partners.com to subscribe to our free ezine: "Power of Partnerships"™... and GROW!

Section Two –
Leadership Development

Create Your Future Today
How to Set Goals that Unleash Your True Potential

by **Mark Victor Hansen**

Y ou have the power to attain any goal you want in life. Do you want to be successful in business? You can be. Do you want a loving relationship with a significant other? You can have it. Do you want a financially abundant life? It's yours–you simply need to know what you want and then ask for it. In fact, you can achieve *any* goal you set for yourself. Your potential is limitless.

Unfortunately, many people don't set goals, and as a result, they never get what they want from life. Sure, they may wish for things and dream about events transpiring, but because they never turn those wishes and dreams into goals, their results are less than spectacular. They simply settle for what life hands them rather than go out and create the extraordinary future they desire.

Most people neglect to set goals because they have never associated with someone who does set goals. They've never had a mentor who believed that goals get results and who could model and teach them goal-setting techniques. As a result, their self-esteem may be low, and they feel unworthy or too inadequate to create the kind of life they want. They don't believe that their goals are worth pursuing.

Your goals are worth pursuing! You can accomplish anything your heart desires. Others have done it before you; now it's your turn. Whether you're just starting your own business and need to jump-start your career or have been employed in a large corporation for many years and want to reach the next level, the following goal-setting and goal-attainment techniques will enable you to turn your dreams and wishes into goals and reality.

Define Your Purpose

Your purpose is the "why" behind all your goals. Why do you want what you want? What's the driving force or the motivation that propels you to want something? What are your values? Whatever it is, your purpose must be bigger than you. As you think about these questions, be sure you answer from your own viewpoint. Your purpose must be yours, not your spouse's, not your children's, not your co-worker's, and not your employer's. If you let other people's perspectives define your purpose, then you never get what you really want and you sabotage your future.

Many people are able to identify their purpose through meditation. If that does not work for you, find someone supportive to join you in a dyad. With your partner, sit face-to-face in a comfortable position. Look deeply into each other's eyes. Your partner's job is to ask you repeatedly for no less than five minutes, "What do you want?" Each time he or she asks, you answer with a statement of something you want from life. At first, your answers may be superficial, such as "I want to be happy," "I want to make a lot of money," or "I want to send my kids to college." That's okay. After your partner asks you what you want twenty or thirty times, your answers will get deeper. You'll enter a sacred space that's not threatening, and you'll hear yourself say some profound statements that define your life's purpose. For example, you may say, "I want to inspire disadvantaged children to finish school" or "I want to help people transform struggling businesses into profit-generating machines." That's purpose! Once you reach that point, keep going. Keep peeling back the layers to uncover the "why" in your life. You'll find that once you define the "why," the "how" and the "what" easily align.

Put Your Goals on Paper

Armed with your purpose, you can begin to define the specific goals you want to attain. To do so, set aside twenty minutes where you'll be alone and uninterrupted. Sit in a comfortable chair with paper and pen, or at your computer. Pretend you're twelve years old again and that the world is yours for the taking. When you were twelve, the future was limitless. Go back to those days and let your mind run free with all the things you want to accomplish.

Write down all the goals that come to mind–what you want to do, what you want to have, where you want to go, what contribution you want to make to the world, what you want to learn, who you want to meet, how much money you want to earn, etc. List health goals, family goals, financial goals, social goals, spiritual goals, and mental goals. Think big. The size of your goal determines the size of your result. Write for the entire twenty minutes. If you find yourself on a roll and unable to stop writing, then write for as long as you can. If the ideas come slowly, then write a few goals for twenty minutes each day. Keep writing until you have 101 goals listed. Whether it takes you twenty minutes or twenty weeks to reach the 101 mark does not matter. What matters is that you actually do it.

This is such an important part of the goal-setting process, because the moment you write what you want and make it clear, it'll be yours. Doubtful? Then consider this: A Harvard study showed that only 3% of the population writes down their goals. It's that same 3% who controls

97% of the world's wealth. Everyone is entitled to set goals. Do so and join the 3%.

Fine-Tune Your Goals

After you have 101 goals written, go back and fine-tune them. You may find that you need to rethink some goals to make them realistic. As you re-read what you've written, ask yourself, "Is this really important to me? Am I prepared to give up something important in my life to make this goal happen?" When you can answer both those questions positively, you will have the energy and the drive to make the goal reality.

Next, make sure your goals are specific. If one of your goals says, "I want to build a profitable business" then define what "profitable" is to you. See the vision of the business in your mind and then describe it on paper. Is your future office in a city skyscraper or a small town setting? How many employees do you have? How much sales revenue are you generating? What does the business look like? Describe the lobby or front office entrance, the furnishings, and the décor. Be specific about every detail down to what type of pens are in your desk drawer. Wishy-washy statements aren't good enough. Give your mind a specific image to strive for.

Finally, add an element of contribution to each of your goals. What are you going to give back to the world as you pursue your goals? Many people get so wrapped up in the "I" of their goals that they neglect the "give" aspect of goals. But remember that in order to get, you must also give. The more you give to others, the more abundant you'll be.

Elicit Support

Any goal worthy of your effort requires the involvement of other people. Form a team of supportive individuals with whom you can share your goals. Choose like-minded people who have specific goals they want to attain and who have been involved with other teams in the past. Meet with these people on a monthly basis, either in person or via phone or Internet, and share your goals with them. This does two important things: 1) It enables you to obtain support, advice, opportunities, and wisdom from people who may have done what you want to do, and 2) It establishes an accountability system so you're sure to work for your goals. After all, if other people know what you're planning to do, you'll be more apt to actually do it.

Be selective of who is a part of your support team. If someone does not contribute to the group or whole-heartedly believe in the goals of each group member, then he or she needs to leave. That person's negativity will drag everyone down. The positive energy you create as a team will help everyone involved reach greater heights. When you reach this state you'll have attained "team enlightenment," which is really one of the meta-goals of every team member, as it allows you to form deeper relationships and help each other in creative ways you may never have thought possible.

Get What You Want

The two most important aspects of any goal are to make sure it is a goal you really want, and to have the belief that the end result is worthy of you. In order to get what you want, visualize the thing or event in your mind. Believe in it and share it with others. Create your own support structure so you can live the better life you deserve.

Keep your goals in mind each and every day. Before you take action or make a decision, ask yourself, "Will this decision bring me closer to or further away from my goals?" Listen to your answer and let it guide you. Your goals are your life's compass. Follow them so you can live to your truest potential. Remember, this is the only life you have; plan it wisely.

About the Author

Mark Victor Hansen is the leading expert in the area of human potential. For more than 25 years, he has focused solely on helping people and organizations, from all walks of life, reshape their personal vision of what's possible. His powerful messages of possibility, opportunity, and action have helped create startling and powerful change in thousands of organizations and millions of individuals worldwide. He is co-creator of the *Chicken Soup for the Soul* series, and a prolific writer with many popular books. His new book, *The One Minute Millionaire* (co-authored with Robert G. Allen), is destined to inspire the creation of one million new millionaires this decade. For more information, please visit www.markvictorhansen.com.

How to Create and Instill a Leadership Mentality Throughout Your Organization

by Douglas C. Adams, Ph.D.

P eople who start and lead privately held companies strive to liberate themselves from the bonds of the past. Personal freedom is often at the root of this desire to "be your own boss." Since it is freedom they desire, then why is it so difficult for leaders to cultivate the value of freedom throughout the organization? Why can't they lead others with this ultimate leadership principle rather than with crushing supervision? The syndrome develops along the following path:

- The individual forms the company and grows it based on the principle of freedom and the enthusiasm that results. The CEO is determined to lead people using different principles than the command and control environment he or she left behind.
- As the company grows, its leaders struggle to create a system of management that supports the ideals of freedom.
- Soon, the leaders lose sight of their original principles and values. As pressures build, they begin to narrow their focus and forget their employees in the rush to augment the bottom line. They become obsessed with control, which in turn stifles freedom, choice, accountability, and responsibility.
- The CEO succumbs to the all-consuming idea that the company's success depends solely on him or her. This causes stress-induced problems for the CEO, along with the corresponding deterioration of health and well-being. Subsequently, the CEO is drawn to a series of leadership and management gurus who promise the cure, but don't deliver.
- Meanwhile costs rise, the best employees leave, and the leaders make excuses as to why it is hard to find "good people." Unable to retain quality employees, the bottom line begins to erode. The advice offered by change gurus sounds wonderful but fails miserably because the company has strayed so far from its ideals.

As this process continues, the CEO allows his or her feelings to guide decisions rather than clear assessments of the business. Both the leader and employees begin to operate from a position of fear, as trust deteriorates. In order to escape from this erosion, company leaders must act responsibly to ensure that they stay true to their original vision.

Command, Control, and Performance Obsession

We can easily see how achievement oriented people, like CEOs of privately held companies, succumb to "Achiever's Disease." The prevalent culture is one where we are rewarded and praised for winning Little League games, for getting "good" grades in school, and for getting into the "right" college. The achiever keeps achieving, yet he or she hears a nagging voice inside that says none of these efforts are good enough.

The roots of this trauma run deep within out culture. We are a society of command and control, and we reward people primarily based on performance. Unfortunately, this cultural conditioning has created a lot of confusion for people. Managers misunderstand their role and attempt to control every employee action, while top performers spend their days trying to please an authority figure who imposes arbitrary demands. Under this type of management, your otherwise cooperative employees will begin to rebel, either consciously or unconsciously.

Fortunately, it doesn't have to be this way. As a leader, you need to overcome this destructive pattern of thinking so you can experience your true mission, which is to enjoy the continuous challenge and positive learning opportunities that come from business ownership. In a well-managed company, leaders value freedom of thought and the freedom to pursue challenges rather than the negatively inspired desire for command and control. Such an attitude of creative leadership allows companies to flourish and fly far above the competition.

A Different CEO Leadership Model

All leaders can take simple steps to introduce the organization to new possibilities and create a culture that increases profitability, reduces waste, and attracts and retains the best talent. The following principles will guide you to a better leadership model.

- Make freedom the number one value in your life and in your company. The practice of freedom is the discipline of being personally accountable and responsible for your thinking and behavior.
- Support employees in the quest to discover their own personal goals for the future, and encourage them to see how that dovetails with the company's vision.
- Change your mindset. Reward yourself for what you learn, what you enjoy, and how you perform. Make sure that the objectives in these three areas are both controllable and measurable.

Breeding Successful Leaders
Throughout Your Company

Once you believe and embrace the previous three guidelines, you can move on to the following four strategies, which will lead your business to sustainable enjoyment, learning, and performance. Simply stated, you will learn where you are, where you want to be, and what methods or values are important for you on your journey. You will then be free to trust your own genius and can begin to unlearn the doubts, fears, and limiting thoughts that haunt you from the past.

- Get a clear picture of how others perceive your behavior. You can use the services of a management expert, or you can consult the people who really know you the best: your family, friends, and other trusted executives within your corporation. Ask, "What stands out for you when you think about my behavior?" Simply ask the question, be quiet until they have finished answering, and then thank them for their thoughts. Just as boat captains need a compass to guide them, so do you. You need to understand the impact of your behaviors on the current situation if you want to successfully implement a new strategic course.

- Identify what you value and make sure your behavior reflects those values. This is a simple concept, yet for many CEOs, their values and behaviors are not aligned. This occurs not through choice, but through lack of awareness. The saying, "It's lonely at the top," is true, and one symptom is the loss of self-aware-ness when others are afraid to tell you the truth. When you consult with others, you foster trust and the free flow of infor-mation, which helps you stay on track with your values and stay connected.

- Decide what you really want and where you want to be in the future. One of the simplest ways to do this is get your favorite magazines, a piece of construction paper, a glue stick, and a pair of scissors. Block out a few hours and find a quiet, relaxing place to cut and paste pictures and headlines that catch your attention. You will uncover many insights about yourself that can change your thinking. Remember the old axiom, "A picture is worth a thousand words."

- Promote and reward business strategies that support account-ability, responsibility, learning, enjoyment, and excellence through-out your company. Initiate these processes with yourself first, then with your executive team, and then throughout the com-pany. These two initiatives often require assistance from a highly skilled coach who practices what he/she preaches. The coach's job is to help you create an environment for your success. His/ her responsibility is to help you become more aware about what learning, enjoyment, and performance mean for you. Once you learn more about yourself and implement the changes in your behavior, others in your company will follow.

Lead the Way for Change

We are a culture in a hurry. Many of us constantly hear one blaring message: "ceaselessly strive for achievements." It is time to let go of this guilt-driven mindset and open the doors to freedom and opportunity.

The tremendous benefits of implementing these strategies will have far-reaching effects for your business and in all areas of your life. The over-arching principle of freedom, which promotes the values of thinking, learning, enjoyment, and excellence, will lead you to increased personal and professional wealth.

Additionally, when you give your employees the same respect and freedom you give yourself, you will find people start to take the initiative to make their departments and the whole business run more effectively. Employees *want* their jobs to be meaningful, and you have the power to make this happen. Learn to listen so that you can identify the motivated people. They are the employees who express a desire to go the extra mile. The bureaucratic environment of the past may have silenced them, but once you unlock their bonds, they will quickly regain trust in your vision.

The solution is to implement these leadership strategies today. Regardless of what happened in the past, it is never too late to start anew. People will respond to your intentions when you show you are committed. Your employees will begin to deliver the superior performance you dream of. Productivity, the skills of the employees, the physical appearance of your facilities, and a focus on key issues will all increase. Overall the attractiveness of your company will improve, thus providing more value to all stakeholders. You'll quickly discover that both you and your employees will win with a leadership model of freedom.

About the Author

Dr. Doug Adams runs Leadership Resources, LLC. He coaches owners and executives of privately held companies to find the freedom they yearn for and to create and implement business strategies that emphasize freedom, accountability, and responsibility in an effort to eliminate waste and create endless possibilities for sustainable revenues. Doug has the experience, presence and intellectual capacity to "create environments for other people's success." He is a player's coach. His years of athletic experience as a player on two Stanford University Championship Rose Bowl football teams, a love of golf, the thrill of snow skiing, and years of being the CEO of several of his own companies is meshed with his passion for lifelong learning. In addition, he has an undergraduate degree from Stanford University, an MBA from Pepperdine University, and a Ph.D. from the Fielding Graduate Institute.

He lives and works with his wife and business partner, Dr. Patricia Qualls. They have a son, Kodiak, and reside in Carmel Valley, California. You can reach Dr. Adams at 1.831.659.8580; via email: coach@dougadams.com, or via the web: www.dougadams.com.

Fifteen Communication Mistakes That Will Destroy Your Business

by Jacquie Damgaard, Ph.D.

E ffective organizational communication is the most critical factor in determining your business's success. Of course, having a needed product, sufficient capitalization, an effective strategic plan, and intelligent and skilled employees are also very important. But if your employees are left in the dark about the company's plans and goals, aren't adequately rewarded for their efforts, or can't respectfully discuss issues with their co-workers, then the best product or service in the world won't help your company succeed.

In order to succeed, each company employee needs to be self aware, able to manage his or her own feelings, be aware of the feelings of others, and have effective social skills. These factors make up what's called "emotional intelligence." Over twenty-five years of research has shown the significance of emotional intelligence competencies in predicting the success of worldwide corporations, as well as the success of government agencies and non-profit organizations.

Further, when it comes to employee satisfaction, effective communication skills within an organization are a key factor in business performance and employee retention. Unfortunately, many managers don't have critical communication skills. When excellence in communication is neglected within a company, performance suffers.

Here are fifteen of the most common communication mistakes that leaders of small, medium, and large companies make. They are mistakes that are lethal to a company's profitability.

Communication with the Company as a Whole

1) **Not communicating your company's vision.** If your company's vision/mission statement is posted on a plaque somewhere and none of your employees know it, it's not benefiting anyone. Without a clear and compelling vision, employees have no standard against which to measure their work, the importance of their specific contribution, their progress toward goals, and how their team fits into the company as a whole. Be sure that you develop your vision with the full participation and support of your employees. Then everyone can communicate it and use it as a reference point in evaluating decisions and outcomes.

94

2) Assuming that saying things once is enough. Just because you've said something once doesn't mean your group will remember it. People sometimes don't listen, sometimes don't understand, and sometimes just forget what you said. When you really need employees to remember something important (like the company vision, strategic goals, or the customer care policy), find a systematic way to say it repeatedly. Repetition leads to retention.

3) Failing to communicate your company's progress. Make sure you regularly meet with your entire staff to discuss current progress toward the company's goals. If things aren't progressing as well as you hoped, be sure to share that with your employees, too. Employees appreciate being informed, even when the news is not outstanding. Let them take some ownership of the results. It may help them develop new ideas to improve the situation.

4) Forgetting to communicate a change in strategic direction. Sometimes it's necessary to quickly change your business strategy to keep up with today's fast paced and changing world. Be sure to keep your employees in the loop whenever changes occur. You don't want them shooting at the wrong target and then wondering what went wrong.

5) Getting scattered in communication with customers. Your employees should know about the 80/20 Rule–that 80% of the business results come from 20% of the customers. They should also know that 80% of their productivity often comes from 20% of their activity. Teach this principle, document it for your teams, and then make sure that they focus their time on the "major" and not the "minor" customers and goals.

6) Overlooking the need to celebrate company victories. How often do you have company-wide celebrations following a key company victory? Reward everyone for a job well done, as that is what keeps the motivation strong for continuing progress. Successful companies often do this once every two or three months.

Communication with Individual Employees

7) Giving vague descriptions of expectations. Make sure your directions to your staff are clear. If you are not specific enough, the employee will not know your expectations. Paint the picture of the result you want and be sure to agree upon a due date. Summarize the desired outcomes in writing; it can be very helpful in tracking the outcomes.

8) Giving too specific descriptions of expectations. Don't outline every single detail in all the steps needed to reach the desired end result.

This will limit the employee's sense of freedom and creativity in coming up with the outcome. Instead, outline the goals and then give the employee latitude and responsibility for deciding how to accomplish them.

9) **Failing to have any systematic follow-up system for tracking progress.** Make sure to have a system for regular reporting from your staff regarding their progress toward their deliverables. While you do not want to "micromanage," you need to establish regular checkpoints so that you can redirect an employee or help him or her with ideas if needed. Decide together with the employee on how frequently this communication needs to happen. Then, make these meetings a priority.

10) **Not giving acknowledgment for desired results.** Some leaders think they shouldn't have to praise their employees for doing their jobs well. Psychologists know, however, that the best way to get a specific behavior to increase is to positively acknowledge it when it does happen. Praise good work. This will inspire employees to consistently do their very best. One of the most effective ways to acknowledge hard work is to give verbal, as well as tangible, appreciations.

11) **Forgetting to give regular performance reviews.** Schedule performance reviews on a regular basis and keep track of when they are supposed to occur. It's not good for your employees to have to remind you that their review is due. These communications are the primary way that employees know what they are doing well, what they need to improve, and how their function is critical to the company's success. Be sure that these occur regularly (at least yearly, if not every six months) and without you needing any reminders.

12) **Overlooking a discussion of the employee's career goals**. Make sure you discuss with each employee what his or her personal career goals are and how they can be met within the company's future plans. This is a major factor in employee retention. If employees feel that they are cared for in this way, they are much more likely to stay with the company and find a way to advance within the organization. They will feel encouraged and more in alignment with their own personal development. Have these discussions a minimum of once a year.

13) **Communicating without awareness of the other's preferred style.** People have different styles in which they communicate. A common system used in corporations is the DISC model, which describes a profile for a person based on his or her relative scores on the Dominance, Influencing, Steadiness, and Compliance dimensions. Other communication assessments utilize different factors, but the idea is the

same—that each person has a preferred style and will respond most comfortably if he or she is communicated with in that style. Your company sales staff can benefit from such training, as it will help them better relate to their customers. It also is a good tool for improving communication within teams and between employees and managers.

14) Giving permission to "vent" at others without respecting them. How do you handle the "charged" emotional states you feel at certain times of the day, especially under stress? Do you give yourself permission to "erupt" at whoever is around? Unfortunately, this occurs too often in some businesses. When this happens, there is often a loss of trust in the relationship, an increased feeling of caution with the offender, and a decrease in employee performance and creativity. Do not let this become acceptable in your company. Bring in a communication coach who can teach all of your staff effective and respectful ways to handle such communication, both outside and within your organization.

15) Failing to distinguish between professional and personal communication. Sometimes employees share details that seem too personal and intimate for the workplace. This often happens because of unusual stress in the person's life. If the employee's home life is truly affecting his or her work, he or she may need to discuss the issue with his or her manager. However, sometimes employees don't distinguish between communications related to accomplishing the task at hand and communication that is best done with a friend. If not managed properly, the situation can greatly reduce the sense of professionalism in the team and interfere with the focus on job results. This is another instance when training in different communication methods would be helpful.

Erase the Mistakes

The fact is that communicating well is a learned skill. If you recognize any of the above mistakes, it's time to make some changes. Immediately institute a coaching program for your company in "best communication practices."

With effective communication strategies in place, you will have happier and more productive employees. They will know where your company is going and what their roles are in achieving company goals. You will be astonished at the positive effect that this skilled communication will have on your bottom line.

About the Author

Jacquie Damgaard, Ph.D. is the President and co-founder of Coaching Solutions International, Inc. (CSI), a Corporate and Executive Coaching firm. Jacquie facilitates corporations in their vision/mission/core values, strategic planning, executive selection, and Board training. Jacquie also coaches corporate executives in the development of leadership skills and corporate teams in the achievement of high impact team functioning. Jacquie is a dynamic keynote speaker and seminar leader. She is especially known for her training in emotional intelligence, high performance teams, communication techniques, and effective habit change technologies. She is a member of the International Coaching Federation. Contact her at jacquie@coaching-solutions.com or 1.404.633.6775.

Energize Your Enterprise for Increased Capacity and Profitability
The Human Economics that Fuels Sustainable Competitive Advantage
by Darwin Gillett

To survive and thrive, every company needs to find and exploit its own competitive advantage. A company that does this well will achieve growth and profitability far beyond the norm.

In the past, companies focused on the "outer" aspects of competence, such as having the best products, best technologies, best market niches, or even best management systems. Today, this is not sufficient to assure success. In fact, a quiet revolution is underway, introducing a new method of winning competitive advantage, one that recognizes and utilizes the "inner" dimensions of the company and its people. This includes the very nature of motivation, work, leadership, and organizational culture.

Tapping the *Inner* Source of Competitive Advantage
Leaders of successful companies are changing their competitive strategy by developing the "internal energy potential" of their organization. This dramatic shift from focusing solely on the external forms of competition to including also the internal human dimension is already producing remarkable results. By addressing the non-material aspects of commerce, both large corporations and smaller entrepreneurial firms are tapping the full range of available inner energies, in the process creating uncommon business success.

Although the external, quantifiable components of business will continue to be important, they will be integrated with something deeper, namely Human Energy Capital, the underlying human energy that is the ultimate source of sustainable competitive advantage. Visionary leaders recognize this trend and are acting quickly to find and draw forth the inner energies of their organizations–and themselves.

Be in the Forefront
In the race to mine Human Energy Capital, companies have previously focused on only one dimension–the mind. Knowledge Workers provide intellectual skills, but they possess so much more to draw from. The

99

company of the future will move beyond treating the human resource as *merely* head and hands and will tap the full range of human energies, including the energies of human emotions, heart, and will. Those companies and leaders that recognize and work with *all* these energies will succeed. Those who wait will be left behind.

This inner dimension of human energy capital will permeate the entire organization, from its purpose and principles to its product and practices.

These six dimensions will characterize tomorrow's leading companies:

1) **Human Economics will guide management decision making.** Material well being and material efficiency, the focus of traditional business, are no longer the primary driving forces of people or companies. The corporation will reinvent itself in ways that honor and integrate both the material and non-material dimensions, thereby fully engaging the whole person in generating prosperity in it broadest sense.

2) **The Human Resource will finally be managed as a true source of wealth.** Leading companies will win by managing as if they truly believe what has been known and claimed for decades–that their people are indeed "our most valuable resource." They will invest in its growth and development and in utilizing it to generate growth and profitability.

3) **A New Work Ethic will feed the soul as well as the bank account.** The "employee contract" will shift from one of "employees provide skills and the employer provides material compensation" to one of " employees bring forth all their gifts to serve the company's highest purpose, and the employer provides opportunities for growth and self-actualization–as well as material compensation." Employers (and employees) that make this shift will see a whole new work ethic emerge that will energize their companies.

4) **Spiritual Capital will augment Intellectual Capital in generating wealth.** The Knowledge Worker will become a "commodity" due to the greater supply of and global access to educated people and the proliferation of highly sophisticated computer technology. The primary fuel of vibrant organizations of the future will be their Spiritual Capital– the energies of human Emotions, Heart, and Will. To thrive, corporations will look to attract, engage, grow, and fully employ this Spiritual Capital.

5) **Energized Enterprises will draw on human spirit to fuel success.** Organizations energized throughout by the human spirit become powerful players in business. In the corporation of the future, organizational processes will be less about just the *action* of efficiency and output, and more about the *energy* of creativity, innovation, inspiration,

and collaboration. These companies will focus on relationships and the energies that flow through them.

6) **An "Energy Infusion" Leadership approach will transform organizations.** Traditional leadership methods focus on extracting effort from existing resources. Leaders will shift to an "Energy Infusion" model that recognizes that their most potent role is to infuse the organization with energy. They will energize people by speaking to what fires their deepest desires, values, and energies, thereby unleashing the huge store of talent and spirit that often lies dormant within organizations.

As employees bring all of their talents and spirit to their companies, they will create vibrant, high-performing organizations. Employees will discover, express and utilize hidden talents and passions. They will approach their work with enthusiasm, dedication, and commitment, taking initiative, collaborating and helping the company generate superior results.

Building the Energized Enterprise

To build Energized Enterprises, leaders will take steps that combine inner energy with outer action. Inner strategies focus on being and relationships. Outer strategies focus on the decisions and actions where most companies still concentrate.

These six steps will help you build an Energized Enterprise:

1) **Create a Compelling Direction** – Most companies run on a fraction of available energy because they do not address the non-material needs and aspirations of their employees, customers, and vendors. By creating a powerful vision and mission that speaks to both material and non-material purposes, you inspire people and bring forth the best of their energy.

2) **Build Values into Action** – When companies select impressive values but don't live them, people become skeptics. Hardwire values into your organization. Include them in your decision-making processes, sales strategies, customer services practices, employee development and evaluation processes, and measurement and reward systems.

3) **Create a Culture of Civility** – When unfair policies and practices are rampant within an organization, people shut down, stop taking risks, and leave their best at home. Or they join the fray, bringing out the worst in others and themselves. Build a culture of civility and respect. Set examples by your personal conduct and your company's practices. Don't tolerate acts of unfairness or incivility toward employees, even from customers. When you build a culture of civility, you reap large dividends in employee commitment, and performance.

4) Hire People with Character as well as Knowledge and Skills – Your employees' character will increasingly be a major part of your competitive advantage. Shape your employee practices to attract, utilize, and promote people with the character you want for your business. By emphasizing character as well as talent, you create an unbeatable company.

5) Balance Freedom and Structure – An oppressive management style prevents a company from using human capital to its full advantage. People need some structure, so provide overall direction. Then, to draw forth your employees' best, give them the freedom to take responsibility, improvise, and lead within that structure.

6) Use Inner as well as Outer Goals and Rewards – Create measures of the non-material that are important in your business, such as employee morale and customer satisfaction. Use these measures to determine strategy, set goals, and measure results.

Supercharge Your Leadership

As the corporation evolves, so too will a new kind of leadership, one that focuses on the underlying energies and non-material dimension of the company as well as on its actions and material dimension. Leaders will utilize and balance both inner and outer "action."

Here are two inner/outer actions you can take to help you succeed as the leader of an Energized Enterprise:

1) Take what inspires you personally and make that a central part of your leadership – In an Energized Enterprise, the leader is the chief energy catalyst. So engage the full range of your *own* talent and spirit. Set high goals that embody your passion and vision. Live your values, especially when times are tough. In doing so, you bring a vibrancy to your own life and also to your employees, your customers, and all those with whom your company interacts.

2) Turn negative energies into positive ones – When management concentrates on finding and fixing problems, the problems may get solved, but often the climate becomes one of fear and paralysis. To break out of this cycle, redesign your role as one of inspiring and uplifting those in your organization. For example, find success and celebrate it, which in turn expands the organization's motivation and capacity.

The Evolution of Business and Society

By attracting and utilizing using human talent and spirit for competitive advantage, you will place yourself in the vanguard of corporate evolution. You will also serve the increasingly important non-material needs of society as well as its material requirements. Your life will be enriched as well, as you release and direct the energies that serve the highest purpose for yourself, your people, your customers, and your community. As new Energized Enterprises achieve competitive advantage, they will contribute to the positive evolution of society into a holistic community of people who thrive not only on a material level, but also on a deeper spiritual level, creating an empowered and interconnected society that works for all.

About the Author

Darwin Gillett, president of Gillett Associates, is a corporate futurist, business consultant and leadership mentor for large multi-national corporations and smaller entrepreneurial and professional service firms. Dar is the creator of the Energized Enterprise Model for Peak Performance. He helps clients build competitive advantage through the human dimension of their companies. He speaks internationally on the leadership of knowledge-based organizations built with human energy capital. The author of numerous articles and booklets on corporate revitalization and leadership, Dar holds degrees from Yale University (BA, economics) and the University of Chicago Graduate School of Business (MBA). Contact Dar directly via email: dgillett@darwingillett.com or 1.207.443.4533.

Lead at a Higher Level
How to Grow Yourself and
Great Leaders With You
by Shelley Holmes

In the command and control organizations of yesteryear, the prevalent style of leadership was that of a Warrior. Warriors expect compliance, rules, and discipline. They focus on winning at any cost and ignore the impact of their actions on others. Warriors fear any sign of vulnerability or weakness. They tune out their emotions and are so indifferent to themselves and others that they become isolated.

Such a leadership style leads to frustration for everyone. It yields average results, ensures you do not reach your potential, and has little hope of bringing out the best in anyone.

Fortunately, this leadership style is swiftly becoming extinct. The emerging style is that of the High Performance Leader–the Heroic Leader. This style delivers great business results and leads to fulfillment for each individual it touches. Heroic Leaders seek success in the physical, emotional, and spiritual worlds.

As you shift from a Warrior to a Hero leadership style, you move to a more heartfelt, connected place. You discover that we are all here to learn soul lessons, and daily life is the vehicle by which we come to understand ourselves and reach our potential. As you change the way you behave and feel, so do the people and the circumstances surrounding you. Your daily battles dissipate and your life becomes more free flowing and rewarding. Your business becomes more productive and co-workers relish the workplace you create.

So, how do you shift from Warrior to Hero? Start with the formula:

Awareness + Self-Responsibility = High Performance

Heroes use this formula to bring out the best in themselves and those around them.

Awareness

You transform neither yourself nor your workplace when you are blind to how your beliefs, emotions, thinking, and behavior may be limiting your progress. That's why the first part of the formula requires you to become aware of what you do that puts the brakes on success.

There are two painless steps to becoming aware:

1) Be Open And Receptive – Awareness arrives in many guises (i.e.: through feedback, the results you achieve, a training program, or reading new information and applying those ideas to your life). Whatever form it arrives, if you are open and receptive, the opportunities to become more authentically powerful are endless.

Many Warriors squander these opportunities, as they do not want to confront their shadow side. Warriors fear that by admitting their flaws, they may need to change, and change brings discomfort. So they deny their faults, shut out new ideas, and blame others for their problems.

Like an old sweater that doesn't keep us as warm as it once did, we often cling to comfortable thoughts, feelings, beliefs and behaviors, even though they may not give the best results. Whenever people blame others and circumstances for poor results, they are drawing on their victim. Warriors deny responsibility and project blame onto others.

Coach's Tip: How to become more aware – Catch thoughts patterns such as, *"Thank goodness I'm not like that." Or, "That doesn't apply to me."* These are both good indicators that your Warrior may be in denial. Another tactic of the Warrior is to project fault on someone else, as in, *"Our business would be more responsive to customers if we could get senior management to change."* The Hero's way is to look within and ask questions such as, *"What can I learn about myself from this?" "What truth is there in this for me?"* and *"If I applied this information how would it change my life?"*

When you are aware, you realize that the circumstances and people around you are merely the characters in a universal play designed for your learning. They are here to help you discover what you need to know about yourself. It takes the courage of a Hero to bring hidden fears and emotions to a conscious level. This leads us to the next step in awareness:

2) Take A Breath...Remember Why You Are Here – Most people ask at some point in their lives, "Why am I here?" One reason for human existence is to learn and grow, not just in a worldly sense, but also at a soul level.

At a soul level, particularly as a leader, your lessons could be to overcome fear and limitation, and to care for others as much as you care for your own goals and ambitions. You may be here to learn how to apply virtues such as compassion, humility, respect, love, honor, patience, and consideration.

Coach's Tip: How to remember why you are here – Consistently ask yourself, *"What soul lesson am I learning right now?"* Each time you ask and answer this question, you empower yourself to look at your life from a higher perspective. Appreciate each situation for exactly what it is: an opportunity to live out the purpose of your life–to be all your soul has the potential to be.

Self-Responsibility

Awareness is the first step to mastering the Hero leadership style. Next you need to take self-responsibility for unleashing all the capability that resides within you. Again, you can do this in two painless steps:

1) **Choose Your Response** – When you view life from the higher perspective of soul lessons you understand and accept your life experiences. This understanding gives you the freedom to choose your response.

Imagine you were once a Warrior and that when things didn't go the way you wanted, you became a bully. In an epiphany, you became open and receptive to the feedback that your hostile nature was derailing your career. Through coaching, you came to understand that your soul lesson was to honor and respect people who are less powerful than you.

With this insight, the next time a situation came up where you could bully someone, you asked yourself, "What soul lesson am I learning here?" Then you made the conscious choice to deny the bully and be heroic–patient, compassionate, understanding, and loving.

Coach's Tip: How to choose your response – In any situation where you find yourself faced with Warrior behavior, take a deep breath and ask, *"What soul lesson am I learning? Do I want to be a Warrior or a Hero?"*

The more you choose to be your best, the more power-filled you become. Inner peace swells within you that other people intuitively feel. Remember, the cumulative effect of the little choices make the biggest difference. This leads us to the second step in self-responsibility:

2) **Honor Self and Others** – One way to honor yourself is to become aware and choose your response.

The second way is to choose the words you use, both within your own mind and aloud. Unfortunately, many of us run into trouble with this because of the control our inner Judge exerts over us. The Judge is the critical voice in your mind that constantly finds fault and rejects. In fact, you are filled with judgments about yourself, your children, your partner, your co-workers, your neighbors, and even the people you pass on the street. The Judge robs you of your peace of mind with endless criticism about what you, or others, should have done.

Have you ever woken up at 2 A.M. thinking, "Why was I so stupid? Why didn't I?" This is your Judge. We often punish ourselves over and over for the same mistake. This sets a belief deep in your sub-conscious that you are not worthy or capable. It is important to understand that how you speak to yourself reflects how you speak to others.

Coach's Tip: How to honor self and others – Monitor what you say to yourself and others. When you hear your inner judge being critical or negative, stop and reframe the words. For example, if you hear yourself thinking, "I am so stupid!" stop and rethink that statement. Are you really stupid? Of course not. So instead tell yourself, "I am a smart person. I may make mistakes from time to time, but I learn from those mistakes, which enhances my wealth of experience and wisdom."

The Hero's Journey

Are you willing to be the type of leader who undertakes a journey of self-discovery to awaken your inner power and unleash capability? If you want to lead a powerful and profitable organization, then your answer should be "yes."

The journey of the Hero leader is one of courage, commitment, and perseverance. It may not be easy, and in the beginning, you may even question your wisdom. You won't complete the journey overnight, in a month, or even in a year. For most, the journey ends with the draw of their final breath.

Yet, the rewards are unlimited. Through a deep awareness of self and a commitment to constant growth, the way in which you lead can only become High Performance. As you grow, so will your people. The more you understand yourself, the greater your power, fulfillment, and success.

Treasure each moment of your heroic journey.

About the Author

Shelley Holmes coaches High Performance Leaders from her office in Australia. She regularly mentors heroes from Australia, the United States, Canada, the United Kingdom, New Zealand, and South Africa to create workplace cultures where people have powerful and productive relationships allowing them to perform at their best. More information about this topic is available on her website at www.performanceoutcomes.com.au or by calling +61 7 55 307 061.

How Great Leaders Wow Today's Employee

Aligning Talent and Passion to Achieve Explosive Productivity

by Paul L. Krass

If you were to follow five successful business owners or company leaders for a month as they lead their organizations, you would begin to see what makes successful leaders stand out. Successful leaders consistently achieve superior results by enabling and developing the intrinsic talent and passion within their employees. These great leaders "wow" the competition across all industries.

Observing a great leader's team in action is a privilege. As the leader operates like the captain of a competitive sailboat–confidently coaching and inspiring greatness–the leader's team responds by consistently achieving near perfect results. Great leaders critique every process, but passionately give recognition for any achievement.

It is evident that great leaders have a deep understanding of what motivates people, but how is it they achieve such explosive productivity, and make it look so easy? One reason is that their approach to the organization and the employee is a combination of expert management tools and inspirational leadership.

The View from Above

Many leaders achieve phenomenal success through a unique management style. For example, they might apply a retail marketing approach when they want to evaluate their workforce. This approach can provide revealing insight into the employee's way of thinking.

A retail customer is defined as having needs, wants, and demands that must be satisfied through something that they attach value to. Your employees operate in the same way. A job may meet their basic needs, but an employee attaches great value to professional development. They will demand job satisfaction, of which professional development is a major factor. Although not all employees have the same level of talent, all bring a complex mixture of skills and abilities to their jobs. It is the great leader who knows how to identify and develop their potential to achieve a remarkable level of productivity.

Raise Employee Productivity

Effective leadership is the means to corporate survival. Advances in technology provide both you and your competition with unlimited options, which equalizes competitive advantage. Therefore, your greatest strength lies in your superior leadership.

Your challenge as a leader is to balance "getting it done," and "getting the best" out of your employees' talent and passion. *Re-Imagining the Organization* is a process for re-thinking motivation, accountability, commitment, and innovative possibilities. Great leaders don't proclaim to have all the answers, but are highly motivated to acquire the knowledge they need to make informed decisions.

Re-Imagining The Organization

Picture a spin top spinning on a desk. Do you know what keeps it upright? It is the energy unleashed when it is put into motion. In physics, this is called a centripetal force, which constantly pulls everything toward the center. This force acts on the spin top just as great leadership acts on an organization. Great organizations thrive on these four principles:

- **Leadership is an energy and influence** that constantly pulls your team toward a center of focus, much like centripetal force. This energy takes the form of your expectations, strategies, and vision. Likewise, in the absence of leadership the team topples, just like the spin top, as centripetal forces diminish.

- **Management is an action** that aligns accountability with expectations, strategy, and vision in order to achieve focus. Imagine our spin top being multiple layers of loosely stacked rings rotating independently about the axis. To maintain the desired shape and balance, each ring must be aligned horizontally but relative to the axis. For the organization, this axis is communication.

- **Communication is a transfer of purpose, strategy, and vision.** Communication within an organization acts as both the prime mover and a guide for expectations, decisions, and results. You can think of communication as a pillar that all organizational actions revolve around. The pillar of any organization is the effective communication of expectations, strategy, and vision.

- **Talent and passion** represent the ability to achieve repeatable, near perfect results. Everything in the organization depends on your people. Regardless of our current responsibilities, we each have natural talents and passions, which we can consistently execute to near perfection. Although we may attempt to master new skills, they rarely meet the same level of success that we achieve through our natural abilities.

A Gallup Survey shows that when employees work at what they do best, there is 50% less employee turnover, 38% higher productivity, and 44% higher customer satisfaction. The most startling fact: only 20% of all employees feel they are able to do what they do best everyday. What if *Re-Imagining the Organization* could increase this from 20% to 40% in your organization? What would another 20% of your employees achieving repeatable near perfect results mean to your bottom line?

Develop Your Existing Resources of Talent And Passion

These statistics validate what every great leader already knows. You can achieve more productivity by precisely aligning talent and passion with organizational objectives.

The complexity and pace of today's organization can make an observer break into a sweat. Technology has created an overabundance of micromanagement processes that weigh heavily on the organization's ability to move quickly and effectively. In fact, today's organizations are often mired in conflict, as employers insist that employees are not motivated or productive. But is it really that employees are not as productive, or is it that your competition knows how to develop and leverage employee talent more effectively? Four primary issues contribute to low productivity:

1) Employees don't know what is expected of them;

2) Employees don't believe they have adequate materials, equipment, and training;

3) Employees don't feel they have the opportunity to do what they do best; and

4) Employees don't feel their supervisor or anyone else cares about them.

One unmistakable characteristic of great leaders is that they never ignore survey results. They place a high priority on determining if the statistics apply to their situation, because they appreciate the long-term implication of reducing employee turnover. They dedicate a great deal of energy to helping employees become more successful, measuring behavioral performance, coaching to develop talent, and maintaining a disciplined approach to accountability.

Seven Steps to Better Performance

When blended with coaching and progressive discipline, accountability becomes the glue that holds highly effective teams together. The following seven-step performance coaching process provides the framework.

Step One – Measure behavioral results

For example, if employees fail to start on time, establish a process for measuring behavioral results. Then through a coaching process, discuss the variance between expectations and observed facts. The key is to measure results associated with expectations and communicate the results to employees.

Step Two – Communicate your expectations in terms employees understand

Employees often don't know what is expected. The use of written schedules, operating procedures, guidelines, and policies makes it easier for you and the employees to validate your expectations.

Step Three – Adjust, adapt, and overcome

If the results aren't what you expect, adapt a new approach, develop a new talent, or even gain an understanding about why it can't be done. The key is continuously *Re-Imagining the Organization.*

Step Four – Inspect the results

You get what you inspect, not what you expect. It isn't that you cannot trust people, but rather people do what they believe is acceptable. It is better to identify a changing behavior when it begins, rather than after you see the year-end report.

Step Five – Ask why

Another issue associated with poor productivity is that employees don't believe anyone cares. When you show interest in your employees, you're perceived as caring. Try asking "why?" and listen to the answers. It will help you interpret what is going on in your organization.

Step Six – Create a feedback loop

Communication is the key to creating a feedback loop. Feedback is the catalyst for creating an environment of continuous improvement. It provides the knowledge necessary to recognize and acknowledge even the smallest achievements. It alerts you to communication that isn't clear, and alerts you to the effectiveness of management and leadership.

Step Seven – Implement an audit program

Identify changes that facilitate an environment of pro-action rather than reaction.

Become a Great Leader

So what do great leaders do differently? They don't view today's employee the same old way. Instead, they build a partnership with the workforce. They ensure management develops and uses employee talent effectively, while holding firm on accountability. Most important, they are leaders who listen to the needs, wants, and demands of their organization. Through *Re-Imagining the Organization*, they provide the intangible energy and force that constantly pulls everyone toward the central expectations, strategies, and vision of the organization.

Is this difficult to achieve? It depends on your skill as a leader. To help you implement these procedures, you can use the services of a professional performance consultant who specializes in coaching effective leaders. Regardless, your greatest return on investment is developing an organizational understanding of the patterns of interaction governing communication and learning. The benefit to you is a better bottom line, less conflict, and a strategically competitive organization. Once you take the first step to *Re-Imagining the Organization*, you can exceed your greatest expectations.

About the Author

Paul Krass is the founder of StrategicHelm, an organizational consulting firm devoted to helping individuals, leaders, and teams discover effective leadership through *Re-Imagining the Organization.* Paul has that unique ability to understand and then ask the questions that bring a flood of answers–answers critical to organizational effectiveness and productivity. His keen ability to inspire highly effective leadership applies to any industry or team looking to achieve extraordinary results through ordinary personnel. Among his academic achievements is an M.B.A. from Rensselaer Polytechnic Institute (Troy, NY). You can contact Paul by visiting StrategicHelm at www.StrategicHelm.com or by phone at 1.518.580.0891.

Five Leadership Keys for Effective Business Change

by Melanie Patrick

"If the machine inspired the industrial age, the image of the living system may inspire a genuine postindustrial age."
—Peter Senge et al., in Sloan Management Review

The industrial business models are linear, mechanistic, and focused on static building blocks. Levers, pulleys, and buttons implement change. The simple brilliance of the assembly line guarantees increased production with perfect control over the system. Unfortunately, this static manufacturing model resists change.

The older industrial model is being replaced by rapidly evolving and rapidly changing systems in the information age. Today, new models help us change our business, resulting in a constantly changing and "living" business environment.

The theme of a living business comes from focusing on global issues, ecology, holistic thinking, sustainability of resources, and a whole systems view. Technology serves as the nervous system of this awareness. We experience this communication network as a "web." The Internet itself is an example of the shift in our language. It is one of our first models of a life mimicry process that responds and reacts simultaneously worldwide.

Nature is the most effective model of change, and in fact, our new business language includes many phrases from nature, including "growing a business," "bio-mimicry," "birth of a new world," "ecology of commerce" and "natural capitalism." So we have learned about business change from life itself. Our words reflect these new patterns of life. Companies "live" and "die." Success in business today requires a shift in perspective, plus a few new skill sets and behaviors.

The shift in perspective is that management cannot "make change happen" in the mechanistic way of the old model. The change in thinking process is still new for business. The new model is "allowing change to evolve" and requires "relationship with change" that includes the manager and the teams involved. Such a shift requires relationship rather than mechanical control. To begin, managers and business owners need to have a healthy relationship with change.

113

What Changes Do You Make Willingly?

"Change is the constant, the signal for rebirth, the egg of the phoenix."
                                                    –Christina Baldwin, writer

Examine the changes you make daily, weekly, and seasonally. You change your clothes before an important meeting, you change your schedule to eat lunch with a friend, and you change your eating habits. Your body changes with each breath. In the course of a lifetime, you may change jobs, cities, and marriages. You have partners, friends, co-workers, clients, and children who change your life. In essence, you are in the continual process of change because change is a necessary and natural part of living. You know how to change, and you do so daily. These changes are typically planned or inspired by choice. The outcomes are expected, self-initiated, cyclic, understood, rational, and patterned. We are involved in a natural process of change.

What Changes Do You Resist?

"If we don't change, we don't grow. If we don't grow, we aren't really living."   –Gail Sheehy, writer

The difficult changes are unexpected, sudden, imposed by others, seen as irrational, or result in unknown outcomes. Random change creates instability. You have no choice and often feel powerless. "Crisis management" change is reactive rather than creative. Change is unwelcome when you experience a loss or you cannot see the potential positive outcome.

Change is easier in a stable system. One element changes first, then the next. Incremental changes are more successful when prioritized. If changes in a business environment seem forced or chaotic, people will resist them.

Change the "Process of Change" Within Your Business

"Things do not change, we change." –Henry David Thoreau, writer

As individuals, we discover openness to change that is planned, expected, self-initiated, cyclic, understood, rational, or patterned and that allows choice or involvement in the process. We know this for ourselves, yet we forget as business professionals that change happens most effectively in known steps and with communication. Within a business environment, the challenge is encouraging individuals to collaborate on necessary changes. This change in perspective accelerates when leaders adopt behaviors that encourage a "living and changing process." Following are the leadership keys that encourage a positive change environment.

Key One – Encourage new ideas

The key to positive change involves risk and experimentation in areas of growth. If the culture does not support creativity and possibility, the old system stays in place. So be open to new ideas others present to you, and develop flexibility and adaptability into the workplace. Reward rather than criticize new ideas. Doing so will solve problems as they arise. Eventually, individual self-initiative will become an accepted group norm.

This concept matches the human need for self-initiative and understood change.

Key Two – Create trust among "change members"

The key to successful change is a group process of accepting new behaviors or learning new systems. Distrust generates negativity and lack of communication, so build respect and cooperation among your team to achieve the goals necessary for change to be accepted. If the group does not trust each other, they spend their energy resisting new ideas. Collaboration and learning requires trust built through communication. Reward positive collaboration and refuse to accept competition, put-downs, and breach of trust.

This concept matches the human need for rationality, planned change, and involvement in the process.

Key Three – Define only the final goal

The key to self-initiated change is the team's involvement in the design. Define only the destination. Allow the team to create the itinerary. For example, challenge the team "to cut costs in manufacturing within 60 days." This tangible goal is given back to the team to solve, and they create consensus by achieving it. They will develop a consensus of the methodology required to achieve the tangible goal.

This concept matches the human need for self-initiated change.

Key Four – Initiate a stable environment with incremental changes

The key to continual change process is clear priorities. Change one element at a time, but not everything simultaneously. When staggered in steps, change is more successful. This requires leadership and clear goals. Complete one series of changes before starting the next. If you try to change everything at once, the result is a dangerous juggling act with unexpected outcomes. The chaos generates resistance.

This concept matches the human need for cyclic or patterned change.

Key Five – Instill a clear mission and values within the company

This is the key for leaders who tend to file the mission statement in the bottom drawer. It requires examining how the mission statement applies to the change at hand. The process of defining values and ethics frames the change and creates an alignment for all the company. The team knows what can be changed according to company values. The overall mission is the long-range goal, and the change process is a small step towards it. Constantly reinforcing the company's values is a clear way of aligning how change happens within the organization. The accepted process of change becomes understood.

This concept matches the human need for rational and known outcomes.

Leadership is the Key to the "Process of Change"

Change is defined as "exchanging one thing for another," and known outcomes are more easily accepted. After all, it isn't easy to exchange one known quantity for an unknown. For a business leader in the process of change, you need to identify what needs to be changed and what must stay the same. Leadership requires knowing what goals to achieve and allowing the team to collaborate on the process to achieve them. Then, define the priorities so the changes are incremental. The team becomes the "change agent." The group can then make changes willingly because they initiate the process for a known outcome.

Additionally, team members must understand why the change is necessary. Convince the change members that the goal is achievable and not a moving target. Delegate choices to the members, and then align with choices, values, and outcomes. Remember, we make changes easily when we create the process and move towards an understood goal or outcome. The more we contribute towards the methodology of the change, the more we align with the goal.

Engage your team members in the implementation process. Ensure that they have trust and good communication to openly discuss the pros and cons of all possible scenarios. You can then address their fears of the unknown and move in the right direction for the best long-term goal. The more positive factors in your business that help the change process, the higher your success rate will be at a designed change.

The result of this new living model is an empowered, flexible, and responsive workforce. The pressures of the current economy match the strength of a resilient and committed business team to achieve objectives. As we learned in the past, human potential is not maximized on an assembly line. We achieve it through involvement, learning, and communication. In fact, we willingly make change in our lives through inspiration and choice. Make it possible within your business as well. Take risks and implement empowered changes in your organization. The rewards are worth the risk.

About the Author

Melanie Patrick's studies in Entomology at UC Berkeley gave her a systems view of the natural world; ownership of a café and bakery for 16 years gave her a grass-roots view of business; consultation with businesses and non-profits gave her a broad range view of the human change process; and life in these times gave her a commitment to conscious, healthy living change. For more information about change process, see www.creativestrategicconsulting.com.

How to Produce Breakthrough Results

In Your Vision, Your Business, and Your Life

by Brenda J. Scarborough

To fulfill the potential of your vision for your leadership and your organization, you must discover and overcome the hidden limitations of your current frame of thinking and leading. To achieve what you are truly capable of, open yourself up to new possibilities and take on a breakthrough mindset. When you engage yourself with others in this way, outcomes that once seemed impossible will be within reach.

A breakthrough mindset allows for non-linear advancement (breakthroughs, quantum leaps, or paradigm shifts) in behaviors, actions, and results for you and those around you. It enables the process of continual learning and accomplishment toward your vision.

Most leaders know their vision, but few succeed at breathing life into it and seeing it through to fruition. Without breaking through the unseen limitations of unconscious beliefs and automatic behaviors, you only achieve within your existing paradigm. You are confined to improvement within the bounds of what you already know. You can work harder, gain information, re-structure yourself and your organization (and in that sense, incrementally improve), but essence will remain unchanged and the same limitations will exist. Your vision will fall short of its business potential and your true desire.

Learning how to produce breakthroughs enables you to:
- Utilize the full intelligence within your organization and consistently innovate.
- Bring about transformation, far exceeding the effectiveness of reorganizing structure or process.
- Engage employees in what is meaningful to them, maximizing quality of output, morale, and employee retention.
- Achieve swifter integration of cultures and systems post-merger, and accomplish greater synergies.
- Develop leadership and accountability within your organization and positively impact careers.
- Improve your own sense of personal and career fulfillment, allowing you to leave the legacies you intend.

118

Breakthrough principles provide a disciplined, reliable, and reproducible method of moving beyond hidden but critical factors that inhibit extraordinary results, consistently expanding what's possible. Outlined below are three fundamental elements of breakthrough thinking that all business owners and company leaders must adopt in order to master the most effective approach to organizational change, leadership development, and lifelong learning.

Personalize Your Business Motives

Breakthroughs, by definition, involve unfamiliar ways of being and new actions. They require risks and "getting outside of your comfort zone." Inspired personal motivation makes the difference. When under-motivated, we take easier, less powerful options. Motivation by numbers or financial rewards alone will prove insufficient, while connection to your deepest personal values and sense of purpose in life provides lasting and powerful incentive. With inspired personal motivation, courage seems obvious and passion flows.

If you have no idea what your life purpose is about, your business vision cannot have its fullest meaning or success. Your purpose, vision and values stem from life experiences. They're rooted in your perceptions of what is needed, or missing, for you. Therein lie your greatest leadership gifts. Investment to uncover your personal life purpose and values pays off in business effectiveness.

For example, one leader had valued relationships throughout his career, but had unconsciously bought in to a belief that there would always be an "us" and "them" and that business results happened at someone's expense. From personal experience, he knew the feeling of unproductively dominating others, of causing resentment, and having antagonistic, unresolved relationships. Realizing that results at any cost were not fulfilling and that what really mattered to him was leading and relating to others in a way that contributed to their careers and lives, he set about building an organization where people love to go to work. His strategy focused on developing people and relationship to achieve business results, aiming to include everyone. His organization now delivers better results more effectively than ever, with far higher morale, retention, and career development amongst employees. He is building a legacy that provides him deep satisfaction and reward, and this gives him energy and strength to face his next challenge.

Expand your sense of what is to be gained through your vision in human terms. What is the cost of *not* pursuing it? Detail how it will affect your life and the lives of others who spend more waking hours and more vital force on the job than with family or anything else. Specify what has meaning to you in terms of the culture or atmosphere you love to work in. Design the inspirational legacy you would love to leave. Put it in your own words so you can convey it to others and inspire them.

Human Relationships Are the Foundation for Business Results

The quality of human relationships directly limits, or expands, the quality and magnitude of results possible in any system or organization. Quality of relationship both flows from and comprises the organizational culture, which can be hard to pinpoint by those within it, because what's normal becomes assumed. Culture forms the background for human interaction and underpins performance. You can often achieve breakthrough business results simply by improving the quality of culture. You can assess the quality of relationships, and thereby the culture, as the:

- Degree of freedom (absence of fear of consequence) individuals experience in raising critical issues, expressing concerns and creativity, or exposing vulnerability.
- Degree of trust and respect present, both in terms of others' competence and their reliability to be supportive rather than undermining. The quality of listening present.
- Degree of alignment in shared vision, values, and goals.

Fear in an organization, subtle or overt (such as when threats rather than straight communication are used as management tools), kills innovation and makes breakthrough impossible.

Take specific steps to build and improve extraordinary relationships by continually expanding the limits of communication and learning. Breakthroughs are not achieved alone, and a trusted core team of allies is essential to a breakthrough leader's success. Build trust, respect, freedom of expression, and your competence in relationships throughout your organization and your life. Without powerful relationships, your vision cannot manifest.

Open Your Blind Spots

We each see the world through our own set of values and concerns, which governs our interpretations. Your reality is a reflection of the interpretations you make about your life experience, education, culture, etc. Reality is based on our beliefs and thinking and this both serves and limits us. Our automatic, unexamined world-view makes us blind to other possibilities and points of view. As such, the ability to take honest "reality checks" with trusted allies is key.

Beliefs and expectations from our automatic interpretations can become self-fulfilling prophecies in profound and costly ways. As adults, we unconsciously behave consistent with limiting definitions we made of ourselves early in life in response to circumstances that changed long ago. Assuming them to be true, they remain unquestioned, untested, and reinforced over time. Likewise, unconscious expectations of others directly influence how you treat them, and again, a potentially insidious cycle of self-fulfilling prophecy sets in motion.

Discover the nature of your own automatic beliefs and expectations—your patterns of interpreting your experience. Become intimately familiar with how you constructed your way of achieving success in life, (the set of values and strengths you have developed), and how that both served and limited you. In a spirit of discovery and with courage, practice observing yourself in action. Then, through dialogue in powerful relationships committed to learning, you can bring outdated and self-imposed limitations to light. Your choices for new action immediately expand, and new actions lead to breakthroughs. Asking others for coaching and feedback—and then listening—may be challenging, but it certainly can make a difference.

When you know that perception equates with interpretation, you can dialogue rather than debate illusions of right or wrong, and the nature of communication becomes infinitely more productive. Commitment to become familiar with your illusory and automatic behavior, plus vigilance to uncover its limitations in service of expanding possibility and breakthrough performance, is a powerful way of life.

Adopt a Breakthrough Approach for Maximum Results

Breakthroughs are achieved through:
- Committing yourself to something that is inspiring and worthwhile to you personally.
- Gathering awareness of your unconscious governing belief structure.
- Testing assumptions and asking powerful questions.
- Being willing to give up the certainty of what you know so you can discover something new.
- Taking specific actions based on discoveries, road testing new behaviors, and establishing new practices.

This can only succeed through partnership and dialogue, and takes courage and commitment. The breakthrough mindset is motivated by values that have personal meaning, knows that success cannot be achieved alone, and knows that reality is perception and that perception is not fixed.

To be successful and manifest vision, we must continually learn and grow, shedding what once seemed certain but no longer serves. The speed of change, technological development, and bombardment of information require us to evolve rapidly as human beings and be more skilled at relating, to become clearer about who we are, and more focused on what is most important to us. At this point in history, sustainable ways of being in our corporations are desperately called for. Human beings connecting with one another in the context of breakthrough thinking and learning offer us perhaps the only way.

About the Author

Brenda Scarborough is president of a consulting firm based near San Francisco, California and serving clients worldwide. Scarborough & Company is a specialized team of inspired individuals who live their life purpose and dreams through coaching and facilitating top leaders in organizations to produce breakthroughs in leadership and performance so that results are accomplished that previously seemed impossible and sustainable corporate cultures are formed. Clients are leaders who have a commitment to achieving greatness, typically in large corporations and across a wide range of industries. Find out more information by visiting www.BrendaScarborough.com, or by telephoning 1.415.331.8601.

Want to Lead More Effectively?
Start With Your Heart
by Dina Silver

L ead from your heart, and you will transform your organization. Lead from your heart, and you will handle professional challenges with grace, honesty, and consistency. Lead from your heart, and you will have the capacity to inspire. Lead from your heart, and people will willingly follow because they know what you stand for.

Extraordinary leaders can be as different as night and day. Some lead with grace and elegance, others with power and speed. Regardless of style, inspiring leadership gives meaning and purpose to an organization. *You* have the power to be an extraordinary leader and to unleash a profound energy and determination within your organization. Whether you run a large or small organization or lead a team within one, the strategies in this chapter will help you transform your leadership so that your organization can thrive as never before.

To effectively lead others, you must first know yourself. All great leaders have an uncompromising commitment to their own core values, which are the elemental forces that define us. Some common core values are passion, freedom, trust, and loyalty. Simply put, our values are who we are. When we honor them, they drive us, help us create joy and satisfaction, and move us to action.

Honoring your own values–both at work and in your personal life–is inherently fulfilling even when it is hard. As a leader, you must establish values and commit to them. If *trust* is a stated core value in your business, and you see Jim slip a proprietary CD into his briefcase, you must address this breach of trust. If *loyalty* is a value, you must reward Fran when she comes in on Saturday and Sunday to solve a customer's urgent problem. A commitment to values creates meaning and purpose across all levels of your organization.

Define Your Own Values
The four-step process detailed below will give you a clear insight into the values that are essential to you and to your team or company.

Step One – A Peak Experience
Purpose: To generate an initial list of your central values
Time: Thirty minutes to one hour
The most effective way to clarify your own values is to discover them within your own life experiences. To begin this process, gather

some of your friends together and give them each a piece of paper and pen. Then, in vivid detail, share a significant story from your life. It can be something dramatic, like the time you were snorkeling among sharks, or it might be a special memory of baking chocolate chip cookies with your dad when you were six. Whatever story you choose, make sure it has deep significance for you. Describe how you felt, what you saw, and what you learned. As you talk, your friends can then list the values they recognize embedded in your tale.

Note: Before you begin, clarify the difference between a value and an activity. For instance, "travel" is not a value, but "adventure" is. "Gardening" is not a value, but "connection to nature" is.

When your story is complete, ask each listener to read his or her list aloud. You will find that some values show up on several lists, while others appear just once. You may be surprised by some of the values that others notice. This is natural and is one of the great gifts of the exercise. Maybe you told a story about a risk you took as a teenager, but from your current vantage point, the word "risk" is nowhere in your vocabulary! Perhaps risk-taking is a key value of yours that lies dormant, waiting to be revived.

As your friends share their lists, write down those values you *know* are an essential part of your being. If someone indicates a value you know is not a core value for you, don't add it to your list.

Step Two – Chart Your Values
Purpose: To refine and rank your core values
Time: Allow two hours

You will now complete your list by adding any other core values you know are central to your life. Once your list is complete, the next step is to determine the relative importance of your values.

The work of clarifying and prioritizing your core values is a private exercise. Find a quiet spot where you won't be disturbed. On a sheet of paper, draw ten concentric circles. Start with the center circle and ask yourself, "What is the single most important value without which I truly cannot live my life?"

This task is not easy, and several things will vie for the number one spot. Sit quietly until the truth becomes clear to you. Make sure you are not selecting a value that you think *should* be number one. (For example, you may think that love of your spouse and children *should* be first, but in fact you may find that "freedom" is actually more important for you.) Do not judge or censor your values, and don't shop for values you wish you had. Name your circles from your most powerful place: self-knowledge.

Once you have completed the first circle, repeat the exercise with the second circle to determine the next value that is closest to your heart. Complete all ten circles in this manner. When you are finished, if you have been honest with yourself, you will have created a value-driven map for both your personal and professional life. When important decisions arise, refer to your circles.

Step Three – Lead With Your Values

Purpose: To select three or four core values for your team or company
Time: Allow one hour

Reduce your ten core personal values to the three or four that will most effectively help you lead your organization to success. They will serve to guide your business procedures, your employee relationships, and your customer satisfaction. The values you select will shape the mission and direction of your company or team.

To trim your list down, eliminate any of your top ten that will not serve to strengthen your company. Although your core value of "spirituality" or "romance" may play a central role in your private life, they may not make the cut at work. Ask yourself, "If this were a core value at work, what are the likely consequences?" Select the three to four values that best serve your business, your employees, and your customers.

Step Four – Live Your Values

Purpose: To incorporate your values throughout your organization
Time: Ongoing

Once you have defined your values, commit to them by living them. You are setting a standard for your organization, and others will be willing to follow that standard as long as you avoid sending mixed messages.

As a leader, you must have the courage to be seen and known for who you are and what you stand for. When you share and maintain your core values, you will make a dramatic impact on the success and well-being of your organization and employees. The following techniques will help you instill your values within your team or company.

Communicate:

- Post your personal values in places where they can guide you daily.
- Ask your top executives or your direct reports to identify their own core values. Discuss which values team members share and which values are unique. Find a solution to any conflicting values.
- Post the shared values in the office. Discuss the link between corporate goals and the organization's key values.

Know Your Employees:
- Make time to get to know the people who work for you. Allocate thirty minutes a day to walk the floors and connect personally with employees. Get curious and ask questions that go beyond work. Your employees are your company's engine. Find out what makes them tick.

Tell Stories:
- Good story-telling is one of the most powerful tools you can use to energize and inspire people.
- Plumb your own life for stories that engage the listener and reinforce the fundamental values you live by. Or, if you prefer, choose a person from history whom you admire and whose values reflect those of your company. Tell stories from this person's life as a way of illustrating the power of your values.
- Integrate the best story-telling of all: Tell stories about the people who work for you who have gone beyond the call of duty. Link the person's actions back to the company's values.

Celebrate:
- Honor individual and group excellence. Describe how the individual or group you are celebrating embodies the organization's values by telling a great story about them.
- Encourage others to write a short vignette when they notice a colleague going out of his or her way to honor one of the company's core values. Print the stories in a regular column in the company newsletter, or post them on a bulletin board.

The Clear Path to Leadership Success

Review your core values every few months to be certain you are acting in accordance with them. If you're not, find ways to bring your actions back into alignment with your heart.

You will find that when you lead from your heart and create a corporate culture that is consistent with your values, you will unleash a commitment, passion, energy, and purpose that can drive your organization to greater success. You will not only create a more productive workplace where people work harder, try harder, and succeed more easily, but you will also have accomplished something that defies measurement: You will have created a place where people understand and can fulfill their purpose–a place that gives them the opportunity for a rich and meaningful life.

About the Author

Dina Silver works with CEOs and senior executives to support them in transforming their leadership, their organizations, and their lives. Her coaching style is holistic, assisting leaders in developing superior management, leadership, and communication skills while living rich personal lives founded on clarity, balance, meaning, and wisdom. Dina holds a Bachelor of Arts degree from Princeton University and is an award-winning feature film and CD-ROM producer. She is a Certified Professional Coach and the founder of Pegasus Coaching Group.

Learn more about her at www.pegasuscoachinggroup.com or contact her at: dina@pegasuscoachinggroup.com or by telephone at: 1.310.393.8082.

From Demoralized to Motivated
The 3-KSS™ Way to Leadership
by Melanie Wilson, Psy.D.

Nearly everyone agrees that performance reviews are crucial to monitor job performance. Yet managers and employees alike dread the annual performance appraisal. In fact, this universal assessment process is quite possibly the most procrastinated event in corporate history. Furthermore, after the unwelcome event is finally over, the appraisal document typically disappears into a file, to gather dust until the next review.

An alternative to the yearly performance review exists, in the form of ongoing, informal feedback. However, while it is a much more valuable and effective process, the informal feedback process has fallen victim to neglect. The result is that the once-a-year review tries to compensate for this neglect, yet ends up providing overly negative feedback that hurts more than it helps. Managers often express frustrations that have been building for a year but haven't been addressed, taking the employee by surprise and causing a rift in the relationship. By the same token, good performance is taken for granted, and more often than not, goes unmentioned.

What They Want

The truth is, everyone wants and needs feedback. Employees want to know how they are doing, and they appreciate constructive guidance that helps them achieve their goals and raise their productivity. Realize that employees are not simply looking for recognition, acknowledgment, appreciation, praise, and support for their achievements; rather, they want direction from someone they respect. People want to grow, develop professionally, and feel that they are making valuable contributions.

But managers repeatedly ask, "How do I criticize an employee yet keep them motivated?" Most employees will agree that criticism almost always causes negative feelings, which can decrease motivation and hurt job performance. Of course, this is the opposite of the intended result.

A common observation by employees is that their managers neglect to clearly communicate what is lacking or to give specific suggestions on how to improve. Employees then become confused because they don't know what is expected. The problem is compounded by fear of retribution if they question the review. A promotion or bonus may be at stake. But without honest communication the company is left with discouraged employees who live in dread of the next review.

The questions then are, "What can we learn from this inadequate review process?" and "How can managers improve employee performance through reviews?" The answer lies in ongoing communication.

The Superior Leader

Superior leaders know how to critique their employees in such a way as to increase employee effectiveness and motivation. How do they do it? They focus on the top priority, which is to help others do their best. They have mastered the art of regular, constructive, and uplifting feedback. These people stand out as the true leaders in any organization.

Constructive criticism guides without negative repercussions. An effective critique process provides continuous feedback that feeds the spirit, instead of merely fulfilling the letter of the performance review requirements. Furthermore, a regular feedback process that is informal and easy to use is more likely to be implemented regularly.

The 3-KSS™ Feedback Tool

The 3-KSS™ Feedback Tool is a quick, simple, cost-effective way to give and receive feedback. The basic process is this: Ask someone who knows you – manager, peer, direct report, even a family member - to write down: "*3* things I need to *K*eep doing; *3* things I need to *S*tart doing; *3* things I need to *S*top doing."

The following example concerns a manager who wants to improve his listening skills. The reviewing employee responded with this evaluation:

Goal – Improve Listening Skills
Please write out the following:

The 3 things I need to Keep *doing:*
- **Ask for others' opinions.** It helps us to feel valued and allows us to make a contribution.
- **Take notes on the others' contributions.** It shows us that you listen to and value our input.
- **You usually make eye contact and nod your head.** This gives others the feeling that you are interested and listening.

The 3 things I need to Start *doing:*
- **Ask for our opinions more often at meetings.** Other managers are concerned about wasting your time and displeasing you.
- **Paraphrase** what someone else has said to show you heard him or her.
- **Relax your posture and facial expression.** It would put others at ease and increase their willingness to speak up.

The 3 things I need to Stop *doing:*

- **Interrupting in an impatient tone**. This contributes to the "wall of silence" that you have complained about from time to time.
- **Looking at your watch.** It appears you're not interested or not listening.
- **Staying in your office.** When you visit the various departments and check in with people in a casual way they feel valued and reassured.

Additional Comments – You are well-regarded by most everyone in this organization. You could leverage this advantage more effectively to improve morale and motivation as we go through the merger. Visit the floor more often to show interest in the employees, ask for more input from managers, and really listen without showing impatience or disapproval. Thanks for this opportunity to contribute. I appreciate that you value my opinion!

You can use this form to create your own feedback process. Keep in mind the tone and the ultimate objective of the review. This example is carefully worded to provide constructive criticism, and to reinforce the positive aspects of the person's performance while giving "food for thought" on how to improve in the future.

Seven Tips For Getting 3-KSS™ Feedback

1) **Create a 3-KSS™ Feedback form on your computer.** Print out and distribute copies to your feedback givers.

2) **Keep an open mind.** Appreciate the feedback, even if you don't fully agree with it.

3) **Be curious rather than defensive.** This may take some practice at first, but you will learn more as a result.

4) **Ask the reviewer to explain the review.** Express thanks and seek clarification where needed.

5) **Share the insights** you gained and how you plan to make improvements.

6) **Ask for 3-KSS™ often.** You will gain confidence as you learn about yourself and how others see you.

7) **Keep this information confidential.** Secure your completed 3-KSS™ forms in a private file so that you can refer to them to review your progress.

Seven Tips For Giving 3-KSS™ Feedback

1) **Only discuss observable behaviors and their impact**, not your opinions about underlying motivations or character.

2) Be kind *and* candid. Make sure that you truly have the person's best interests at heart. Then have the courage to tell the truth about what you see and what the impact (positive or negative) of the behavior might be.

3) Respect confidentiality. Don't share appraisal information with others.

4) Be an exceptional role model yourself.

5) Put yourself in the other person's place. Empathy will help you to communicate more effectively.

6) Help the person develop a plan of action and to practice the new behaviors. Offer follow-up coaching, advising, and support.

7) 3-KSS™ is based on subjective perceptions, and is not valid as a formal, objective measure of performance. It should not be used for bonus or promotion decisions. It works best when freely sought out by employees.

The Benefits of 3-KSS™ Feedback

3-KSS™ is a dynamic approach to employee appraisals. It gives employees the opportunity to seek continuous feedback, rather than waiting for the annual review. You will find that it offers the following benefits:

- Increases self-awareness, which is the foundation of personal and interpersonal effectiveness.
- Is "off the record," which increases candor.
- Is written, which encourages thoughtful, responsible expression.
- Transforms defensiveness into curiosity and open-mindedness when feedback is delivered in a genuinely helpful way.
- Recognizes accomplishments and reinforces beneficial behaviors.
- Eliminates the dread of yearly performance reviews. Feedback becomes a routine, commonplace *practice* in your organization.
- Increases morale, motivation, productivity and bottom-line results, when practiced on a regular basis.

Character Strength = Leadership

Don't passively wait for the yearly formal performance review. Performance reviews too often give lip service to helping people develop and advance in their careers. The recipients are mostly interested in how it will affect their bonus and chances for promotion. Traditional performance appraisals rarely help people get the valuable career development information and coaching they need.

Instead, make feedback a routine part of the review process. Start small and easy. At first, you could just ask for the "Keep Doing" feedback. Later, you can add the "Start Doing" and "Stop Doing" components. Eventually, it will grow into a value-added process for the good of the individual and the organization. When you use 3-KSS™ often, you become expert in getting and giving feedback on a regular basis. You'll soon start to look forward to the improvements that result.

It takes a positive attitude and strong qualities of character to ask for and receive feedback. How you handle it and what you do with it will speak volumes about your leadership qualities. You'll be admired and respected as a role model. By following your example, others can gain the confidence to try 3-KSS™ for themselves. Now, that's leadership!

About the Author

Dr. Melanie Wilson is a psychologist, executive coach, business and leadership consultant, speaker, and writer. She is CPO ("Chief Psychological Officer") of Executive Consulting Group, based in the Philadelphia region. Her specialties include leadership development, performance enhancement, career success and overall health and well being. She can be reached at mwcarly@aol.com or 1.610.526.9111.

Section Three –
Marketing and Sales

Getting to First Base
The First Step to Scoring More Sales
by Robert Middleton

Networking events and social gatherings pose great opportunities to build business relationships and get the word out about your company and the services you provide. The scenario is familiar: a room full of people mingling and discussing business, trying to make connections. When a potential client approaches you and asks the ultimate question, "What do you do?" your answer is crucial. This is your chance to put yourself in position to score a sale, but you must respond in a way that attracts their attention, or the opportunity will pass and the person will move on.

The key is to make a good first impression and appeal to your prospective clients' needs. But how do you do this? Is there a reliable way to get attention with just a few words and avoid the "glazed-over look" from prospects?

You can get this attention and interest by knowing *exactly* what to say. It's like swinging at a baseball – you either strike out, go foul, or make a solid connection. Your response to their question about what you do, when phrased properly, will get you solidly on first base. Let's look at how to do that.

Play Marketing Ball

Marketing Ball is a model based on a diagram of a baseball diamond. It takes some of the mystery out of the marketing and sales process.

Start at home plate, go around the bases, and then back to home. Getting home means you've "scored" by winning a new client. But before you score, you need to get to first base–where you have your prospect's attention.

First base is where every business needs to get to before anything else–in a brochure, an advertisement, a website, or a simple verbal introduction. If you don't get to first base, you're out of the game. After you're on first base, it's easier to get around the diamond. Second base is where a prospect is ready to explore working with you. Third base is when a client is ready to buy from you, and home base is when the sale is actually consummated.

First base is the most crucial and is deceptively simple. Just like in a baseball game, it is the initial hit of every sale. In networking situations, the hit comes when the person you're speaking to shows some interest and wants to know more. You have four different ways to get onto first

135

base, and some are more effective than others. In fact, the first two hardly ever result in a hit, but people persist in using them.

Label

The majority of business people use labels to get attention. When asked what they do, they respond with: "I'm an accountant (or a management consultant, an executive coach, or a widget salesperson)." Those labels may be accurate, but they sure aren't very attention-getting.

People develop their own pictures of what those labels mean. What stereotypes can you think of for lawyers or used car salespeople? Are these pictures always accurate? Of course not. Let's take accountants, for example. People tend to think accountants are boring. So when you reply to the question about what you do with the label, "I'm an accountant," in the back of most people's minds they think you're boring. Not much of an attention-getting marketing impression.

So forget labels. Don't ever lead with your label. It makes people pigeonhole you and it works against you almost every single time.

Process

When people stop using labels to introduce themselves, they often start using a process to describe what they do. Again, consider our intrepid accountant who, rejected every time he used the accountant label, now tells people that he prepares taxes and does financial statements.

This is a little better, but not much. A process doesn't answer the question on everyone's mind: "What's in it for me? You prepare taxes and do financial statements. So what? What's the advantage, the thing that will help my business?" When you talk about what you do in terms of a process, you become a commodity. After all, every accountant prepares taxes and does financial statements. There's nothing to distinguish you and, once again, you fail to get attention.

Solution

Undeterred, our persistent accountant learns that he must speak in terms that mean something to the prospect. Now he emerges with the statement or "Audio Logo": "I help people in the restaurant business reduce their taxes and increase their cash flow."

This is a whole lot better. Mr. Accountant has targeted his market and clearly expressed a desirable result or solution he can accomplish for his clients. Using a solution-oriented response will get the accountant and you on first base more often. To spark interest, say who you work with and the solution you provide for them.

Here are some examples:

- "I work for high tech companies to improve the communication skills of their technical managers."

- "I help writers who want to get their first book published quickly."
- "I offer training for leaders who want to beat the competition more often."
- "I provide equipment for hospitals that gives a six month return on investment."

If you're speaking to the right person, all of these are likely to get you onto first base. And this is usually as far as most business people go.

However, solution-oriented Audio Logos don't always yield maximum interest. When you tell someone the solution or result you provide, it often sounds just too good to be true. The inward response goes something like, "Well, of course he's promising that, but can he really deliver?" People are, by nature, skeptical, and it's easy to arouse skepticism with a solution-oriented Audio Logo. To a writer who's been trying to get a book published for years, the promise of getting it published quickly isn't even close to reality. So they can't hear what you're saying.

Problem

Let's go back to the accountant example. He's been getting some results with his solution-oriented Audio Logo, but not enough to satisfy him. So instead he tries a response based on a problem: "I help people in the restaurant business who are tired of paying too much taxes and having terrible cash flow."

When you use a problem-oriented Audio Logo you communicate to your prospect that you understand their suffering. You don't even have to tell them yet what you can do for them. They'll automatically understand: "Yeah, I'm paying too much in taxes and my cash flow is terrible. I wonder what he has that can help me?" This invariably leads to a "that's for me" response. The accountant is immediately on first base. With a problem-oriented Audio Logo you hit nerves that none of the other approaches can touch.

Create Your Own Problem-Oriented Audio Logo

What is the big difference between the solution-oriented and problem-oriented Audio Logo? The solution-oriented response is about what the accountant will do. The problem-oriented is about how the prospect is suffering. In the second, 100% of the attention is on the prospect. The accountant is actually out of the picture. And what are people most interested in? Themselves.

To develop a problem-oriented Audio Logo, start with the problems, issues, and challenges your clients face, and express them in simple terms. Don't talk about how you do what you do or even how you can help them; talk about the pain they're going through. This approach may seem negative, but people will respond positively because your words will go to the heart of what's not working in their business. They will immediately want to know what you can do to make things better.

Here are the previous solution-oriented Audio Logos turned around into problem-oriented ones:

- "I work for high tech companies whose technical managers are alienating their staffs."
- "I help writers who are frustrated that it's taking so long to get that first book published."
- "I offer training for leaders who are discouraged that they keep getting beat by the competition."
- "I provide equipment for hospitals that are anxious about return on investment."

You may be amazed by the interested reaction you get from a problem-oriented Audio Logo. People will often respond by telling you in great detail what their problem is, which then gives you the opportunity to discuss your solutions.

Perfect Your Swing

Identify the struggle, frustration, discouragement, or anxiety your prospects experience, put it into an Audio Logo, and test it on several people to gauge their reaction. Fine-tune it until it clicks and you'll get a whole new level of attention and interest. You'll be on first base and ready to move towards second.

Keep practicing, but don't worry about getting a home run. Imagine using an Audio Logo and getting this response: "Wow, you help people with that problem? That's incredible! I've been looking for someone like you for years! We have a half million-dollar budget to solve this problem. Is that enough? Can you come over right away?"

Yes, that would be nice, but it's a fantasy. It's not going to happen. Instead, be satisfied with getting prospects onto first base and gradually working them around the bases until you bring them home.

About the Author
Since 1984 Robert Middleton has offered marketing coaching, consulting, and workshops to thousands of self-employed professionals who need to attract more clients. Robert is the author of the *InfoGuru Marketing Manual* (available on his website) and his main work today is Marketing Action Groups conducted virtually by bridge conference line with clients all over the world. You can contact Robert by visiting his website at www.actionplan.com. There you can subscribe to his free weekly eZine, More Clients, and get a free Marketing Plan Workbook plus several other freebies such as a Marketing Scorecard, audio programs, articles and reports.

The Fastest Way to Increase Your Sales

Four Steps to Develop the Most Compelling
Answers to Why Your Prospects Should
Buy Now!

by Michael Cannon

At the heart of your prospect's decision to buy or not to buy from you are two questions:

> **1)** Why should I change what I currently do and buy this product/service?
>
> **2)** Why should I buy your solution rather than a competitive offer?

Consider your company's sales messaging. What buying questions does it answer? If it is like most, your sales messaging may be answering one of the buying questions and leaving the other unanswered, or it's answering both questions poorly.

Most sales messaging is developed in a product-centric manor. It's a feature and benefit description of what your product or service does and the value your customer receives. Compelling sales messaging is developed in a buyer-centric manor. It answers your prospect's primary buying questions. Your use of product-centric sales messaging results in fewer customers, slower sales cycles, and higher sales costs.

Why Buyer-Centric Sales Messaging?

If you identified all the reasons why your company's sales performance is not optimal, they would fall into six problem categories. Listed in increasing order of time, cost, and difficulty to fix, they are:

> **1)** Your sales messaging does not answer the prospect's buying questions in a compelling and persuasive manor.
>
> **2)** Your employee's goals and compensation are not optimized to company objectives.
>
> **3)** Your sales processes are not clearly defined, repeatable, and measurable.
>
> **4)** Your employee's skills and knowledge are not matched to tasks.
>
> **5)** Your offer's price-to-value equation is not compelling.
>
> **6)** Your offer does not generate meaningful value for the target market.

The easiest and least expensive option is improving how you answer your prospect's buying questions. Thus, developing and deploying compelling, buyer-centric sales messaging is often the fastest way to profitably increase sales. The following is a proven four-step process to help you accomplish this goal.

Step One – Determine Your Prospect's Primary Buying Questions

There are eight primary buying questions. Select the appropriate ones for your firm's market and sales plan:

1) **Why should I buy your solution rather than a competitive offering?** This question is important in an A Opportunity Market, also known as a pull or late majority market. Buyers have already decided why they want to buy your product or service. Often, an impending event is in place; the company has allocated money for the purchase, and it is actively evaluating potential suppliers. The majority of the sales effort is focused on satisfying demand.

2) **Why should I change what I currently do and buy your product/ service?** This question is important in a B Opportunity Market, also known as a push or innovators/early adopters market. Prospects do not know about your offering and thus do not know why they might want to buy it. The buying process is educating prospects as to why they might want to invest in your company's offering. Once prospects agree, they become an A Opportunity. The majority of the sales effort is focused on creating demand.

   In between the A and B Opportunity markets is the push/pull market or the early majority market. This market contains a mixture of both A and B opportunities so buying questions one and two are in play. The key to success in this market is quickly qualifying which type of opportunity you are selling to and then adjusting the sales effort appropriately.

3) **Why buy now?** Do not confuse this question with, "Why should I change what I currently do and buy your product/service?" "Why buy now?" is not a market specific question; it is account specific. It is about comparing what other purchases the prospect is considering to your offer, and then validating that yours is the best solution to buy now.

4) **Why buy by buyer roles?** This question is important in markets where a group of people must agree on a purchase. The typical attributes of this market include complex and or high-priced goods and services, like business software, manufacturing equipment, a fleet lease, etc.

5) **Why buy by vertical market?** This question is important in the early adopters market as a way to gain critical traction for your offer. It also

becomes important in the late majority market as the market splinters into highly customized niche solutions.

6) Why buy by competitor? This is a version of "Why should I buy your solution rather than a competitive offering?" question customized to a specific competitor. It's most important in a pull or late majority market to help prospects evaluate potential suppliers.

7) Why should I meet or talk with you? This question is the most ignored buying question and the one that causes the most pain, since nothing happens until a buyer and seller talk. The prospect's unstated question at this step in the sales cycle is, "What am I going to get in return for my time?" If the prospect can see clear value in meeting, then he or she will allocate the time. No value means no meeting and no sale.

8) Why should I distribute your product or service? This question is important in a Distributor or OEM sales plan. It's primarily associated with an A Opportunity or commodity market, where prospects are pulling the market faster than a company can satisfy demand. In addition to the primary distributor buyer question above, there are two associated questions to consider: *Why should I distribute your solution rather than a competitive offering? Why should the sales rep sell your offering instead of other products that the distributor carries?*

Step Two – Identify Improvements to the Customer's Condition

Having selected your prospects primary buying questions, you now must develop the material needed to answer the questions. Employing the Use Case Methodology is the best way is to do this. It will help you identify the ways in which your company's offering improves the customer's condition. To be meaningful, the Use Case must be limited to a single offer focused on a specific buyer. If your company sells multiple products or services you will need to develop a Use Case for each offer.

A Use Case compares what your customer's condition was like before your company's solution was purchased to what it is like after your solution was implemented. The more your company's offer improves the customer's condition, the more valuable your solution becomes and the more likely the prospect is to buy it and buy it from you.

An effective Use Case contains the following seven sections:

1) The current solution.
2) The problems with the current solution.
3) The impact of these problems.
4) The value of reducing or eliminating those problems.

5) The problems your solution reduces or eliminates.

6) How your solution reduces or eliminates the problems.

7) The problems not solved by your competitors.

The Use Case Methodology identifies both the ways your company improves the customer's condition and how you do it better than competitive solutions. A solid set of Use Cases will contain the keys to your company's sales and marketing success. If your company's Use Cases are weak, it's a sure sign that you a) were not able to obtain meaningful informational interviews with prospects and customers, b) that you need outside help to develop them, or c) that you have some major product or market problems to overcome.

Step Three – Answer Your Prospect's Buying Questions

Create compelling and persuasive answers to your prospect's primary buying questions using the summary format below:

- Create three to five claims that appeal to the buyer's emotional reasons for buying and provide an intellectual justification for the decision.
- Develop a meaningful list of evidence for why your three to five claims are true.
- Summarize the answers on one page.

Using this format is based on the principal that most people will only remember three to five points from a conversation. The format makes it easy for prospects to understand and remember your key three to five points. It also makes it easy for your sales team to communicate the points necessary to win more business. Once you have created your summaries, conduct a few more informational interviews with prospects and customers. As compelling as you think the buyer-centric sales messaging might be, your opinion does not count. Only the prospect's opinion does.

Step Four – Deploy Your Sales Messaging for Optimal Results

Infuse the sales messaging into your company's sales and marketing efforts using a sales process and tools map. The map contains three columns: Role, Steps, and Tools. Role is the primary buyer type in each step in the sales process. Steps define the process for converting a suspect into a prospect, a prospect into an opportunity, an opportunity into a customer, and a customer into a repeat customer. Tools are the specifics needed to move a contact through each step in the sales process such as a website, call guide for getting an appointment, demo scripts, presentations, proposal, etc. The sales process and tools map will help you identify the optimal sales processes, the correct sales tools, the goal of each tool, and the sales messaging needed to make each tool effective. It will also give you a roadmap and set of best practices for how your company wins customers.

The Fastest Way to Increase Sales

The fastest way to increase your company's sales is to use the proven four-step process for developing and deploying buyer-centric sales messaging. The methodology will help you create compelling and persuasive sales messaging, accelerate sales cycles, attract more customers, and increase your company's bottom line.

About the Author

Michael Cannon is a sales consultant, speaker, author, coach, advisor, and board member. He has over 20 years of sales, management, and founders experience in the enterprise software, telecommunications, wireless, training, and professional services industries. An expert at increasing sales, he has helped more than 20 companies, as big as SBC and as small as a three-person garage start-up, make dramatic improvements in sales performance. As Founder and CEO of the Silver Bullet Group, a sales consultancy, Michael created the *Why Buy? Now Sales Planning System*, a proven methodology for increasing business-to-business sales. More information about this topic, including examples, are available at www.silverbulletgroup.com or by calling 1.925.930.9436.

Brand Delight
How to Stay Alive in a World of Commoditization
by Allan Gorman

O ver 3,000 marketing messages bombard us each day. You encounter them everywhere: on billboards, on television, in magazines, on the radio, in newspapers, and even on the Internet. So many ads scream, "Look at me! Look at me!" that very few have the power to get noticed at all.

Successfully marketing new products and services is a challenge for any company, especially those aspiring for quality and leadership. Investing money in advertising, public relations, promotions, package design, product design, and graphic identity used to be the ticket to a brand's success. Not anymore. Media costs continue to spiral higher and higher with less and less evidence of their effectiveness. Additionally, good press is hard to control, and a public relations campaign is often incapable of sustaining positive awareness and product preference over the long haul.

Too Many Choices

Thirty years ago, only a handful of television channels existed. We could choose from a dozen or so major consumer magazines and just a few radio stations and newspapers. Yet, these options satisfied our needs for entertainment, diversion, and information.

Back then, just like today, ads and publicity campaigns vied for our attention. The difference is that in today's new information age we are seeing an absolute explosion of commercial data, with more venues and outlets than ever before. Today, with a customer's ability to access information instantly, consumers want to know how fast your company can deliver and how much you charge rather than what level of quality and value you provide.

Despite this shift, many modern companies achieve considerable success—and stay leading brands—even while their competitors are struggling to survive. For example:

- Starbucks has become a welcomed sight on every city street corner, with almost no traditional ad expenditures.
- Mercedes Benz brand cars are everywhere, as are Mini-Coopers, while other car companies all but beg for sales with 0% financing and thousands of dollars in factory incentives.
- Target has redefined its image to one of a cool, low-priced household product haven that offers "cheap chic."

- Washington Mutual is changing the banking landscape with a highly visible ad campaign that champions "the little guy."

Brand Delight Makes the Difference

While everyone else is fighting off commoditization, the leaders stay above the fray. They command premium prices, sell to better and happier clientele, and continuously create irrationally loyal "brand fans" who become their best salespeople through word of mouth.

Each of the previously mentioned successful brands had the vision to fill a void. They also had an understanding and knowledge of their market, a commitment to adding value, staying power to wait for the public to accept that value, and a healthy dose of luck. And they've discovered how to continually nourish innovation and excellence.

The marketplace leaders have capitalized on a profound shift. They have moved from simply offering goods and services to delivering a true "brand experience," leaving their competitors in the dust. Consider these examples:

- Universal Studios and Six Flags/Great Adventure cannot hold a candle to a Disney vacation experience.
- Honda, Yamaha, and Suzuki all sell great motorcycles, but none can compete with Harley-Davidson. None will offer the psychic connection that HOG devotees have to their bikes, to the company that makes them, and to the community of which they feel a part.

Most Companies Don't Really Understand Marketing

Most corporate managers—especially in a pressured economy—consider that their job's primary purpose is to help the business make more money and that the common sense way to make more money is through more sales. However, this sales-driven orientation creates a marketing philosophy that exploits product advantages and makes comparisons about the product's practical values—the features, systems, and practical benefits of use. They employ hard-selling messages designed to overcome their prospect's resistance to buying and then they resort to manipulative appeals, incentives, and gimmickry to push and close "the deal."

But this isn't marketing at all—it's selling. By comparing their product to others, this "sales" mindset instantly commoditizes the product. So, at best, this strategy only appeals to that small portion of the buying universe who happens to be shopping for a product like that at any given moment.

To Change Your Brand, Change Your Thinking

Suppose we suspend the notion that the primary purpose of the business is to make money, and think, instead, that the primary purpose is actually to make more customers? Now our mind has turned to true marketing, not just selling. We begin to understand that what's important isn't our company—what we make, what we do, how we do it, or the special incentives we're offering. Rather, it's all about the customers—what they need, how we can meet their needs, and how the product or service we provide can add an experience of delight to their life.

The question then becomes, "What can we do to turn our own product or service into a delightful brand like a Harley or a Disney?" While there's no exact science to answer that question, we do have some ideas about what works. In fact, modern super-brands have learned the value of employing a rigid system of standards that helps them stay focused and on track. You can employ them too. Here are eight tips you can start using immediately to make your brand stand out:

1) **Develop a clear identity**. Do market research on a regular basis to learn what your identity is in the eyes of your best customers. What is their perspective of your product or service's value? Use what you learn to distinguish yourself from your competitors in a meaningful way. You must build your brand's identity and story on a platform that intentionally sets you apart from everyone else. Everyone who comes into contact with your brand is going to pigeonhole you. How would you like them to do it?

2) **Offer a relevant benefit**. Why should a customer do business with you? Your product or service is going to solve a problem (maybe one the customer doesn't even know he or she has), and your customer is going to be delighted by the results. Build your premise around a great benefit that your prospect can easily understand and relate to.

3) **Appeal to your prospect's emotions.** How do you want prospects to feel after listening to what you have to say? How do you want them to feel after using your product? Align your story and creative marketing techniques with the desired emotional response.

4) **Help them remember your name and what you stand for.** Employ a unique device to help prospects recall who you are when they're ready to purchase what you're offering. You can accomplish this through an appealing graphic, a turn of phrase, or a combination of the two. Whatever you decide, make sure it's meaningful, memorable, and identifiable with your company. It should remind prospects how delightful it will be to do business with you.

5) **Penetrate their "noise" barrier.** Find out how to penetrate your prospects' resentment and resistance to sales. Face it; your message is an annoyance to them. People will tune you out unless you're offering

some information they can actually use. Measure all your marketing efforts by your prospects' standards, not yours.

6) **Be all you say you are.** Make sure you support and sustain all your claims and promises. If you make claims you can't support, your prospects will see right through your words and do business elsewhere. If you must, change your products and services to support your claims.

7) **Over-deliver on promises.** Make the experience of using your product or service a joy. Find ways to extend your desirability by adding extra value and extra reasons for your customer to return again and again. Offer free advice and support. Follow up and ask for feedback. Send a timely handwritten and personalized "thank-you" note. Do what you must to make their interaction with your products and service "human" instead of cold and matter-of-fact.

8) **Teach current customers how to become your ambassadors.** Use word-of-mouth to extend your message by giving loyal customers the tools to become "brand ambassadors." Reward them for referrals. Lavish them with extra "perks" for coming back to you. Introduce your customers to others who use your product or service so they can create mutual relationships.

Commit to Becoming a Provider of Brand Delight

Keep in mind that you will need courage to be unique and to resist the market pressures and advisors that will try to lure you back into that old "sales by comparison, commoditizing, me too" trap. You may even need to take a few steps backward to learn new skills, attitudes, and techniques. Doing so will require an investment of time and funds. It will demand change, and it will take ongoing work to remain on the leading edge. But in the end, the investment will be worth it. In fact, once you've begun the journey to market leadership you won't want to stop. You'll become forever committed to delivering the true experience of brand delight…something that your new loyal customers will go out of their way for and gladly pay a premium to get again and again and again.

About the Author
Allan Gorman is owner of AGCD —a Montclair, NJ based creative and branding consultancy that specializes in helping clients who won't settle for parity realize market leadership. His creative talent has been cited and showcased in *Graphic Design USA* and *Adweek*, as well as in numerous weekly and monthly publications. He has also been the recipient of over 400 industry accolades and awards. Download a complimentary copy of Mr. Gorman's informative and helpful report: "Ten Marketing Secrets for Building a Sexier Brand," and sign up for his "briefs for building better brands" newsletter at www.agcd.com. Contact Mr. Gorman at 1.973.509.2728.

Give Customers What They Want
How to Win Their Loyalty and Boost Your Sales
by Dan Grandstaff

What is the secret to gaining loyal customers? Many business owners, managers, and executives think the key is to be friendly, attentive, responsive, persuasive, and sincere. While that answer is not completely wrong, the real secret goes far beyond personality and attentiveness.

If you want to win with people, especially your customers, you need to focus on only one thing–helping people get what they want. This may sound simple, but in today's society, individuals and companies tend to lose sight of this focus. Rather than helping customers get what *they* want, we focus on how the customers can help us get what *we* want.

The Sales Experience

The two most important questions for most customers are "Can I trust you?" and "Do you care?" When they can answer those questions with a solid "Yes," they relax their resistance, trusting they will get exactly what they want by working with you. They know you will help them find the features, benefits, and requirements they need.

We have all experienced high-pressure sales tactics where the salesperson is friendly and positive about the product, but obviously more concerned with making the sale than meeting our needs. What is your typical reaction to these types of situations? Chances are, you won't trust the salesperson, and you will take your money and your loyalty elsewhere.

On the opposite end of the spectrum, can you think of a time when a salesperson helped you decide which product to buy based on your current needs? Perhaps the salesperson even encouraged you to postpone the purchase until you could find exactly what you needed. Such experiences create customer loyalty. When salespeople are truly intent on helping us get what we want, we become loyal fans, going back to their company again and again, and recommending their services to everyone we know.

Putting the Ideas into Practice

The fact is, when you help people get what they want, you get something more valuable than an immediate sale or their passing appreciation. You win their ongoing loyalty. By putting your customers' needs before your own, you virtually guarantee that they will be back for further business. Following are a few guidelines to help you win with your customers and create long-term relationships that will drive your business to success.

1) **Make it a priority to help customers get what they want.** Make it your mission to help people get what they want. Write it down. Post it where you and your people will see it throughout the day. Tell your customers that your most important goal is to help meet their needs. Before you call a customer, remind yourself of this goal. Ask yourself at least three times during the day, "Am I focusing on helping people get what they want and need?" Doing so will keep you in a customer-focused mindset all day.

2) **Ask customers what they want.** You may not be able to call your customers and say, "We'd like to know what you really want from us," but you can ask them to tell you what you need to do to make their experience better. If you don't ask, you'll never know. Ask them to give feedback in conversations, suggestion cards, surveys, and focus groups. When customers believe their input will be used to serve them better, they will be happy to oblige.

3) **Listen to your customers.** How many times have you had a restaurant server ask you, "How was everything?" as he or she dropped off your check, only to hurry away without giving you time to answer? While the server may have taken the time to ask, he or she did not take the time to listen, which is the most important part. When people give you feedback, listen to them. You can get some of the most powerful ideas for growing a business from your customers.

   Many executives and owners choose not to listen to their customers because they do not want to hear negative feedback. Granted, no one likes hearing negative news, but your customers are revealing issues you need to address. Company after company has turned their business around when they finally stopped avoiding the hard to take feedback and started making the changes the customers requested. Listening to your customers is crucial to your future success.

4) **Study customer behavior.** Even though people are unique, their behavior and motivations follow certain patterns. By learning those patterns and what they mean, you can communicate and respond much more effectively to customers and everyone else in your life. When you understand how your customers see the world, you are better able to meet and even predict their needs.

   Two popular tools for understanding people's behavior are the DISC and the Myers-Briggs Type Indicator (MBTI). You can learn the basics of these tools in a couple hours from a certified consultant. Behavioral assessments like these can teach you how people prefer to communicate, what turns them off immediately, what their primary motivators are, and how they make decisions. They're valuable tools for any business.

5) **Analyze and optimize the customer's experience.** When was the last time you took a serious look at your business from your customer's point of view? Make a list of every point of contact a customer or prospect could have with your business. List every contact, including driving into the parking lot, walking in the front door, being greeted as they arrive, making an appointment, visiting your website, etc. Beside each point of contact, briefly describe the customer's needs and possible wants at that stage. Ask questions like "What is the customer's probable state of mind?" and "How likely is it that the customer's needs will be met by this contact with the company?" The answers to these questions will help you discern between the ideal and the reality. Once you are able to see the reality, you can develop priorities for improving your customers' experiences.

You can do this simple analysis on a legal pad in a couple hours, or you can work with a consultant to do a more in-depth analysis. Either way, what you learn will put you miles ahead of any competitor who has not carefully considered their customers' needs and experiences.

6) **Learn how to deal with dissatisfied customers.** If you are lucky, your customers will tell you when they don't get what they want. Learning to consistently and effectively deal with dissatisfied customers will help you keep many good customers from taking their business elsewhere. Not only will you keep those customers, but you will also turn many of them into your most enthusiastic supporters.

Dealing with a dissatisfied customer, or "service recovery," does not come naturally. Our initial reaction is usually to get defensive and irritated. That is why you need to develop and practice a system for service recovery, and make sure every employee in your company learns and practices the system as well.

A good method for dealing with people who are upset is to use the acronym **LEARN** (**LEARN** from your customers and **LEARN** from your mistakes).

   L– Listen. Don't try to answer or calm the person down. Just listen. Give the customer time to vent. If you're in a public space, invite the customer into an office where you can have some privacy.

   E– Empathize. Tell the customer you understand why he or she is upset and frustrated. Above all, do not say that the customer is wrong, even if he or she did contribute to the problem. Do not blame the customer or anyone else for the problem.

A– Apologize. Tell the person you are sorry the problem happened. Do not say, "I am sorry you are upset." This implies that the customer's feelings or perception of events is the problem. Saying you are sorry is not taking the blame or admitting guilt. It is often the only phrase that will calm things down enough to move toward a resolution.

R– Take **R**esponsibility for addressing the situation. Tell the customer that you want to understand what happened and that you will work toward a resolution. Again, you are not taking responsibility for the problem. You are taking responsibility for resolving it.

N– Take **N**eeded Action. Handle the problem yourself. If you have to hand it off to someone else, make sure it is taken care of. The key is to follow through until the problem is resolved.

Everyone is a Valued Customer

By following these strategies, you not only win with your customers, but you also win with your employees, co-workers, suppliers, and partners. The key to winning with people is to treat everyone you meet as a valued customer. Help them get what they want. See things from their point of view. You'll find that what people want most is often easy to provide – acknowledgement, courtesy, respect, attention, appreciation, and trust. Find ways to give people more of what *they* want, and your business will soar to the level that *you* want.

About the Author

For over 20 years, Dan Grandstaff has been helping companies and individuals achieve greater success by improving their effectiveness with people. His firm, Win With People, Inc., provides coaching, consulting, and training services to companies in customer focus, employee selection and retention, team development, and performance improvement.

More information about improving people effectiveness, including the award-winning newsletter "Win With People," is available at www.winwithpeople.com, or by calling Dan Grandstaff at 1.800.490.5637. He is based in Chapel Hill, North Carolina and works with companies all over the world.

ee Factors that Make or
ak Your Business

by William E. Jackman

Many brave individuals with ideas and vision give small business ownership their all for the passionate possibility of living the entrepreneur's dream: achieving time and financial freedom while remaining healthy long enough to enjoy the experience of having created a meaningful life and business. However, studies show that 80% of small businesses in North America fail within ten years. A quick trip around the globe reveals this storm of dismal results has swept across many other continents, leaving a wake of dreams broken and spirits shattered.

As with most things, if you fail many times and still believe you can do it, eventually you'll find a way to succeed. According to research, at least 20% of small businesses find their way to increased levels of business success. While it may take them ten years or more to figure it out, they eventually make enough mistakes, learn enough lessons from them (emotional and logical), and finally achieve long term success. This simple pattern is the true foundation of your entire life's education. It is an inseparable part of your original programming and your key to creating the business success you desire.

Unfortunately, the question, "How do 20% of small businesses succeed?" will not get you the answer you desire. In fact, many times we get the wrong answers (results) simply because we ask the wrong questions to begin with. Instead, consider the question: "Why do 20% of small businesses succeed?" The answer ultimately makes or breaks your business and is shockingly obvious: **Your success in business is a direct result of your ability to focus on a single, definite purpose while taking action in a way necessary to achieve your desired outcome.**

When you look at this in reverse, it simply means that if your business has yet to produce the results you want, then either you have not taken action in the most effective way, *or* you have not focussed your business on a single, clearly defined purpose.

At this point you should resist the natural temptation to defend your past efforts. Instead, allow yourself the opportunity to contemplate and accept the powerful simplicity of this idea. When you are ready, embrace it with the firmness of a bear hug. You'll take a quantum leap towards the success you and your business deserve. In fact, you will have aligned yourself with the winning mindset shared by the successful 20% of small businesses.

Consider Three Critical Factors

Now that you are on the right road and are prepared to head toward your ultimate destination, you need to be aware of three critical factors that will cut your journey short and stop you in your tracks. Ignore these at your own peril, because that's exactly what the unsuccessful 80% of small businesses do. They fail to understand these critical factors and apply them correctly. In order of priority, they are:

1) You Must Make A Genuine Promise

2) Your Business Must Consistently Make Good on Your Genuine Promise

3) You Must Promote The Fact Your Business Consistently Makes Good on Your Genuine Promise

You'll find these critical factors at play in 100% of all businesses. Your current level of business success, or lack thereof, reflects your understanding of them and your enthusiasm to make them a reality. The 20% of small businesses that succeed use the three critical factors, knowingly or unknowingly, as their ultimate business strategy. The other 80% generally:

- Do not define or make a "genuine promise." Instead, they allow customers to create their own version of what they believe the business promises. This sets up a no-win situation because customer expectations in a competitive world are a moving target. Establish a target of your own worthy of customer demand. Successful business owners define and satisfy their customers' expectations.

- **OR** – Partially define a promise (although in most cases not a "genuine" one) and do not have sufficient organization to consistently "make good" on it. The inability of their business to meet their own partially defined expectations means their customers are likely to have inconsistent experiences. Inconsistency is the enemy of trust. It eats away at it like rust, until one day it completely falls apart. Therefore, you need to protect and cherish your customers' trust. The best way to do this is to consistently "make good" on your "genuine promise."

- **OR** – Promote their business before ensuring critical factors #1 and #2 have been adequately addressed. They actually end up advertising their weaknesses instead of their strengths. This is extremely counter-productive and rapidly lethal. Competition in the marketplace will eat you alive if they get wind of your weaknesses. Your competitive weakness becomes their competitive advantage. This nukes your customers' trust. Why would anyone in their right mind pay to advertise to their potential/actual customers the fact they cannot be trusted?

Using the three critical factors as your ultimate business strategy will allow you to clearly focus on your customer and make better marketing, management, operational, and financial decisions.

This is why 20% of small businesses succeed–they consistently make better decisions in all areas of their business because they use this strategy as a "decision making framework." In turn, they yield sustainable, long-term, positive results. Are you interested in seriously doing the same?

Apply the Factors to Your Business

Start by considering the three critical factors and how they apply to your business. After determining the area(s) you need to address, simply follow the order of the ultimate business strategy as you take the actions required. This order is the key to achieving maximum results.

Understanding the nature of your "genuine promise" is also extremely important. Your "genuine promise" *is* the single, clearly defined purpose your business was created to achieve. It is the primary reason for the existence of your business. Defining and communicating your "genuine promise" requires you to:

- Determine the *single* category your business predominately belongs to (i.e. specialty foods, cellular communications, retail giftware, new vehicles, etc.).
- Define the core customer of your category (age, income, needs, expectations, etc.).
- Identify the biggest problem your business category solves for the core customer.
- Survey core customers of your business category and determine which businesses they think of first and second (leading competitors) when faced with the major problem your business category solves.
- Determine what your business does to help the core customer with their biggest problem that your leading competitors do not.
- Define the greatest emotional benefits (the most positive feelings) your core customer will receive from a long-term relationship with your business versus your leading competitors.
- Define the greatest logical features your product or service offers your core customer that your leading competitors do not.
- Determine the risk-free guarantee your business offers your core customers that your leading competitors do not.

- State the greatest emotional benefit(s) your business offers your core customer followed by the greatest feature(s) your product or service offers followed by your risk free guarantee.

This is the foundation of your "genuine promise."

Develop Your Business Identity

Once firmly established, allow your "genuine promise" to act as the one non-negotiable constant of your business. All future business decisions should then be held accountable and made in careful alignment with fulfilling or "making good" on it. For example, when considering your business identity elements, you should make sure they all serve to communicate and enhance the value of your "genuine promise" as perceived by your customer.

In particular, pay special attention to these identity elements when projecting a consistent professional image to your customers:

- Logotype
- Primary Business Color
- Your Location
- Days and Hours of Operation
- Employee Attire
- Inside and Outside Signage
- Window Displays (if applicable)
- Business Cards and Stationary
- Website Design
- Brochures and Presentations
- Community Involvement

Strive for Consistency

With a defined commitment to your "genuine promise" and "business identity" you must then strive to "make good" on it 100% of the time. You can accomplish this by systematically organizing your business operations. Consistency is the biggest benefit for developing and using systems in your business because results are measurable and predictable. You can develop highly effective operational systems for your business by:

- Establishing the minimum operational goals needed to ensure that customers who take you up on your "genuine promise" expect what you have told them to expect.
- Outlining the entire process required to make the minimal operational goals a daily reality.
- Documenting the "step-by-step" procedures necessary to execute the process in a way that guarantees your employees' success at delivering consistent, satisfactory results.

Through consistent practices, your business builds an image that customers trust.

Make or Break Your Business

When you take the time to develop and provide proven systems for your employees to follow, you give them the powerful ability to consistently make good on your genuine promise. Everybody win–your customers, employees, suppliers, and you. Take pride in the fact that you do what you say you will do, and then constantly promote how your customers feel about their satisfying relationship with your business. Do this and you will have created a "genuine" successful business–a business worth sharing with the world.

About the Author

William E. Jackman, PMP, MCPM is President of Jackman BrandMarketing Inc., an innovative Canadian based consulting firm with the single focus of helping small to medium sized enterprises achieve their success by effectively "brandmarketing" their business operations. William is also the creator of the "Jackman BrandMarketing System" (JBMS) – a revolutionary "step-by-step" system designed to help business owners achieve measurable, profitable results from their marketing activities while turning their business into a successful brand. Explore how the "Jackman BrandMarketing System" can benefit you and your business at www.jackmanbrandmarketing.com or by calling 1.709.687.8828 or 1.866.676.8654 and requesting your complimentary JBMS information portfolio today.

Three Secrets to Successful Selling

How to Get the "Yes" You Deserve

by Michael Johnson

Did you know that whether you sell a sophisticated high-tech system, a piece of heavy equipment, or a service that offers a better solution, your prospect stereotypes you as a sneaky used car salesperson? It seems unfair, but it's true. In the prospect's eyes, any person connected with sales is perceived to have the characteristics associated with the stereotypical used car salesperson: pushy aggressive, manipulative, and self-serving.

Like it or not, this is the preconception prospects have upon meeting you. In essence, they don't trust you or respect you. They feel justified in using you; they have a "do it to you before you do it to them" attitude. This distrust is the basis for a familiar problem facing salespeople: giving presentations, quotes, samples, time, etc. that should win the business, only to come away with, "I want to think it over."

As a sales professional, you need to develop a mutual trust and respect before you proceed, otherwise prospects will treat you like any other salesperson. Following are three secrets successful salespeople use to develop trust and respect.

Secret One – Build Rapport Through the Magic of Matching

Most of us believe that what we say has the most impact on people. However research conducted by Dr. Albert Mehrabian, Professor Emeritus of Psychology at UCLA, found that our words only account for 7% of our communication. In fact, the other person is not listening to what we say, but rather to how we say it (tonality accounts for 38% of our communication) and how we move (physiology accounts for 55%).

For example, have you ever met someone for the first time and felt like you had known him or her forever? Chances are the person had similar tonality and physiology to you. Conversely, you've probably met someone that you just couldn't get in sync with and couldn't get away from fast enough. Perhaps he or she spoke too fast or loud, or seemed nervous to you. Maybe the person seemed too laid back and disinterested. Again, his or her tonality and physiology were likely different from yours.

Matching occurs when people are comfortable with each other. Normally this takes several weeks, months, or years to occur. This secret allows you to reduce it to several minutes.

The next time you meet with prospects, pay attention to the volume and tempo of their voice, and then match them. If they speak soft and slow with a gentle rhythm, you do the same. If they are loud, fast, and clipped, then match that.

Matching the prospect's movements is even more important. Notice how the other person sits. Are they leaning back or forward? Are their legs crossed? What are their gestures or head movements? Match those. If they move in the chair, wait a second or two and then do the same. The idea is to match, not mimic.

The better you become at matching, the more comfortable and trusting the other person feels. You can gain their trust in a few minutes, rather than a few months.

Secret Two – Have it Your Way

We all have fears ranging from cold calling and meeting with a senior executive to asking about money and rejection. In fact, fear is the biggest obstacle to sales success. The reason is simple: if you project your discomfort or lack of confidence during the sales call, your prospect receives that message loud and clear and plays into it.

For example, if you are uncomfortable discussing money, then you put it off until late into the cycle, only to discover that the prospect was unwilling or unable to pay a fair price for your product in the first place. He or she knew you wouldn't talk about price, so the prospect let you go on without mentioning it either.

Wouldn't it be great if you could make all your fears disappear? You can! Here's how:

1) Find a quiet place, close your eyes, take a deep breath and relax. Once relaxed, pick a fear–let's say cold calling.

2) Imagine yourself making a cold call. Only this time, everything is going well. You are relaxed and happy; your voice is strong and resonant. Make that image big, bright, and colorful. Hear and feel your sense of confidence as you talk with the person. Make the image as inviting as possible. Really see yourself confident, unflappable, and having fun.

3) Once you see it, step inside the image and experience the scenario as if you were really doing it. Hear the person's voice on the other line. Imagine the prospect responding positively. Feel your confidence and resonance as you hear the sound of your voice.

4) Repeat steps 1-3 until they become automatic.

5) Now imagine the same scenario, only this time the person is irritated by your call. See yourself handling the situation as before: confident

and unflappable. If the person is upset, that's okay. It's not personal; they don't know you. See yourself calming the other person or thanking them for their time and moving on.

6) Now, as before, step into the image and experience the scene first hand.

Repeat steps 1-6 several times per day. Soon you'll find yourself confidently making cold calls and wondering how this was ever a problem. Do this process for any fear you may have.

Secret Three – Stop Closing!

In sales, everyone is taught that getting the prospect to say, "Yes," is the key to success. We present our features and benefits, discuss pricing, and then close, close, close. We're taught to ask for the order early and often. "Selling is ABC...Always Be Closing," noted Alec Baldwin as the tough executive motivator in the movie *Glengarry Glen Ross*. Of course he meant closing a deal. This is dead wrong!

Customers expect you to push for the close. As such, they have developed an elaborate defense system, requiring proposals, presentations, samples, or demos without any commitment on their part. They want you to give them your best shot, and then they'll get back to you. This is a losing situation.

You are forced to guess at the opportunity drivers, budget, decision-makers, etc. It's like going to a doctor, demanding a prescription without an exam, and telling the doctor not to worry. The physician wouldn't go for it and neither should you with your prospect. You must become the doctor of your product/service and recognize that you must diagnose the problem *before* you can prescribe a solution. Begin by following the Hippocratic Oath of Selling:

1) **Realize that you, your company, and your product/service are valuable.** They are not free. Prospects must qualify for your time. They must be willing to fully discuss their need, budget, and their decision making process. Otherwise, it is not a good fit and you move on with no hard feelings. This is business and not every prospect qualifies.

2) **Let prospects know that you want them to say, "no" if they don't see a fit.** Tell them that if, at any time during the process, they don't want to continue, just say "no" and it is okay. You will do the same for them. You will say "no" if you find there is not a fit. Obviously, "yes" is preferable. "Yes" means the prospect is willing to move the process towards an order. Don't allow a form of "I'll think it over." "No" is okay, "yes" is great, but "I'll think it over" is really a "no" in disguise, so move on.

The secret is that your prospects really don't want to say, "no." They really want to know that they *can* say "no" without getting browbeaten. Give them permission and free them to say "yes."

3) **Instead of ABC, try ABQ – Always Be Qualifying.** Ask lots of questions. Find out what the prospects' challenges are. Is their program funded? Are they willing to spend the money you require for your solution? Will they make a decision to buy if they are satisfied with your solution? If the answer to any of these is "no," then move on.

Help the customer say "no." Let them know it is okay. You are not a stereotype; you are a professional businessperson and advisor. Your time and products/services are valuable, but not suitable for everyone. The only way to determine whether a fit exists is to have an honest and open dialog. You respect the prospect's time and expect the same in return.

Sales Success Can Be Yours

As a successful salesperson, you know your profession inside and out. You have likely spent years learning your skill. These long hours give you the confidence that you can help many, but not all, of your prospects. Some prospects simply won't value your advice and services, and are a waste of your valuable time. They are best left for others to handle.

A successful salesperson refuses to prescribe a solution before a thorough diagnosis. Therefore, you must understand the prospect's problem, its impact, the budget for fixing it, and the decision process. Failure to do so could cost you the sale.

Always remember that the relationship between the salesperson and prospect is built on trust and respect. As such, always have the prospect's best interest at heart. Your prospects will in turn respect you for your knowledge, integrity, and professionalism. You will then get the "yes" you deserve.

About the Author

Mike Johnson, principal of Michael Johnson Sales Solutions (www.MJSalesSolutions.com), helps technology companies achieve revenue growth. Before starting his sales consulting business, Mike enjoyed a successful sales career for over 25 years, in which he received many top sales honors. He is a Master Practitioner and Certified Trainer in NLP and lectures at the Haas Graduate School of Business at U.C. Berkeley on entrepreneurship. Mike is an officer of the Association for Corporate Growth; hosts "Control Your Destiny," a motivational series designed to help professionals move out of their comfort zones and achieve new levels of success on TAZA Radio; and is a popular speaker throughout Northern California. Mike holds a MSEE from U of K. Contact him at mike@MJSalesSolutions.com or 1.877.862.4000.

Your Advertising Could Be A Waste Of Money

Three Simple Questions Can Reveal The Truth

by Dennis Kunkler

D o you know specifically how much and what kind of business your advertising is bringing in to your company per year? Most business owners and senior level executives do not. However, if you were to make a capital equipment investment for the same amount as your advertising budget, you would certainly perform some kind of Return On Investment study. So, why then do so many companies see advertising as an expense rather than an investment that produces returns?

Thousands of businesses that sell to other businesses (B2B companies) through trade publication advertisements are wasting their money. Shocking, but true. These companies create "ego" advertisements by only talking about themselves. If you look at the ads, you'll read: "We have everything," "We do it all, and we're the best," and "We have great facilities and exotic equipment." As customers read these advertisements, they can't help but ask themselves, "So, what does that do for me?"

It's the classic W.I.I.F.M. (What's In It For Me) principle. These companies miss the fact that advertising is about what the customer wants and needs, not about what they like about themselves. Bragging is not advertising. The customer wants to know, "What do I get or what problem will you solve for me? Do I know what that exotic equipment will do for me? What does 'doing it all' mean to me?"

W.I.I.F.M. is widely used in consumer advertising, but is often missed in trade ads. As a result, B2B advertisers are wasting money and missing opportunities because they don't focus on the customers' needs. Whether you're a manufacturer or the owner of a professional services firm, if you advertise to other businesses, you need to think critically about how you may be wasting your advertising dollars.

Start By Looking At Your Customers

Using Pareto's 80/20 Principle, (where 20% of efforts produce 80% of results) chances are that about 80% of your company's income is produced from about 20% of your customer list. Inversely, the remaining 80% of your customer list brings in only 20% of your income.

The following formula can help you determine your best customers:

1) Create a list of all active customers in descending order of their year-to-date sales and total it. (Largest first)
2) Calculate 80% of this value. This amount represents your major revenue.
3) Start with the first customer on the list. Add each customer's total sales until you reach that 80% figure. Every customer above this point represents your best accounts. (The breakdown isn't perfect; 80/20 is a statistical average like a Bell Curve.)
4) Repeat this process to find the customers providing 80% of the income from the lower group as well.
5) Analyze the rankings and ask critical questions like, "What do the kind of customers versus the breakdown of products and services tell me?" and "Which group am I catering to?"

This process is important. Suppose you budget a modest $35,000 per year to attract more customers. Shouldn't you know how much and what kind of business that $35,000 brings in per year? If you're not specific to whom you're advertising, you may be just attracting more customers similar to the bottom 20% of your income producers.

Rather than spending your money to attract non-ideal customers, why not just give your top salesperson a $35,000 bonus for attaining one more customer just like your best one? Granted, that may not be realistic for your business; however, the point is to analyze how you allocate your advertising dollars and determine what you're getting for them, and then decide if your money is well-spent.

Realize that this is about smart advertising, not less advertising. Madison Avenue advertising agencies and the largest advertisers in the world use a proven process before they develop any concept, design any package, or produce any ad. Because millions of dollars are at stake, they engage in a proven system called "positioning." This is a process that's done first, and then all subsequent communications are governed by it. All major companies do their positioning homework before they develop any program or product.

Many manufacturers have adopted quality programs such as QS-9000, QOS, ISO Certified, SPC, Six Sigma, and TQM in their operations, but they often fail to realize that strategic positioning actually guides many of these programs. In fact, strategic positioning can have just as profound of an effect on how business is done within a company as these other programs have. Just as each one of these quality strategies elevates a company to a new paradigm, a positioning program will redirect the way your customers see the value of your business from the outside looking in.

The Secret to Smarter Advertising

Three simple questions will help you quickly discover where you may be wasting precious advertising dollars. Once you fully understand the magnitude of these questions you will see the world through new eyes. Just imagine, by understanding the principles behind three simple questions, you can easily determine how savvy your competition is and how to out-maneuver them in your market.

Ask the following questions about any ad (yours or another company's) and reveal for yourself who's enlightened and who's not.

1) Does the ad identify its intended audience?
2) Does the ad communicate what the buyer gets?
3) Does the ad indicate why the buyer should purchase from the advertiser and not from someone else?

That's it. Simple, yet profound.

Let's test the principle. Pick up one of your industry's trade publications. Close your eyes, open it up, and point to a page. Look at the closest ad and ask the three questions. Wishy-washy answers are not allowed. It's pass or fail. Was each point clear or not clear? Most ads fail the test. However, advertisers who understand the concept of positioning will ace all three.

To better comprehend the secrets of positioning, you need to "reverse-engineer" the three questions so you can understand your own company's unique position in your market.

Reverse-Engineering the Questions

Question One – Do you know specifically to whom your ad is talking?

If you can answer yes, that means you've defined the customers who fit your company and you know where to find them. You know their job titles, their problems and concerns, how they get their pats on the back, and what they want. You know how to get their attention by addressing the things important to them.

If you want to find those specific, top 20% ideal customers, you must identify them first. Create a profile of your best customers.

Question Two – Do you know exactly what your customer gets from you?

This is critical. Never forget that it's all about your customers and what they get, not what you have to offer. You need to identify what they really get when they purchase from you, whether they save time or money, solve a specific problem, or simplify a process. You should also understand the emotion that is satisfied, like peace-of-mind, safety, security, or prestige. It could be as simple as getting an "attaboy" from their boss.

Ask your best customers why they buy from you. Then, make sure every employee understands what your customers are really getting from you.

Question Three – Why, specifically, do your customers come to you and not your competition?

Know your unique value. It could be price or quality. You may have a unique expertise or special service no one else offers or you may deliver faster. It could be your great location or even your salesperson's personality. List all of the special reasons your customers buy from you. Even if you think you know what they are, ask your best customers. They know exactly why they come to you.

Once you define your unique value, create even more reasons, so your customers couldn't possibly consider going elsewhere.

Money Well Spent

Now you know how to identify your ideal customer, what they get, and why you're the best source to provide it. Understanding this basic positioning will help you look closer at your customer list and see the types of customers you serve the best and want to attract. You may reveal that the lowest, least-profitable tier diverts precious resources and attention away from your most important accounts.

This process pinpoints your preferred market(s) and identifies, specifically, who you want to reach in your ads as well as what you want to communicate. By using the information you uncover, you will strategically position yourself within your niche, thereby using your advertising dollars much more wisely.

Create your own positioning statement based on the three questions above and use it as a basis for all your advertising. Soon you'll be communicating directly and intelligently to the right customers, for the right reasons. They will know specifically why you're better than anyone else. Your business will grow, and focus on your customers' needs, which will enable you to generate higher profits. You will be on your way to "World Class" because you will be one of the few who can readily answer the three simple questions for effective advertising. At that point, your advertising will never again be a waste of money.

About the Author
Dennis Kunkler, a designer and creative director, has 28 years experience designing consumer packaging, sales promotion, and advertising materials. Mr. Kunkler now develops strategic positioning and branding programs for Business-to-Business marketers who are either struggling with market share, or who need to enter new markets. He can be reached at 1.413.786.9911 or www.positionedtosell.com.

Ask the Right Questions to Create Powerful Marketing Materials

by Neroli Lacey

If you want a terrific business, you need to be a terrific salesperson. You must know how to persuade and build trust, whether you are on your feet, in print, or online.

The problem is that your marketing materials are so-so. They focus on the features of your service or product instead of the benefits your prospect will gain.

They say, "We offer business process digitization" (a feature), instead of, "We can double your revenues without increasing your overhead" (a benefit). They don't lead your prospect from emotional to rational reasons to buy. Your PowerPoint has too many slides, and each slide has too much data.

Worse still, you may not have marketing materials. You can't describe what you do for your prospect in a few sentences because you haven't prepared what to say. You don't have a company or product brochure to leave behind after a sales call or trade show. Your website is outdated.

It doesn't matter how good your service or product is, success depends on presenting your case well. Whether you are pitching for $100 million of new business, asking the Board to approve an acquisition, or raising second round funding, everything hangs on how you present how much money you have, how much influence you have, and how you feel about your life.

Success means knowing what to say first and what to say next. Success means using language that your prospect understands. It means having superior materials to leave behind because your prospect needs to review your argument several times before he or she understands and remembers it.

You cannot afford to fail. And yet you probably write your presentation, brochure, or website the same old way as before, because that's the only way you know how.

You talk about your industry, your company, and your service, instead of focusing on your prospect and what he or she wants and needs. And you write your materials at the last minute, because you are up to your neck running the business.

The trick to creating great content is to have someone ask you the right questions. Here's how you get started.

Step One – Create Sizzling Content

You need to communicate the kernel of your industry experience. And you need to say it in a way that people outside your industry can understand. It needs to be authentic, persuasive, and clear.

The content for your marketing materials is within you; you just have to discover it. Ask a trusted friend who isn't involved in your business to interview you. The interviewer must understand the importance of this process. He or she should listen to your responses carefully and encourage you to expand on your ideas. Make sure the person is comfortable enough to challenge your inconsistencies and press you for better answers.

Below is a sample list of questions that will guide the interview process. Have the interviewer record your answers so you can go over them and find new material and fresh ideas. Work extra hard on the questions involving the clients' problems and your specific solution. These sections will form the core of your marketing materials.

Let the telling detail emerge. Also, avoid using industry jargon in your answers, because clients may not understand what you're saying. Use this exercise to move from phrases like: "We are a leader in the emerging category of Enterprise Marketing Management," to "Do you want to know how your customers like to buy? We deliver the knowledge and power you need to sell in the Internet economy."

The Questions

Adapt these questions to fit your business, and don't be afraid to get excited about your answers.

What is the business problem?

1) What is your client's business problem?

2) Who exactly has these problems?

3) When and how did the problems start?

4) Is your client worried about service, cost or both?

5) Give me some examples of real client problems.

What is your solution?

6) What is your solution?

7) What does that mean?

8) How is it different than your competitors' solution?

9) How is it similar?

10) What is unique about your solution?

11) How did you come up with this solution?

12) What are the benefits of your solution? Make a detailed list.

13) Which benefit is the most important?

14) Why is it urgent for your client to have your solution?

Why should a prospect trust you to deliver this solution?

15) Who are your key executives?

16) How long have you been in business?

17) Where are you based?

18) What are your services/products?

19) Who are your clients?

20) Provide client testimonials.

As you think about each question, delve deep to uncover new answers. When you know what your customers are struggling with, you also understand the nuances of your solution. And this is gold; it is your unique contribution and it shows you a new strategy for your business. Next, use your answers in your marketing.

Step Two – Use Your Answers Wisely

Read the transcript of your answers. Here you'll likely find fresh, authentic raw material for your marketing materials. Underline what is new. It should leap off the page. You will discover a deeper, more precise understanding of your clients' problem and your solution every time you do this exercise, because as markets change, so too does your particular place in them.

Based on your answers, use the following template to structure your marketing piece.

- **First,** what is my audience's business problem?
- **Next,** how do I solve that problem?
- **Last,** why should they trust me to do it for them?

Use this structure for most of your marketing pieces, such a brochures, sales letters, and in-person presentations. For example, if you are a senior executive presenting your division's results for the latest quarter, you might be accustomed to using a "what happened in the past, what is happening in the present, what we plan for the future" structure. Don't. Your audience has a problem, which is, "How are we going to grow this business?" You need to show how you are going to solve this for the corporation and why you are the ideal person to do it.

Realize that every good piece of marketing material sets out the business problem or opportunity. Reading this, your client will say, "Finally, someone who understands what I am struggling with." This is your "hook." You "hook" your client by showing empathy. Later you apply logic by explaining why your service is the ideal fit for the client's problem.

Defining your client's problem is often the hardest part of marketing, because we don't spend enough time putting ourselves in our clients' shoes. What do they struggle with? We tend, instead, to focus on our solutions.

For example, we say, "We sell network management software." Using this formula, it would be more powerful to say, "Are you worried about the vulnerability of your IT systems today? Do you dread losing your information assets? Our network management software has worked wonders for clients just like you."

Or we say, "We are a business-oriented law firm." Again, using the formula, a better approach would be: "Are you thinking of expanding your business? Are you looking for a team best experience and knowledge of your industry in the country? We don't just deliver wordy legal contracts; we deliver cost-effective business solutions."

Use this exercise once a year to continually update your message, to keep a strong presence within your market niche, and to position yourself accurately. "Positioning," means defining exactly who your ideal client is, what they want, and what you are good at. When you position yourself correctly, you knock your competitors out of the game.

Follow this method and you'll have marketing materials that are clear, authentic and persuasive. When you focus your marketing on your clients' needs, you can get out and sell on your feet, in print, and online. Then you can sleep easy, follow your dreams, and retire rich.

About the Author

Neroli Lacey has helped executives transform their businesses and their lives with outstanding marketing materials since 1995. Her company, Beyond Communications Inc., is based in Minneapolis, MN. She has worked with clients such as VISA, 3M and Perot Systems. Lacey used to be one of the top journalists in Britain writing for *The Times, The Sunday Times, The Daily Telegraph, The Independent, The Guardian, The Evening Standard, New Statesman, Vogue and Tatler.* Before newspapers she was an investment banker. Do you want to sell more on your feet, online, or in print?

For more information please contact Neroli Lacey at 1.612.215.3826 or email: neroli@beyondcommunications.com. Claim your FREE 20 minute consultation or sign up now for her FREE e-zine by visiting www.beyondcommunications.com.

Simple Steps to Cold Calling Success

by Ron LaVine, MBA

When doing cold calls, do you find it difficult to reach the decision-makers in a large corporation? Maybe you know who you need to talk to but have trouble getting past the gatekeepers. Or perhaps you keep finding yourself in an endless loop of voicemail.

Rest assured, you're not alone. Every day, sales professionals and small business owners pick up the phone to make cold calls, only to hang up discouraged and confused. But it doesn't have to be this way. While it may seem near impossible to make a successful cold call, you *can* do it successfully. Cold calling may present a challenge, but it doesn't have to be difficult.

The main complaint made about cold calling is that it is hard to get a response, and sales training is often to blame. Reps are trained to start selling *before* they even determine whether a need for the product or service exists. To make matters worse, many times, salespeople try to make the sale before realizing they aren't speaking with a decision-maker. Add in the urge to speak about their solutions rather than ask questions and listen, and what could have been a successful sale usually turns into nothing but wasted time.

The key to making a successful cold call is to change your manner of thinking. Switch from the old idea of "If I make enough calls, I'll sell something," to "If I speak with the person who has the authority to buy and if I have a solution to fit the company's needs, then the company will buy." Rather than focus on yourself and what you need to do to make a sale, focus on the company and how you can help meet its goals. Before you attempt to make a sale, gather information on the organization so you know if there is a need for the company to buy. This knowledge will help you tailor your presentation to fit the organization's needs. The more you know about the company, the better your chances of landing a deal.

Whether you're selling a product or service, the following steps will help make cold calling easier and help you go above and beyond your sales goals.

Establish Call Objectives

The first step in making a cold call is to determine what your objectives are and how you will meet them. Your first objective should be to locate the "Who," or the decision-maker(s). Second, you need to find out if a

169

need for your product or service exists within this particular corporation. If a need does exist, your third objective will be to suggest a solution based on the information you have gathered. Once you have presented a solution to the company's problem, ask to set up a date and time to take specific action steps. If you take the time to plan your calls before you dial the number, chances are you will yield more positive results.

Find the Decision-Maker(s)

Trying to find the "Who" can be much like trying to find your way through a maze. If you don't know exactly who you need to speak with, you may easily get sidetracked by someone who says he/she has the authority to buy, but really doesn't.

To locate and find out who the decision-makers are, you can use three different approaches: Top Down, Sideways In, or Bottom Up. Generally, the most effective of the three is the Top Down approach, using the power of referral from above. Start by calling the organizations' receptionist. After confirming the address, ask the following questions: "Maybe you can help me. Who is responsible for...?" Follow that immediately with: "Do you have a CIO, CFO. CEO, etc...?" This is not the time to talk about your solution. Remember, your initial goal is to find the "Who." Beginning the conversation in this manner will keep you out of sales mode and help you stay in information mode. The questions will also diminish your fear of rejection and build your confidence, since most people are usually willing and able to answer them. You'll also find that people are less defensive and more helpful when they don't feel like they are being sold something.

Once you have the name and correct spelling of the CEO, ask to be transferred to his/her assistant. The advantage of speaking with the CEO's assistant is twofold: 1) the assistant deals with the higher level people (C-level, VP's, etc...), and 2) if the assistant refers you to the "Who," that person or their office's gatekeeper will usually take your cold call. It is very difficult for a subordinate to refuse a call coming from a superior or a superior's office. After you have been transferred, the first thing you should say is that you were referred by the CEO's office (or the CEO if you actually spoke with him/her).

If you prefer to use the Sideways In approach, instead of asking for the CEO's assistant, you will begin by asking for a particular department, such as Investor Relations, Purchasing, or Sales. As with the Top Down approach, your main objective is to find the "Who." The Bottom Up approach begins by calling people who work in the mailroom, an outlying factory, retail location, or customer service, and then working your way up.

Ask Permission to Speak

From a business perspective, nothing is more valuable than a person's time. So before using your opening statement, let people know you respect their time by asking, "Is this a good time to talk?" or "Do you have a few minutes?" Not only is this a more professional approach, but you'll also find people will offer their full attention since you've been given their permission to speak.

If you have called at an inconvenient time for your prospect to talk, schedule a follow-up call and hang up the phone. Why waste their time, or your own for that matter? If someone is busy, you certainly will not have his/her attention. Make a good impression by being polite and respectful.

Use Direct, Open-Ended Questions

When you finally do speak to the "Who" person, start by using direct questions, such as "How do you currently handle...?" or "What are you doing in the area of...?" or "When do you plan to make a decision on...?" or "Why do you think that is?" Direct questions demonstrate that you are in control of the conversation and you know what you are doing. Also, if you listen carefully to the answers to these questions, you can learn a lot more about the organization and its needs.

Avoid using weak statements or questions like: "Could you possibly...?" or "Might you be able to tell me...?" or "I was hoping to find out..." These types of statements imply a lack of confidence and may have a negative impact on your results.

Summarize Your Conversation

At the end of any conversation during which specific action items were discussed, you should verbally summarize the important points and clarify times and dates when specific actions will take place. After you hang up the phone, follow up the verbal summary with an e-mail, and then call back a little later to make sure the information was received.

A summary e-mail helps you move forward towards the close of a sale. It should provide a detailed summary of your conversation and an outline of the next steps to be taken in order to complete the sale. Here is a list of points to include in the e-mail:

- Prospect's Company Background (Describe the past and current company situations);
- Current Challenges (List the needs, problems, pains, or challenges and why they are occurring);
- Timing (Specify the evaluation completion and decision dates you were given);
- Evaluation Process (Identify who will conduct the evaluation and the criterion to be used);

- Decision Process (Note who will be involved in making the decision and how these people will decide);
- Budget (Establish that a budget has been set or that the person/department has access to funds from another source or department);
- The Next Step (Lay out the process of who will do what and by when);
- Signature (Include your complete contact information and a tag line explaining the benefits of your solution).

Don't Make Cold Calling Harder
Than It Really Is!

You *can* make successful cold calls without fear of rejection. Think of it as an informational puzzle. Your goal is to see how many pieces of information you can get on every call. When you gather information you didn't have before, you've already achieved part of your goal. If you've achieved part of your goal, this means you were successful. By speaking to the right people and listening to what they tell you about their company, you can maximize your valuable selling time and your results.

About the Author

Ron LaVine is president of the Oak Park, CA based Intellworks, Inc. Ron specializes in delivering live cold call sales training workshops for companies in the technology industry.

To learn more about Intellworks, Inc.'s revolutionary live cold call sales training workshops, call Ron LaVine personally today by calling 1.818.991.6487 or email: liveworkshops@intellworks.com or visit our website at www.intellworks.com and sign up for the no charge Sales Tips for Selling Success email newsletter while you are there.

Magic of Selling
How to Make Your Competition Disappear
by Randall Munson

R emember the good old days, when your clients impulsively bought all the hottest technology products and complex business services without question in order to stay ahead of the competition? Now that the "dot-com" boom is over, the glow has worn off high-tech. Although your company offers innovative ideas and excellent products, your sales force faces the cold, harsh reality of selling expensive technology amidst tough competition to skeptical prospects. The days of the "easy sale" are over.

You may have an energetic, well-trained sales team that has read the great sales books and attended seminars to refine their natural knack for selling. But how ready are you to beat your competition? Just like you, they also have quality products and services (otherwise you wouldn't consider them competition) and a comparably trained sales staff. The truth is, most companies find themselves on a level playing field with their competition.

However, a valuable pearl of opportunity lies hidden in this sea of competitive equality. With the right focus and a little effort on your part, you can achieve dramatically better sales results and leap ahead of your competition. CEOs of top technology companies around the world already enjoy success from the three magic secrets of selling highly technical and highly complex items. Like master magicians, these successful CEOs want to keep the secrets to themselves, amaze their competition, and delight their stockholders. But you and your team need to learn what the masters realize. The three key secrets to the magic of selling technology are simple but spectacular, and once you implement them you will be amazed at the results:

Justify for the Brain, but Sell to the Gut
Sales are not logical–they are psychological. A common mistake sales professionals make is to sell complex and technical products by throwing facts and features at the prospect. While technical information is important, it is not sufficient. If it were, you could just post your product specifications on the wall, pull up a chair, and take orders. But it doesn't work that way.

Car salespeople have perfected the technique of the psychological sale. The automobile is a complex machine. But when you walk into the showroom, the salesperson doesn't plunk you in a dark room and narrate

173

a slide show on the technical specifications. If they did that, you would most likely lose interest and walk out. Instead, the salesperson encourages you to admire the gleaming car, experience the comfortable seats, and inhale the new car fragrance. You react by visualizing how fabulous you'll look in your new car, enjoying years of driving excitement. By that time, the salesperson usually has you hooked.

All sales, including technical sales, are emotional decisions. Information causes people to think, but emotion causes them to act. People decide to buy based first on desire, and second on logic. Your job is to make them want it and then give them enough technical information to justify what they want.

To magically "sell" your prospects, you must think differently than your competition. For example, most salespeople accept the following as a typical sales process:

INFORMATION ⟶ DISCUSSION ⟶ DESIRE ⟶ BUY

This means they provide information to the prospect, which generates a discussion and leads to a desire for the product, and ultimately a decision to buy. Unfortunately, the steps of the sales process rarely progress in a straight line to the decision to buy. The more likely scenario is that information leads to discussion, questions, then challenges, requests for clarification, and more information:

INFORMATION ⟶ DISCUSSION ⟶ DESIRE ⟶ BUY

The whole cyclic sales process lasts much longer than necessary, and too often results in a missed sale.

A more effective approach is the following:

DESIRE ⟶ INFORMATION ⟶ BUY

With this approach, you can manage the entire selling process much more effectively by first giving your prospect a desire for your product or service. To create desire, show the prospect how their business, their success, and their life will be better with your product. When they have a desire for the product, when in their gut they want it, then give them the detailed information. At that point, instead of using information to challenge you, they will use it to justify their desire for the product, and the sales cycle will be significantly faster.

Sell them SUCCESS

People desire success. They want to achieve their goals, have a good life, be with their family and friends, make the world better, and enjoy the rewards of their efforts.

Knowing this, you should show them how they can be successful because of the product or service you sell. As demonstrated in the California gold rush of 1849 and the silicone valley "dot-com" rush of 2001, people will happily invest like mad when they see an opportunity for success. Once they conclude that your product will help them achieve success, they will be eager to buy it. The three keys to selling success are:

- Sell to the person who will benefit most from your product or service. Often the direct users are not the greatest beneficiaries. While your competition is wasting time selling to direct users, who may be resistant to change, you can be getting approval from the high-level decision maker who will succeed with your product or service.

- Emphasize the ultimate worth your product or service will provide, instead of focusing on the technical features. If you develop your ability to communicate the highest level of benefit to your prospects, namely your product's worth, you are much more likely to make a sale. To understand the four levels, consider an example: a paper shredder.

  - **Level One:** The Description – In the case of a paper shredder, the description would include the shredder's size, weight, power consumption, reliability, capacity, sound level, and control options.

  - **Level Two:** The Use – The shredder can be used to shred personal papers, bills, canceled checks, and credit card receipts.

  - **Level Three:** The Value – With the shredder, you can make sure the papers you discard will not be readable by others and protects your privacy.

  - **Level Four:** The Worth – The worth is the ultimate impact it will have on your life. The shredder prevents the theft of your identity from your trash. If someone steals your identity they can run up huge bills, disrupt your life, steal your savings, destroy your credit, take your home, and even get you arrested or thrown into bankruptcy.

The ultimate worth of the paper shredder lies in the potential financial loss it can prevent. A prospect is much more willing to invest in your paper shredder out of fear of bankruptcy than because it has a 1.3 cubic foot waste container capacity. No matter what the product, the key to selling success to your clients is conveying value and worth, because they are what matters to the decision maker.

Present your product as a business investment, rather than as an expense. People avoid expenses but they are anxious to invest in their success. Technology is usually considered an expense, but if you sell it as a means to business success rather than as a product or service, your prospect will see it as a positive investment with enduring benefits.

Deliver a GREAT Presentation

Your sales presentation has far more influence than you might imagine. Your presentation is the single most powerful element in the sales process so don't scrimp on it. Following are the six most important actions you can take to ensure an effective sales presentation:

- **Use visual images** – Don't rely on text and generic clip art. The more complex or abstract the information is, the more important it is for you to use props, illustrations, and diagrams to explain the product.
- **Use stories and analogies** – People learn faster and retain more when you engage emotions and relate your information to something interesting and familiar.
- **Hire an expert** – Have a specialist create your presentation. Hire someone who can comprehend your product, understand your market, and apply professional experience designing presentations that deliver a powerful sales message.
- **Sacrifice volume for clarity** – It is far better for your prospect to genuinely understand your primary message than be bombarded with volumes of detail.
- **Be consistent** – Consistent colors, styles, fonts, and transitions tell your audience the presentation is important to you and worth their attention.
- **Present well** – Get the personal coaching and presentation skills training you need to deliver a great presentation.

Investing in a great sales presentation gives you tremendous leverage over your competition at the most critical point in the sales process. Your audience consists of those people whose decisions can make or break your business. A great presentation is therefore essential.

The Magic

Regardless of the ups and downs of the economy or the intensity of your competition, these simple secrets of sales magic will place you ahead of the competition. When you create a gut level desire for your product based on the success it will bring to your prospect, you are already halfway to making the sale. Creating desire, combined with a powerful presentation, can make you irresistible in the eyes of your client. This is the magic that will make your competition disappear.

About the Author

Randall Munson is president and founder of Creatively Speaking®, based in Rochester, MN. He is the sales expert that Fortune 500 corporations and technology companies across six continents rely on to increase their sales. Merging the experience of two decades with IBM and 25 years as a professional magician, Randall is the expert that creates powerful sales programs and helps executives deliver great presentations. Randall is an author and Certified Speaking Professional that presents international award-winning programs to audiences in more than 30 countries.

For additional information, please call: 1.507.286.1331, e-mail: Randall@CreativelySpeaking.com or visit: www.CreativelySpeaking.com.

Cultivating Market Perception

by Debra Murphy

Many entrepreneurial business owners try to navigate a sea of prospects with only a set of oars. Like the ship's captain, you need a map to get to your destination successfully. Your marketing plan is the map that guides your efforts and helps you establish value in your customer's mind. But to many, developing a marketing plan is perceived as complex and costly. Ask most business owners about their marketing strategy, or whether they have a marketing plan, and you will see their eyes glaze and their face turn pale with anxiety.

One way to simplify marketing is to develop your marketing plan as a contractor develops a building–follow a logical series of steps beginning with the foundation. Your marketing foundation is comprised of several elements–strategy, positioning, messages, and brand–each critical to the success of your marketing effort. If you develop the marketing foundation one element at a time, finishing one before moving on to the next, you will achieve the stability you need to get the most from your marketing. This process removes the intimidation factor, gives you a sense of accomplishment, and enables you to take small, manageable steps that offer benefits.

Build Your Marketing Foundation

The first element of the foundation is your positioning statement. A positioning statement expresses how you want customers to think and feel about your solution relative to the competition. It describes the single most important aspect of your business that you wish to instill in your customer's mind. By developing your positioning statement prior to executing any marketing program, you create clarity and consistency in the way you speak to the market. This ensures continuity throughout all of your marketing and makes communications less complex and easier to manage. Without a positioning statement to guide your marketing effort, you sail aimlessly through your sea of prospects, shoot at random, and waste time and money.

Elements of the Positioning Statement

The following template helps you create a two-sentence positioning statement that tells people what your solution is, how they will benefit, and why your solution is different than others.

For **<target customer>** who **<statement of problem>**, our product/service is a **<solution>** that **<key benefit>**. Our solution **<unique competitive advantage>**.

- **Target customer** is the specific audience with a need for your solution. Good positioning requires sacrificing some customers to better serve a more appropriate segment.
- **Statement of problem** clearly expresses your target's frustration or pain. Show that you understand their concerns and they will listen to what you have to offer.
- **Key benefit** illustrates how your solution will improve your target's situation. Offer your target results, solutions, and answers for the pain and they will take action.
- **Unique Competitive Advantage** (UCA) is the uniqueness you offer your target customer that sets you apart from your competition. It must be meaningful, measurable, and defensible.

Probe for Positioning

To determine the positioning that attracts your ideal client, probe your thoughts, feelings, and passion about your business. The process is enjoyable if you enlist an objective friend, business coach, or mentor to help you. You need to investigate your business, your ideal customer, your solution, and why they should do business with you.

Working with a colleague gives you an unbiased view of your business through their eyes. Information you think is insignificant may be important to your ideal positioning. Having an impartial third party ask questions, listen carefully, and take notes can reveal hidden treasures that help you refine your strategy. You need to answer the questions instinctively, from the heart, and without pretence. Your answers will unveil your strengths, unearth your passion, and uncover the precise positioning that your perfect prospect will hear. The questions to answer are:

1) **What is your business?** Begin talking about your business to get the conversation flowing–why you got started, what excites you, and why you do what you do. Describe what really gets you energized. Your colleague should especially note what you say when you get passionate or enthusiastic. Most often, passion is a key indicator of what you enjoy the most in your business, helping you identify your unique strengths and ideal markets.

2) **Who is your ideal customer?** Identify your target market by talking about your clients, what problems they have, what skills they lack, and what determines your ideal customer. Although you may have many different clients, talk about the ones that gave you the greatest satisfaction. Is there a pattern that puts these clients in a segment and attracts them to your solution more than others? Is there something

you do specifically for them that makes them more successful? Pinpointing your target market and understanding what keeps them up at night allows you to distinguish how you eliminate their pain or satisfy their needs better than anyone else. This laser sharp focus on your sweet spot enables you to differentiate your solution such that it appeals to those customers who have a need and are ready to buy.

You must sacrifice some markets to be successful in others. This is the hardest concept for many business owners to accept because they think they will leave money on the table. When one business owner described his product's sweet spot, his response was that he did not want to limit the product's success by selecting only one market. What he failed to realize was that he already did exactly that–limited its success– because it is impossible to market a product to a broadly defined market for multiple purposes. Buyers will not take the time to figure out what it does and why they might need it. So although you think you appeal to everyone, you actually appeal to no one.

3) **What is your solution?** Discuss how your solution solves a particular problem, alleviates a pain, or adds value. Put all the benefits of your solution, no matter how minor, on the table for discussion. (You will not use all these benefits in your positioning statement, but they are valuable for developing your core marketing messages.) Then ask how these benefits appeal to your client's feelings, emotion, or state of mind. A retired veterinarian who developed, and now sells, pet nutritional supplements appeals to the emotions of pet owners by helping them keep their furry friends healthy. The supplements may be good for the animal, but the appeal is that the owners do all they can to help their pets live long, healthy lives.

Your customer does not buy what you sell; they buy what they get from what you sell. They don't buy employee relations; they buy improved morale and increased productivity. They don't buy pet nutritional supplements; they buy their pet's health. They don't buy computer services; they buy increased reliability for critical business tools.

4) **Why would I do business with you?** Describe how your solution uniquely differentiates you from your competition. This is actually the most difficult task because you must ask from the client's perspective, "What's in it for me and why do I care?" Ask yourself why you can promise a benefit better than the competition. Begin with a statement that describes the benefit, and then explain how you achieve that benefit uniquely. If you can't, then it's probably not your differentiator. Your benefit must be measurably better than your competition or unique to your business. Once you have something, test it with your clients to be sure it is true.

Determine the Results

Once you've gathered all the information from this exercise, ask your colleague to point out the patterns. Does one type of customer give you the most satisfaction? Are you more satisfied because you did the best work, or had the best relationship? Did clients from one segment appreciate your solutions more than others? Let the information guide you–try not to affect the answer based on your current beliefs.

Now you have the information needed to put together your positioning statement. Let's look at an example for an executive coach.

For executives **<target audience>** whose career is stagnant **<statement of problem>**, our coaching service **<solution>** removes the obstacles that interfere with success **<emotional benefit>**. We help clients identify the behaviors that sabotage success, and recommend specific action plans that can be easily implemented **<UCA>**.

Positioning for Profit

Now you have the beginning of your marketing foundation. Your positioning statement is where you develop the messages for any marketing campaign. A clear, defensible, differentiated positioning statement ensures that you deliver consistent and credible information every time. It can help improve your networking introductions, your presentations, your marketing collateral, and your website home page. You can avoid losing customers because they don't quickly understand the compelling reason to do business with you. You have provided answers for what you do, where, and for whom, and what makes you different. And, consistent repetition of your positioning has a cumulative effect, strengthening the market's perception every time it is heard and effectively building your brand.

About the Author

Debra R. Murphy, founder and President of Vista Consulting LLC, brings more than 20 years experience in marketing to entrepreneurial business owners to help them attract and retain new customers. After many years in high technology marketing, she started working with small business owners to help them market their products and services. Debra created the VistaPlan™ Framework, a visual guide that simplifies developing a marketing plan, removing the stress usually associated with this process. She is based in Massachusetts and can be reached at 1.508.303.0766 or email at dmurphy@vista-consulting.com. For more information, visit her website at www.vista-consulting.com.

Attracting Loyal, Profitable Clients
Learn How Successful CEOs Do It
by Barbara Payne

Y our clients have a choice. They can get products and services much like yours from a lot of different vendors. And the Internet gives them faster access to more options every day. So why do they come to you?

Is it price? Businesspeople do sometimes change suppliers to get a better deal—and they often compromise quality in the process. But your most profitable clients don't buy on price alone. If they did, all you'd have to do is be the cheapest guy on the block.

Is it convenience? Certainly that's important. But few clients will return if you muddle their orders or treat them poorly—no matter how many options you offer or how easy-to-use your website is.

Today's Secret to Success

Let's face it. Though prospects do care about price and convenience, to get your bottom line up today you need more. Only one thing guarantees success in today's fiercely competitive marketplaces: having clients who trust you. And the best way to create trusted relationships with your clients is to tell them—clearly, powerfully and frequently—that you care, you understand their needs, and you offer solutions they want.

Using your *true voice*—that is, expressing your highest values in all your communications—automatically attracts others and inspires trust. Great leaders in industry, politics and religion have always understood this. Now it's your turn to attract loyal clients by tapping this power.

Step One – You Have the Answers

Your highest ideals and deepest desires spring from a part of you that's separate from ordinary consciousness—a place that houses vast stores of wisdom your conscious mind isn't always aware of. Great minds freely admit the existence of this inner wellspring and acknowledge it as their source of creativity. Often called your higher self, it's where you'll find your true voice.

Use this exercise to help you access the wisdom of your higher self:

Go to a quiet spot. No interruptions. If you like, put on a CD of some quiet soothing music or other comforting sounds. Get pencil and paper. Stretch out; get comfortable. No crossing arms or legs and scrunching your neck up (a recliner chair works well; if you lie flat, put a pillow under your knees). Keep warm with a blanket.

182

Close your eyes and begin to gradually tense and release the muscles in each part of your body. (Practice this technique until you can get to a fully relaxed state.)

Focus on your breathing; breathe slowly and deeply. Let your stomach expand as you breathe; don't worry about how you look.

Imagine yourself in a huge banquet hall. It's ten years from today. The place is packed to the rafters with people in your business, including your clients. You are at the head table. How are you feeling? Pulse racing? Perspiring a bit?

Glance down the starched white linen tablecloth. See some of the most important leaders in your industry. Hear them talking quietly with each other. Are you smiling? Are your hands fidgeting? Feel your body reacting.

Now hear the MC saying it's the ten-year-anniversary of the Nobella Peace-and-Prosperity Prize for your industry. Tonight we're here, she says, to celebrate the first decade's winner of the prize. As she reads your name, the crowd stands and breaks into thunderous applause. Are getting goose bumps? Do you feel humble perhaps?

Now the tall, handsome white-haired CEO of the Universal Trade Association rises from his seat, walks over and reaches for your hand. Placing his other hand firmly on top of yours, he nods gravely to acknowledge his respect and admiration. Then he walks to the podium and clears his throat. You and the audience are riveted in silent expectation as he begins... *"On rare occasions in the history of this industry, a star arrives on the scene..."*

He's talking about you.

"...a star that shines new light on solving the problems we all face every day..."

What does he say now? Listen carefully as he tells the audience how your company is helping make things better...

See yourself at work doing the things that made that happen.

Hear him, in his deep and dignified voice, name all the important things you've done for your industry.

Take your time. He has a lot to say.

When he's finished speaking and the audience finally stops clapping, open your eyes. Get a pencil and write down what you saw, heard and felt. Don't think about how; just write.

If you like what you read when you're finished, but it doesn't seem like enough, do the exercise again on another day. If it doesn't make sense, you may have gotten distracted. Try this exercise before you go to bed at night; write down what comes to you when you wake up. You might be surprised—your subconscious is often hard at work while you're asleep.

If you actually *don't* like what you write, ask yourself why. Is it possible you might be happier in a different business? Or do you need to change your approach to this one? Your answers will guide your voice.

Step Two – Ask and Listen

Now that you know how you feel and what you most want for your business, it's time to find out *how others perceive your company*. Ask your clients. Ask third-party vendors. Ask your family.

Other people often see things about us that we can't see ourselves, so get feedback from people who know you fairly well. That can include colleagues, employees, your wife or significant other and/or friends. Adult children, by the way, are often ruthless observers of the truth about their parents.

Ask how *they* perceive you and your company. Ask how you're delivering on expectations. Be prepared; their responses might surprise you. But trust their perceptions; what people *believe* is what's real to them. If necessary, consult with an expert on how to ask the right questions.

Once you've learned about your own attitudes and assessed the feelings and reactions of clients and other people with whom you have close relationships, you can convert that knowledge into winning communication strategies for your business.

Step Three – Put It All Together

The next step is to synthesize the information from your research into a coherent whole. You may find it effective to use an experienced third party to help interpret your ideas—the words you use and how you put them together are critical to expressing your true meaning.

This person can help you understand how to apply all that you've discovered. Together you would answer questions such as these:

- How did you come to be in this business?
- What did your clients say when you asked how they think of your company?
- How did it match what you came up with? Where are the differences?
- What did they say about your customer service?
- How does that differ from the ideal you heard described in your Nobella award scene?
- What did your salespeople or your colleagues say?
- How did your front desk people describe their relationship to your company?

- What do you really want your clients to know about you?

Step Four – Communicate!

Next, craft a communications plan that projects the ideals you identified and *reflects what your clients want.*

Build those trusted relationships by communicating through your website and with newsletters, blogs, letters, and e-mails, in any combination that makes sense. Deliver your messages frequently and consistently. Use your true voice—which means communicate with flair, and share information that gives value, reassurance, and recognition to your clients. People don't want to be "sold." Invite them to work with you to build that trusted relationship ever stronger and more valuable.

As you build your trusted relationships, keep these points in mind:

- Be true to your voice. When your motives match your true voice, you can trust that in all that you do, you will produce what you intend.
- Be honest. When you speak in your true voice, you need never doubt yourself. Remember the old adage: "I always tell the truth. That way I don't have to remember what I said." Even unpleasant truths are more readily accepted when you say them in your true voice. People recognize and trust authenticity.
- Be consistent. Be reliable. Your clients do not hear the whole truth in a single instance. They need constant reminders and reassurance.
- Be generous. Forgive your clients when they are not authentic in return; eventually they will follow your lead. Or at least you can part ways without fighting.

Into The Future...

Using the power of your true voice is guaranteed to attract loyal, profitable clients—and success in every area of your life.

Using that power may even cause you to start viewing your work as a sacred mission. When you believe that, challenges are simply invitations to grow, and success means far more than money. Now, armed with the best-kept secret of great leaders, you can step into the future.

Go ahead, find your voice. The world awaits...

About the Author

Barbara Payne is the managing principal of the website www.ReallyGoodFreelanceWriter.com. She helps consultants and executives at companies of all sizes find their true voices and create authentic communication programs that attract loyal, profitable clients. Her site, www.blogforbusiness.com, explains how to use one of today's most powerful communication tools to help you "Find your true voice...and grow your business."™

Increase Retail Sales Quickly And Easily
Without Spending Another Dime on Advertising
by Chris Philippi

I
f you are a small retailer, then you have likely already discovered the frustration of buying advertising that doesn't even bring in enough business to cover its cost. Is advertising a worthwhile investment? Over the long term, yes. However, implementing a few simple strategies today will increase your sales immediately and cost you close to nothing.

The biggest mistake small retailers make is failing to maximize business with their existing customers. It's really a no-brainer. They are already in your store, so why not help them buy as much as possible?

The fastest and most cost-effective way to grow your business is to sell more to the shoppers you have already attracted to your store. To grow your business using this "internal marketing perspective," you will focus on two key success factors.

Key One – Increase Your Conversion Ratio
Conduct a simple experiment for your store. During a typical retail day or week, silently observe at least 100 of your customers. Do this when you are not running any major sales that would encourage customers to buy more than usual. Also, keep this study a secret from your employees; you want to observe how they normally behave around customers.

The purpose of this exercise is to discover 1) what percentage of your store visitors currently purchase goods from you, 2) what prevents this ratio—buyers compared with total numbers of browsers—from being higher, and 3) what you can do to improve.

Your conversion ratio holds the key to unleashing massive hidden profits. What would happen if your current ratio of 30 buyers to 100 browsers improved to 40:100? This is a 33.3% improvement from what you were doing before! So no matter how busy your store, there are always opportunities to increase sales by converting more browsers to buyers.

Key Two – Boost Your Average Ticket Sale
It is very useful to understand what your average customer spends per purchase. Your average ticket sale represents what your customers spend without receiving any incentive, push, motivation, or rationale to buy more.

Your goal is to increase this figure, while keeping your customers' best interests in mind.

When you set goals to increase your average ticket sale, do it based upon a percentage. So if your average customer spends $30, aim to sell $36 to achieve a 20% increase. It's no secret that the easiest sale to make in retail is the add-on sale. Yet every day in retail stores across America, add-on opportunities are wasted or never even explored.

Time for Some Action

This all sounds good, right? But where do you begin? Start with any powerful insights you made during your secret observation of your customers. What is blatantly obvious that you need to change right now? In what areas is there room for improvement?

To help you grow your business, here are some proven strategies to convert more browsers to buyers and increase the amount customers spend with you.

Adapt Your Policies –

Are you accidentally scaring customers away or making it difficult for them to buy from you? Consider, for instance, a women's apparel store in a major shopping mall. The retailer reports that sales are down, walk-in traffic is almost non-existent, and any visitors that do enter rarely buy anything. Who or what is to blame? Is a competitor beating them on price? Are they selling clothing that doesn't appeal to their customers?

The real culprit is the big, obnoxious sign that you can't miss from 100 feet away:

NO REFUNDS. EXCHANGES ONLY WITH RECEIPT
WITHIN 7 DAYS

What does this policy say to the customer? We have no faith in our products? We will take your money and be out of business tomorrow? Or we just don't care about you?

Review all of your policies to determine if they are store-friendly or customer-friendly. Update these policies to be more customer-friendly, and your customers will reward you with their hard-earned dollars. You can transform a strong guarantee into a competitive advantage. If your return policy is more generous than the competition's, you give the message that your products are of higher quality and you are trust worthy. Will your rate of refunds rise? Maybe. Will your increase in sales far outweigh your refunds? Absolutely!

Update Your Signage –

A sign marking prices down 25% may move more products off the shelf. But if your idea of a sign is to just list the product and its price, then your signs are grossly under-performing. Case in point: A menswear retailer selling wrinkle-proof dress shirts posted a sign that read, "Wrinkle

Proof Shirts - $39." These shirts sold moderately well. After changing the sign to read, "Wrinkle Proof Dress Shirts – So you look just as sharp at 5 as you did at 9 – Only $39," the shirts sold out in one day! The sign appealed to the business professional who was conscience of his appearance and willing to pay to look good. If your signs clearly state the benefit of owning the product, they will do half the selling for you.

Offer Good, Better, and Best Pricing Options –

You may be unaware of this, but your customers would probably give you more money if you just encouraged them to do so. Offer more irresistible deals and your customers will almost always opt for an upgrade.

Try this experiment: Pick a popular product, one that already sells well and that your customers may buy again in the future. Offer good, better, and best pricing options. The higher volume they buy, the greater the savings. Use signage to promote the value in the upgrade, and instruct your staff to remind customers at checkout that they can save $X by buying a higher quantity. While your margins may decrease, your gross profit can actually double. Plus, this approach turns inventory around faster, improves cash flow, and builds goodwill with your customers by providing added value.

Is this one of the oldest tricks in retail? Of course it is. Are you using it to the greatest advantage in your own store? Probably not.

Take this strategy a step further by identifying two or more products that compliment one another. Chances are, if customers buy one item, they could use the other in the near future. Your objective, however, is to encourage them to buy all the accessories right now. Save your customers a trip and secure those add-on sales now by bundling products together. Then, pass along savings to customers if they buy your package today.

Invest in Sales Training –

Depending on how well they treat your customers and their ability to sell, your employees will make or break your business. Unfortunately, too many retailers refuse to invest in sales training for their people. Failing to adequately train your sales force will end up costing more money in lost sales than would an investment in a professional training program.

Here are some things your salespeople need to know to better help customers and encourage additional sales:

1) **Always greet customers warmly.** The primary reason shoppers leave without buying is that they were ignored.

2) **Avoid using the boring greeting, "Can I help you?"** Otherwise, you will only receive the conditioned response, "Just looking." Get

creative. Get personal. Comment on the weather. Say anything to lower their guard and you will increase the likelihood of them opening up to you.

3) **Ask open-ended questions to learn what customers really want.** It's one thing to know your customer wants tennis shoes. It's another thing to know she has a match this weekend and needs a pair with better traction to improve her game. Suggest the right shoe, and she'll buy. Suggest the wrong shoe, and she'll take her business elsewhere. In order to effectively sell, you must know your customers' true intentions.

4) **Ask for the sale.** Sixty-two percent of all salespeople will take the time to answer questions or conduct a product demonstration and then walk away without closing the sale. Encourage your team to follow through and avoid this unfortunate mistake.

5) **Remember that customers pay your salary.** A very successful retailer gets this point across by asking all job applicants how they define great customer service. He hires people with the best and most sincere answers. The only condition is their understanding that the day they stop treating customers this way, they are out of a job.

Your Higher Sales Guarantee

These are just a few proven methods to grow your retail business. Use them to constantly stay one step ahead of the competition. Remember, the shoppers in your store right now are looking to buy something. The only question is whether you—or your competitor down the street—will sell it to them.

You owe it to yourself and your customers to make every attempt possible to ensure that their shopping experience is a memorable one. Make it easy and fun for customers to shop your store, and they'll spend more, leave happy, and return often. Guaranteed.

About the Author

Chris Philippi is president of Philippi Marketing & Associates, LLC, a northern New Jersey-based retail consulting firm. Chris specializes in helping small, specialty retailers increase sales and improve profits with low cost marketing strategies that "get more customers to spend more money with you more frequently. Period!" Chris's proven marketing system for retailers focuses on 5 key areas: 1) Increasing store traffic, 2) Improving conversion ratio, 3) Increasing average ticket sales, 4) Increasing frequency of repeat purchases, and 5) Gaining more referral business. To contact Chris, call toll-free 1.866.391.5727, email him at service@philippimarketing.com, or visit his website at www.philippimarketing.com.

Publicity for Growth and Profit
Discover the Most Credible Way to Increase Competitive Strength

by Shelley Smith

In today's business environment, positive publicity and on-going media coverage create familiarity, enhance credibility, and foster trust. Failure to cultivate these key ingredients in a world full of skepticism, fear, and doubt can limit business opportunities and ultimately short-circuit long-term success and profitability.

So how can organizations and professionals establish name and brand recognition, while also building and maintaining credibility and trust? The answer lies in creating familiarity through an on-going, well-planned publicity program based upon truth and value—not on the hype or empty promises often associated with advertising.

Publicity is More Credible than Advertising

Unlike advertising, publicity is free media coverage based upon news you provide. It has the power to spread the word rapidly and increase the desirability of your product or service. The 2003 Edelman Survey on Trust and Credibility showed that earned media coverage from publicity is more credible than paid coverage by a margin of eight to one. Additionally, the study found that a story appearing in media outlets generates higher levels of trust than a single-outlet story. Clearly, the media should be an important target for your communications goals.

Many people incorrectly assume that getting publicity is a simple matter. They contact a few media outlets or blast out e-mails to everyone they know and hope that something will eventually get covered. This approach wastes a lot of time and generally produces few, if any, results—except for angry replies regarding all the Spam received.

In order to get coverage in newspapers, magazines, television, radio, or the web, you must understand the intricacies of the process. For the best chance to gain on-going, *free* publicity that builds credibility, trust, and profitability, take the time to learn the following guidelines.

How to Pump up Your Publicity

Step One – Write a Great Press Release

Your press releases should contain valuable news and information. Write them often, and share them with the right people.

When using publicity as your communication strategy, identify stories that are truly unique. Brainstorm ideas about everything in your organization that's new and different. Are you announcing a new product? Do you have an unusual service or approach to business? Ask yourself these questions, and consider the following news angles to see if any apply:

- **Is your company, product, or service the first of its kind?** Be objective. Don't lose your credibility right off the bat by making a false claim. Do some research to determine whether what you do or what you sell is, in fact, unique. If you're not the first, then consider another angle.

- **Do you, your organization, or your employees have interesting contributions to the local community or to charities?** If not, consider how your organization can make a difference through volunteering or pro bono work.

- **Does your organization or its management style tie into a global or national trend?** One example is the new age trend to offer employees massage and yoga classes to lessen workplace stress. Read business news magazines and industry trade publications to find other examples. Be creative and you'll find activities that already tie in to trends, or some that can be implemented relatively easily.

- **What is the latest change with your organization?** Have there been executive management changes or significant employee hires? Did your company move or open a new office, store, or branch? If the change is significant to your industry or local community, then it may be news. A company event that only provides a benefit to your organization usually doesn't qualify.

- **Does your company have experts who can write articles that will benefit your target audience?** Providing helpful information will demonstrate your expertise and show the value of your product or service.

Once you have identified your news angle, begin gathering information to use in a press release, which is your primary tool for communicating with the media. Before you start writing, research industry trends, survey results, economic reports and other information relevant to your company. The more facts you use and cite properly in your releases, the more you will bolster your organization's credibility.

In addition, seek out industry experts to provide objective statements about your organization, product, or service. Gather customer comments and get permission to use them in your press releases and marketing materials.

Once you've written your release, send it only to targeted contacts. If you're planning a national campaign, consider purchasing a subscription to an online database. If you build your contact list yourself, identify all types of media outlets that could be interested in your news, including:

- Local daily and weekly newspapers;
- Local radio and TV stations;
- Local business and news magazines;
- Industry trade publications, both print and online.

You'll also want to send out your press release announcements to the following non-media industry contacts:

- Industry association members;
- Board members;
- Investors;
- Contributors;
- Associates.

To find proper formatting and distribution guidelines, check the resource list at the end of this chapter.

Step Two – Build a Publicity-Friendly Website

The media is a deadline driven business, so immediate and easy access to important information will greatly improve your chances of getting on-going publicity. The best way to ensure 24/7 access to information is to create a Press Room within your website. Make sure it is as user friendly as possible. Inside your Press Room, post documents, images, and presentations that are easy to view, download, and print. Consider including the following items:

- Company fact sheet;
- Management profiles and photos;
- Product photos;
- Logo files;
- Historical milestones;
- Short presentations;
- Video clips;
- Previous press releases.

Together, these items create your online media kit, so be sure this information remains current. Also, include this link in your marketing and publicity materials.

Step Three – Create a Professional Visual Image

One of the most common mistakes made by small organizations and entrepreneurs is using an unprofessional identity mark or logo. A poor corporate image leads to poor publicity results. In fact, any kind of unprofessional communications—website, brochure, or spokesperson, for instance—can and will drive away business.

Your image directly affects your chances of success because it communicates your competency, skills, and attention to detail. It's important to have a robust and memorable identity that will attract the right clients and, in turn, facilitate company growth. If your company mark doesn't convey the essence of your business in a simple, yet memorable way, it's time to re-evaluate the design. You may even consider getting a professional image "make-over."

Just as wearing a crisp white shirt for a meeting conveys an aura of professionalism, motivation, and competence, your corporate identity will also convey a message. Make sure your visual communications reflect professionalism. The bottom line is this: If you improve your organization's image, you will increase your impact and credibility—all of which lead to profitability.

Step Four – Align Publicity Goals with Company Culture and Vision

All organizations have unique goals and strategies to achieve them. The more a publicity program parallels the company vision, the greater the support from the CEO's office on down. Further, the publicity program should fit into the culture so that the budgets are available and the results are meaningful and measurable.

An important study conducted for the Council of Pubic Relations Firms in 1999, still relevant today, demonstrated the relationship of public relations or corporate communications spending to corporate reputation. Results clearly showed that *Fortune's* Most Admired Companies spent proportionately more on corporate communications than those lower in the rankings.

When you also consider the results of the earlier-cited Edelman study, the importance of company communications becomes clear. Nine out of ten people agree that a corporation's reputation strongly influences consumers' opinions of its products and service. Also, eight out of ten people are willing to pay more money for goods and services from a company with a well-regarded labor and environmental record. A majority of those interviewed will also turn to companies that consistently engage in philanthropic activities.

Clearly, notable activities that align with corporate values and benefit others can also produce positive benefits to an organization's bottom line. Examples of newsworthy programs to consider implementing include the following:

- Community events tied to your product/service;
- Charity fundraisers involving dedicated employees;
- Sponsorships for beneficial products, services or information;

- Scholarships/grants for education;
- Charitable donations of equipment, services or employee assistance;
- Food, blanket, coat, or toy drives;
- Conservation activities and organized recycling efforts;
- Strategic alliances with non-profit organizations.

Publicize Profitably!

Publicity is an effective communications strategy that creates familiarity, enhances credibility, and builds trust for organizations, products, and services. The key to success, however, is an on-going, well-planned program.

Begin today by developing your publicity plan. Determine target audiences, outline clear goals, and assign resources to achieve them. Establish measurement criteria and budgets and be prepared to invest time and effort to work the plan. By consistently providing truthful, newsworthy information to your audiences, your organization will obtain meaningful and measurable results. Over the long-term, organizations that adopt this strategy will have the best chance to build a strong reputation and reap the rewards of sustained profitability.

About the Author

Shelley Smith, founder and president of Stellar Agency, is an award-winning communicator providing marketing and public relations services. She has a proven track record in creating or revitalizing brands and perceived images and assists organizations in communicating clearly and profitably. Shelley has implemented successful programs for Fortune 500 companies as well as small businesses and start-ups. Shelley has won numerous industry awards, is a published writer, an adjunct instructor at JFK University and a speaker on publicity, corporate branding and profitability. Contact her by email at shelley@stellaragency.com, or by phone at 1.925.829.9600.

For an in-depth resource list of marketing and publicity tips, tools and news, or for more information on how to foster credibility and trust for greater organizational profitability, visit: www.StellarAgency.com.

The Science of Persuasion
The Surefire Ways to Win the Hearts and Minds of Any Audience (And Thereby Advance Your Career!)
by Karyn J. Taylor

T he phone rings. Your boss or the senior partner is on the line. The next industry confab, board meeting, or high profile case is approaching and he wants *you* to make the presentation. Inwardly you gulp. Public speaking is not your "thing." But refusing is not an option; you have a product to launch, investors to "woo," or a verdict to win. Stifling your urge to say, "Sorry, wrong number," you say, "Sure." Your career, after all, depends on it.

Millions of entrepreneurs, sales professionals, and trial lawyers step up to the plate every year. Many do so brilliantly. Many more fall flat on their faces. Yes, they're prepared–sales projections, evidence, *PowerPoint* slides and all–but around the room or in the jury box, people are doodling on their notepads or dozing off.

All too often, we use presentations merely to present facts and information. That serves a purpose but it usually leaves our audiences disengaged. Worse, it does nothing to advance our careers. If we aimed instead to inform and *inspire*–to position ourselves as leaders and persuade our listeners to follow our lead–our sales team might actually boost sales, the board might vote for the merger, or the jury might award our client millions. Isn't that what we truly want–to get *results* for our bosses, our clients, our companies, and our careers? Absolutely.

So how do we inspire our listeners to action? Social scientists have spent billions to provide the answer. Madison Avenue calls it market research; the legal community calls it jury research. The venues are different but the lesson is the same: there is a *science* to persuading people to think and act a certain way, and we can *use* that science to reach our goal.

Make it Visual
The primary tenet of the Science of Persuasion is surprisingly universal: seeing *is* believing. People forget what they hear, but remember what they *see*. Research shows that an audience that merely *hears* a presentation will remember only 10-15% of what it heard three days later. What if three weeks or three months pass before your audience must *use* that information? Your sales pointers will be forgotten before your sales team's

next sales call or the evidence you presented at trial will be forgotten long before jury deliberations begin.

Luckily, social scientists have discovered the solution: an audience that both hears and *sees* a presentation will retain 70-85% of what it has seen and heard. That's an increase in retention of 60-70% just by using graphics! So the first step in making both you and your presentation memorable is to use visuals. But not all visuals are alike. Some, stuffed with too many fonts, too many colors and/or an overwhelming amount of text or information, are difficult to understand. "Busy" graphics undermine your presentation—and your image—and in the end, are unpersuasive. What's a presenter to do? Remember that less is more.

Deliver Only One Message Per Graphic

A good graphic is visually clean and uncluttered. It focuses your eye on the most important piece of information on the page. More important, its design doesn't upstage, confuse, or overpower your Bottom-Line-Take-Away Message™—the one message you want your audience to "get" from seeing that particular graphic.

Maybe your message is that sales rose 12% in the third quarter, that the merger will eliminate two offices in Ohio or that the LAPD overlooked three pieces of evidence during its investigation.

Whatever the message, express it in simple, visual terms. Then express it verbally in the title of your graphic: "Third Quarter Sales Up 12% Over 2002." "Consolidation of Youngstown and Oberlin Offices Saves $3.2 Million." "LAPD Ignored Three Key Pieces of Evidence." Make your title as short as a newspaper headline or it will be hard to remember and defeat your purpose: people cannot be persuaded by what they can't remember.

Use the "Ten-Year-Old Rule"

Broadcast journalists use this rule when writing for *60 Minutes, 20/20,* or the six o'clock news. They choose language so simple a ten-year-old child can understand it after hearing it once. For them, they have no chance to clarify: when the broadcast ends, that's it.

Public speakers only get one chance too. Sure, you can provide handouts, but if your handouts are as wordy, complicated, and as hard to fathom as your *PowerPoint* slides, you're doomed. Your opportunity to make that all-important career-advancing impression has been lost.

Here's a solution: practice your presentation before an audience of eight- to twelve-year-olds. If their eyes glaze over, you'll know your job isn't done. Better yet, ask them what they *understood.* Their answers may surprise you but will be worth their weight in gold.

Appeal to the Heart

Using "clean" graphics that deliver simple, easily understood, *Bottom-Line-Take-Away Messages™* is your first line of defense in delivering a career-altering presentation. But those are just the mechanics of reaching an audience. To *inspire* your listeners–to reach them "where they live"– you must appeal to them *emotionally.*

Social scientists, experienced sales professionals, and skilled trial attorneys all know this simple truth: people *think* they think with their heads, but they really make decisions with their *hearts.* Dale Carnegie knew it. His best-selling book, *How to Win Friends and Influence People,* was a monument to this principle. Johnny Cochran knew it too. He defended O.J. Simpson with the understanding that a jury doesn't reach a verdict on the basis of facts and evidence alone.

No matter the circumstances or the issues at hand, people act on the basis of how it makes them *feel.* To move a sales force, a jury, or *anyone* to the point of action, you must give them an emotionally compelling reason to act.

What emotional "hook" gets *everyone* motivated? Personal gain (i.e., "What's in it for me?"). Tony Robbins proved it. He built a worldwide following coaching people to find their *Personal Power™*. To inspire your listeners, figure out what matters to them most (i.e., what's in it for *them*) then tailor your keynote address, sales pitch, or closing argument to give them what they want.

If you're in sales or marketing it's easy. Use a graphic showing that for every 5% rise in sales, employee bonuses rise 3%. Your sales force will work harder for you to make more money for themselves.

If you're a trial attorney defending an insurance company against an elderly patient claiming non-payment of her medical bills, your task may be harder. Few jurors will vote against grandmothers in favor of large corporations. But use a graphic identifying your client as a mutual insurance company owned not by fat cats in Armani suits, but by ordinary people like themselves, and you'll get the jury's attention. Add a graphic showing that when insurance companies pay for elective surgeries, the cost of insurance premiums rises and the jury will vote against the grandmother to keep *their own* premiums low. *How* you deliver your message is just as important as the message itself.

Tell an Emotionally Compelling Story

By nature, people tend to organize disparate facts and information into stories. Given a choice, research shows 95% of us will use a story format over any other. That explains why public speakers or trial attorneys who merely offer fourty minutes of facts and information leave their listeners or their juries cold. What people want is a *story,* and the best orators, be they entrepreneurs, corporate executives, college professors, or litigators, always give them one.

Imagine making your sales presentation the form of a story about "Joe Q. Employee," an average guy with an average performance record. Joe has brought newfound happiness to his family by implementing the five new sales tips you are now introducing. You show pictures of Joe beaming as he hands new car keys to his college-bound son; Joe getting a big kiss from his wife when the new dishwasher is delivered; and Joe's entire family (Fido included) on a trip to Disneyland–all made possible by the huge bonus Joe earned implementing your five new skills.

Would your audience be entertained? Probably. Would they remember your presentation? Undoubtedly. Would they be motivated to acquire new skills in order to take *their* families to their own version of Disneyland? You bet. The key to persuasion is in the story you tell.

The Secret to Persuasion – Give the People What They Want!

To win the hearts and minds of an audience, give them more than mere facts and information. Galvanize your listeners to action by appealing to their self-interest. Deliver your message in an emotionally compelling story that informs and entertains. Use simple language to ensure your message is understood. Use visuals to make it stick.

Will the boss remember your resulting jump in sales at promotion time? Will the insurance company re-hire the litigator who won the "impossible" case? Absolutely.

Congratulations! Mission accomplished.

About the Author

Karyn J. Taylor is president and founder of The Strategic Image, a business communications and trial consulting firm based in Los Angeles. A former award-winning producer for *60 Minutes* and *20/20* with 25 years of experience, she helps trial lawyers increase their odds of winning in court and helps business executives reach their target audiences through sales and marketing presentations, advertising collateral, infomercials, training videos, and websites. Karyn lectures frequently on the science of persuasion before legal and business groups and trains clients to use communications strategically to enhance their careers.

For more information please contact Karyn at 1.310.821.1776, email ktaylor@thestrategicimage.com or visit www.thestrategicimage.com.

Make Your Website a Strategic Marketing Vehicle

by Karilee Wirthlin

E very company starts out with grand plans for using the web to solve problems and completely transform the way business is done. As a marketing executive of a large corporation, you get the funding, hire the finest people, and tell them, "Create the best."

Why, then, does your website fall short of your expectations? How did you end up trying to coordinate so many websites—your external site, your partner extranet, and your sales intranet—to meet your sales and marketing objectives?

The question comes down to this: "Who owns the web inside a company?" Ask a dozen people and you'll get a dozen answers. The correct answer is: everyone. A web team may be responsible for delivering the finished site, but product marketing managers, salespeople, services and support, and engineers are *all* responsible for delivering content that drives sales and customer satisfaction.

Enterprise content management systems have emerged to help companies solve this problem. Without knowing HTML, multiple people can contribute to company websites while ensuring consistent design and user interfaces. Unfortunately, however, technology alone will not solve your problems. The ultimate success of this technology depends on the foundation on which you build these systems.

Buying a technology solution too early can divert your attention to the details of building the system—and away from the overarching vision that guides development. Think of your content management infrastructure as a house. If you start building the walls without laying a solid foundation, the structure will crumble, no matter how great the construction materials.

You can minimize or avoid many of the headaches associated with large-scale website implementation by following five principles for building a solid website foundation.

1) **Tie your website goals to the overall business objectives.** Are you focused on increasing your sales reps' effectiveness? Then incorporate the sales intranet site with current or desired sales processes. Do you want your partners to promote your marketing message over others? Then treat partner extranets as an extension of your sales force, and make it easy for them to connect with your company. Do your

marketing programs aim to generate sales leads by driving customers to your website? Then ensure easy follow-through on your program's "call to action" from your site.

While this advice may sound elementary, web teams often get tangled up in the design or technical details of implementation. Tying clearly defined goals to overall business objectives will keep your team on track. A website will be a waste of money—no matter how pretty it looks—if it doesn't embody your company's strategic goals.

2) **Involve your target users from the start.** Many web teams are far removed from the customers that they ultimately serve. Some teams perform usability testing, but this usually occurs just before the site goes live. To ensure that your website adequately serves its users, consult them before any design and coding begins.

You can involve your users in several ways, including one-to-one interviews, group interviews, or surveys. Observing people at their jobs or watching them use your current site may help you obtain a true picture of users' needs. This is especially important in companies with a global presence. The further your target user is geographically from corporate headquarters, the less likely you are to fully understand your website's value to them.

Users are eager to provide this kind of feedback. Don't get caught in the trap of thinking that user participation will delay web development. If you incorporate user feedback into the overall website objectives, you will reduce implementation time. Focusing on user-stated priorities will also produce very happy—even proud—users when it's time to launch the site.

3) **Create a sense of ownership outside of the web team.** Many people outside your web team provide site content, and they often get frustrated when they have a hard time delivering the content they've created. If, for instance, providers must rely on an overburdened web team to publish content to the sales intranet, they may instead design and maintain their own internal websites. This makes it difficult to create a consistent reference tool for the field sales organization. Conflicts also arise with partner or customer content. Often, content providers develop material without involving the web team from the beginning. As a result, your web team may end up in a time crunch, delivering important content at the last minute.

While editors may need to review content before it goes live, the web team can instill a sense of ownership by showing content providers what part of the site or page belongs to them. Tell them, "You own this section of the website," or "Your content goes on this section of the page." Ask how they want that section set-up and delivered. You can still do this within branding and design guidelines, and you'll get more cooperative content providers by giving them more control of their product.

4) **Invest in user interaction before design and programming begins.** This is one of the most important steps for ensuring successful and cost-effective website implementation. Draw on your stated business objectives and utilize user and content provider feedback for pre-implementation planning. In this stage, you will work out elements of design and system requirements on paper.

Simple card sorting exercises are effective ways to involve users in the design process. Present users with typical information found on the website. Ask them to sort the information and name the resulting categories. Conversely, present users with category names and instruct them to sort information into the pre-existing categories. Both tests allow you to truly understand how to organize your site from a user perspective. While these exercises are typically done using 3x5 cards, you may instead employ online meeting technology, which allows global users to participate.

After completing these exercises, use wire frames (skeletal line designs showing where elements of the website will appear on the page) to outline the website design. Creating wire frames before graphical or technical implementation is both timesaving and cost-effective. People may easily make changes in web functionality or design with a few line and text alterations, rather than expensive programming time. Well-developed wire frames will also reduce the amount of back-and-forth between your graphic designer and technical team, saving you time and money when you start employing these resources.

5) **Think of the web as a two-way interaction with employees, partners, and customers.** The true value of the world-wide-web is in creating connections with people. If you use your website only to push information out to customers, partners, and employees, the true potential of the web remains untapped. Enterprise content management systems transform users into additional content providers who share feedback with you and the rest of the user community. This constant flow of user feedback allows you to continually refine marketing messages and programs. In this manner, your website becomes a veritable strategic marketing vehicle.

Create Your Own Online Marketing Machine

The ultimate goal for an enterprise content management system is to create a single sales and marketing repository where content can be easily re-purposed to meet customer needs. Ideally, content providers would store and classify various versions for sales reps, partners, and customers—all in one place. Your external website, your partner extranet, and your sales intranet would draw from this single repository to create specific interfaces to these target audiences. Thus, you will have achieved the supreme objective of any marketing executive: Delivering a consistent marketing message, both inside and outside the company, that drives sales and customer satisfaction.

Maintaining this vision throughout website planning and implementation is tough. When you hire vendors for this large-scale effort, make sure you have a trusted member of the team who focuses on the big picture and coordinates the efforts of your in-house team and vendors. This way, you ensure that your vision is not lost. The average large-scale website may cost upwards of $250,000 to $1 million in content management software and implementation. Be sure that you do not throw that money away.

While enterprise content management systems may not immediately deliver on the promise of a single sales and marketing repository, you can take a giant leap toward this goal today. Start with a single website: your sales intranet, your partner extranet, or your external website. Apply these five principles before you implement a content management system. If you already have a content management system in place, test your organization's application of these principles. It's never too late to start. A solid website foundation will go a long way to making the web a strategic marketing vehicle for your company.

About the Author
Karilee Wirthlin, principal and founder of KL Consulting in Silicon Valley, California, is a leading website strategy consultant. Combining her sales support experience with her technical background, Ms. Wirthlin produces innovative, targeted, and effective web content management programs. She has worked with companies such as PeopleSoft, Business Objects, Adobe, NVIDIA, and SGI to apply best practices to large-scale, strategic web efforts. Ms. Wirthlin has worked with web content management systems since their emergence in 1998. More information about this topic is available on the KL Consulting website at www.klconsulting.com or by calling 1.650.947.4986.

Section Four –
Personal Growth

Improve Your Results Through Personal and Spiritual Growth

by Bob Proctor

D o you ever not do something because you're worried what the neighbors (or your employees, or your spouse, or anyone else) will think? If you're like most people, chances are you were raised to fear what others think about you. Maybe you're afraid they think your business is too small, your car is too old, or your house is in the "wrong" neighborhood. Such a fear controls many people.

The truth is, other people don't even notice such things about you. While you're worried about what everyone else thinks, the only person whose thoughts really matter are your own. Therefore, you must follow your heart. Step out of the position that you think is secure and do what God is telling you to do, because that is where your heart leads. If you follow your heart, that urging inside you, you'll live a fulfilling life. Follow your own counsel by going inside and listening to your inner, quiet voice.

Whether you are a business owner, a student, or a senior executive, it is simply human nature to be unsatisfied with your present situation. Dissatisfaction is a creative state that urges you from inside. So don't be upset about being unsatisfied. In fact, you should always be unsatisfied; you should always strive for improvement. Unfortunately, most people get stuck at some level, despite their efforts.

The key to improvement is personal and spiritual growth. You must change what's inside, rather than what's outside. No matter how successful you think you are today, if you are not committed to a daily program of personal and spiritual growth, then you are cheating yourself out of something very rich and meaningful. With an organized program, you can compound your success and improve the bottom line of your financial statement. By following three secrets to personal and spiritual growth, you will improve your results in every aspect of your life.

Secret One – Decide What You Want

As the ancient Greeks described, our spirit, our heart, and the subject of the mind where our being lies are forever pushing us to greater things. This is what makes us want to do better. For example, if you are a marathon runner, you want to run faster; if you are a salesperson, you want to sell more; and if you are a painter, you want to make a perfect picture. Such a desire for greatness is inherent in all people.

205

In a world filled with so many material things, it is easy to want everything. In fact, you may find it difficult to weed through all the "stuff" and identify what you really want out of life. Many times, our wants surface in the form of an idle wish, like "I wish I had a better car," or "I wish I was making more money." You don't take these wishes seriously because you don't yet have a conscious plan on how to make the wish reality.

To know what you really want, you must learn how to be quiet, how to be still, and how to put yourself into a relaxed mental and physical state. You can do this through prayer, meditation, or by listening to soft music. Operate with the understanding that you are a spiritual being, and spirit is always for expansion and full expression, never for disintegration. Your responsibility is to be the best possible instrument for spirit to work through.

As you allow what you want to come into your conscious, you must be aware that you won't know how to get it or where the resources will come from. It surfaces as a fantasy, and that is where all the work begins. The more you focus on your vision, the sooner it will go from fantasy, to theory, to fact. Let the fantasy move into your consciousness and nail it with the point of a pencil by writing it out. Now look at it and say to yourself, "This is what I want." It takes some understanding, but through personal growth, it will come and liberate you to succeed.

Secret Two – Stay Positive

Laws are a uniform and orderly method of the omnipotent God. There are laws of gravity and laws of nature, and the whole universe operates around these laws. Another law, the law of polarity, states that everything has an opposite. That is, there is no up without a down, no hot without a cold, and no negative without a positive.

Building off that polarity law, everything "just is," and if you don't like it, you can change it. Your thoughts and reaction make a situation positive or negative. When you become aware of your negativity, you have the power to change it. So if you're depressed because one of your top employees resigned, you are focusing on only the negative side of the situation. Instead, focus on the positive side. Maybe that person wasn't as right for your company as you had originally thought. Now you have the opportunity to find a new person, with new ideas to fill the position.

The same concept applies when dealing with negative people. When you see the negative aspects of your friends, your employees, your co-workers, or your spouse, you are being negative yourself. Realize that you can never change a person, nor should you ever try. If your spouse has a negative outlook that brings you down, make a list of ten things you admire about his or her personality. When you feel the person's attitude getting you down, flip to the list and read over it. If someone affects you with his or her negativity, then your positive outlook will rub off on the person as well.

Realize that every situation comes into your life to make you grow, and a positive side to everything exists. You simply must seek the positive side of everything. While it may be impossible to stay positive all the time, it is possible *most* of the time. The truth is that you don't have to stay negative. What you focus on is what you attract, so if you focus on negativity, then you will attract negativity. But if you focus on the positive side of things, you'll attract more positive results in your life. This means that you are in total control of every negative and positive situation.

Secret Three – Have the Confidence to Take Risks

In this unprecedented time, a paradigm shift is taking place globally. As technology and communications advance, business and industry change. In this unstable environment, there is no job security, and you must step out and take some risks.

This is harder said than done, as early in life most people are taught that it is better to be safe than sorry. We're conditioned to avoid risk and to fear failure. But imagine what a tragedy it would be to reach the end of your life, look back, and wonder what would have happened if.... What would have happened if I had started that business? What would have happened if I had moved to the new city? What would have happened if... It would be better to look back and view some failures, because we learn from our failures. Remember that it is better to learn from failure and look back on it as an enriching experience than to never take a risk and always yearn, unfulfilled, for something more.

If you're not living on the edge, then you're taking up way too much room. You should always reach and stretch for the best in everything. Step out and take action toward your dreams. If it excites and scares you at the same time, then you're probably going in the right direction. You're excited about it because that is what you want, and you're scared because it isn't in harmony with the security you're used to.

Many people feel secure in their job or their relationship because of outside factors, but the security to take risks really comes from inside. True security or confidence comes from an awareness that you are one with God. You may get some of this confidence through genetics or the environment you grew up in, but the only way to master it is through study that leads to understanding. You have to become aware that you're in connection with an infinite source of supply. Everything you'll ever want is there; you just have to be aware of it. For example, the ability to fly has always been there; the Wright brothers just became aware it.

Personal and Spiritual Growth for the Future

Personal and spiritual growth are essential if you want to improve your results and live a full and balanced life. Sure, you can have great success in business and be totally out of balance in your personal life. But when you get to the end of the road, do you think you'll look back and wish you spent more time in the office? No; you'll wish you developed better relationships and lived a personally and spiritually fulfilled life.

So take a close look at your dreams. Listen to your heart and decide what you really want out of life. Stay positive about issues that arise on your path to success and learn from each mistake. Look inside yourself and discover the true source for the confidence and security to take risks.

You already have the keys to better results in all areas of your life; you simply need to look inside yourself and make them work for your success. When you do, your results will be amazing.

About the Author

Bob Proctor has spent over 40 years focusing on helping people create lush lives of prosperity, rewarding relationships, and spiritual awareness. With the help of personal growth training, he went from being a high-school dropout with a resume of dead-end jobs and a future clouded in debt to a six-figure income earner, eventually topping the $1 million mark. After rising to the position of Vice President of Sales at Nightingale-Conant, he established his own seminar company. Bob Proctor now travels the globe, teaching thousands of people how to believe in and act upon the greatness of their own minds. For more information, please visit: www.powertohaveitall.com.

How to Navigate the Grey Areas of Your Thinking for Greater Success

by Opher Brayer

E ven the most successful people feel the need for improvement in their lives. They do well, but don't feel it's good enough. If you ever feel this way, and you can't identify the problem, chances are something in your subconscious holds you back.

Everyone has abilities that lead them through life. You have a model in your mind that leads your actions as a manager, as a parent, and as a person. In every model, you have grey areas, or hidden drivers, causing problems. The problems are symptoms of these grey areas. This means that the problems you have in your personal life and your professional life are connected. They are all symptoms from the same grey areas in your mindset.

For example, a person who has experienced a failed marriage and a failed business has a driver that's causing the failure in both areas of life. Somewhere in that person's mind is a grey area that leads to failure. The failure itself is not the problem; the failure is a symptom created by this grey area. Something inside the person's thinking model leads him or her to make different mistakes, which are different symptoms that all come from the same place.

Fortunately, a step-by-step approach can help you identify the grey areas in your model that cause problems in your life.

Step One – Identify the Problem

To fully understand how problems are really symptoms, imagine a car driving in the snow. This situation is a closed cause and effect loop. The driver pushes the gas pedal (cause), the wheel spins (effect), and throws mud and slush (symptoms) all over the sidewalk. All cause and effect loops create symptoms. The first step of solving these symptoms is to identify and connect them.

- First, define one problem or symptom that you see in your life in general.
- Second, define another problem, this time related to your profession. Ask yourself, "In my work, what's the main problem I have to solve?"
- Third, identify a problem you have that appears habitual, in all areas of your life.

These three items make you look at you in three ways: 1) you as yourself, 2) you in your profession, and 3) you in the world. Let's say, for example, you identify the following three problems, or symptoms:

1) Lack of communication with your family.

2) Unorganized at work.

3) Unbalanced life.

Use a Venn diagram as shown to illustrate the model.

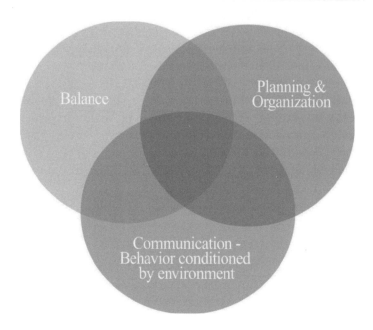

At first, you may not see any connections among these three symptoms. But, you have drivers behind each of these problems that drive the cause and effect loop.

Go through the symptoms and find the connections between #1 and #2, #2 and #3, and #1 and #3. What is the driver between the lack of communication with your family and your unorganized work? It may be difficult at first, but the connections are there.

Keeping with the example, let's suppose the driver between communication and organization is stress. You can't communicate and you're unorganized because your stress level is too high. So, if you eliminate the stress in your life, you will be able to communicate more effectively with your family and you will be more organized. The driver (stress) now becomes the key to the solution (eliminate stress), rather than the problem. Now you are in a grey area of your model. Go through each symptom and connect it with the others and write the answer on your Venn diagram as shown. As you work through each combination of symptoms and identify the drivers, you go deeper into the grey area.

Ask yourself, "When I look at the three drivers I identified, where do they lead me?" In this case, by connecting the three areas, you may find the main driver behind the three to be consistency. Place this on your Venn diagram as shown.

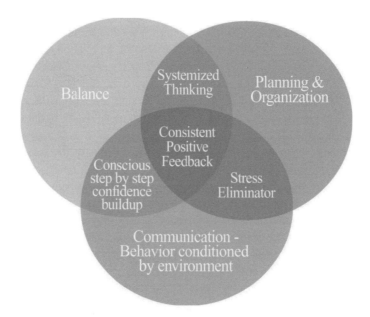

This first step allows you to actually go into the model of your inner system. It is not the systems, but the connections between them that you need to understand. When you understand the connections within the inner system, then you begin to see yourself as a system where everything is connected.

Step Two – Analysis
In the first step, you identified the symptoms. In our example, #1 was communication, #2 organization, and #3 unbalanced life. Then you connected them to each other with drivers. Let's say the drivers you found between #1 and #2 was stress elimination, between #2 and #3 was confidence building, and between #1 and #3 was a systematic approach. These are now your key areas for development.

Once you've identified these areas for development, you can move to the next level of exploration. Use another Venn diagram and label each circle as one of the areas for development.

Stress elimination becomes key area #1, confidence building becomes key area #2, and systematic approach becomes key area #3. Each of these areas is connected and the cause and effect loop continues. For example, stress elimination builds confidence and confidence eliminates stress.

Just like in step one, look for the grey areas between each of the key areas. Compare #1 with #2, #2 with #3, and #1 with #3. Brainstorm ways to solve the key areas. How are they related to each other? Probe each area with open-ended questions, such as "Why do I think variable #1 has an impact on #2?" You'll answer, "Because of X." Then ask yourself, "Why does X have this kind of impact?" You'll answer, "Because of Y." Continue, "Why does Y have the ability to perform this way?" And so on. A coach may help you go deeper into these new grey areas. A good answer will never be more then eight words in length. Look at the answers and find the most important element in each sentence. Keep questioning the causes of these problems until you find the links, or the second level drivers.

Let's say that through questioning, you found the balance of needs and capabilities as the driver behind #1 and #2, initiative behind #2 and #3, and objective diagnosis and distinguisher behind #1 and #3. By balancing your needs and capabilities, taking more initiative, and objectively distinguishing and diagnosing, you determine that you will be more open.

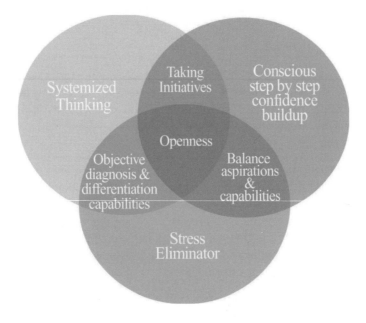

Use the same question process as before. From consistency, the main driver in the first step, to openness, the main driver in the second step, we see another loop forming. If you cannot be more open, you cannot be more consistent, and that is cause and effect.

Step Three – Build Methodologies

In the second step, you identified the following three drivers: #1 balance of needs and capabilities, #2 initiative, and #3 objective diagnosis. Now these three drivers become your new key areas. As you did with the others, find the links, or drivers behind each of these. Look for the grey areas between each of the new key areas. Compare #1 with #2, #2 with #3, and #1 with #3. Go through the same questioning process and try to identify the main driver behind the three of them.

Let's say you identify courage as the driver between balancing needs and capabilities and initiative. Then you find leveraging your level of experience as the driver between initiative and objective diagnosis. Last, you find practicality as the driver behind balance of needs and capabilities and objective diagnosis.

For the third step, you must determine where these three drivers take you. If you have courage, would you be able to leverage the level of your experience? If you are more practical, more courageous, and leverage your level of experience, where do these things take you? Let's say, for example, your answer is recognition. These three things would give you a higher level of recognition. This becomes your third level driver.

To be more consistent, you need to be open. To be open, you need recognition. This is your new model, your third level model.

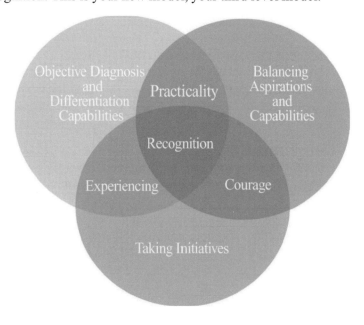

You have identified the main drivers. The first was consistency, second was openness, and the third was recognition. Now you have closed the loop. This is what constructs your mind when you define your problems.

Now, you're ready for the final step of moving deeper into the gray areas–to the inner system that drives you. Take the three inner drivers you identified in each of the steps (in our example, openness, consistency, and recognition), and put them in your final Venn diagram. Do the questioning process once more. What do each of these items have in common? For this example, self-esteem may be the answer. This fourth level connects all previous sub-systems.

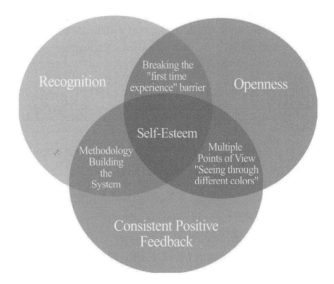

Each problem will be unique, but there is some value behind each one that you must locate and connect in order to find solutions. There are common denominators between drivers. These are the tools that will solve your problems. Use these tools to build problem-solving methodologies.

Begin Your Journey

The value in this process is to focus on the internal driver for where your actions originate. In order to focus, you must know how the system works in your mind. Each problem for each person is different. Take these steps to discover the inner values that hold you back from success.

By embarking on this journey, you peel back the layers of your self. You can find the clarity and the path to the good things in life by identifying your inner drivers. Realize that you have the tools for success within you; you just have to know how to make them work for you. Only then can you have the success you desire.

About the Author

Opher Brayer, Founder and President of Mega Language Ltd., is a Business Consultant and Corporate Coach currently based in Israel. For the last 25 years, Opher has conducted independent research in the multidisciplinary field of creative development. Based on this research, Mega Language Ltd. was established to enable corporations and individuals to increase their creativity quotient, and thus their effectiveness. Opher has developed over 60 new and inspiring methodologies for enhancing creativity, problem solving and innovation. He specializes in developing structured processes for the generation of new and valued ideas and solutions.

For more information, please contact Mega Language Ltd., # 2 Simtat Harav, Ramat Hasharon, Israel; megalang@netvision.net.il or opher@mentorsmind.com, Office: +972 35406993; Fax: +972 35470328.

Don't Sweat It
How to Thrive Under Pressure
and Come Out on Top

by Linda Brockbank-Curtis

Pressure is a constant force in our lives. While it's easy to think of pressure as a negative element, in reality, it is a positive one. Because of pressure, unlimited possibilities exist. Pressure is that tension we feel when there is a big gap between how things are now and how we wish them to be. In other words, it is our motivator to "get things done." When you learn to deal with pressure effectively, you open up hidden corners of your soul and perform better than you ever imagined.

When channeled correctly, pressure can redefine your limits. Too often, executives let pressure tyrannize them, which often leads to communication breakdowns with co-workers and staff, ill-conceived business decisions, low morale, and physical dis-ease among employees. Instead of leaning into the pressure, some people react by withdrawing, reducing communication, and stewing in low-grade panic. But to be a powerful, resilient, and inspiring leader, you need a working strategy for embracing pressure.

When you follow the next sequence of steps, you will be able to use pressure to your greatest advantage.

Step One – Quiet Your Mind
Every day our senses are assaulted with noise, images, and data. Information overload makes us tired and stale by choking our creativity and cluttering our mind with other people's ideas instead of our own. Therefore, we need to find deliberate and creative ways to build openings for silence into each and every day. Here are a few ideas:
- Experiment with eating one daily meal without talking, reading, or watching TV.
- Spend the last five minutes of your commute in silence, without distraction.
- Take five minutes to pray, meditate, or just quietly listen to some music. Just make sure you schedule 'quiet' into your day.

You can only fully realize the depth of your internal resources when you create an opening for them to surface. This opening occurs when you stop input (i.e. listening to the radio, reading) and output (i.e. talking). Silence also creates an invitation for gratitude and appreciation to surface in your mind. You will then be able to notice what IS working in your life

216

and what support is already in place. This is bound to put you in a more positive mindset. When you practice silence consistently, you will come face to face with the reality that doing nothing is actually doing something.

Step Two – Activate Your Intentions

Prior to any interaction or event, set your intention. Ask yourself what outcome you are seeking and what behaviors will make that outcome a reality. For example, when you ask a question, do you want to gather information, play devil's advocate, make a powerful request, or persuade and gather support? What qualities–compassion, courage, and vision– will best serve you in reaching your desired outcome? Examine your intentions before you start speaking.

This advance inquiry only takes a few minutes, but it will transform your results by taking the wind out of pressure. In a world where few things are controllable or predictable, establishing clear intentions is 100% within your control. It brings purpose and clarity to each moment and eliminates time spent in reaction mode.

One executive who used this tool began to realize he was participating in too many meetings. By reviewing his intentions, it became clear that certain meeting topics were better suited to other members of his staff. When he delegated meeting attendance, it freed up his time for more pressing tasks.

Step Three – Slow Things Down

Early in his tennis career, Andre Agassi noticed his tendency to rush when under pressure. This resulted in reactionary plays, unforced errors, and defeat. Many of us also have moments like that.

Agassi developed a simple technique to slow things down. Reflecting inward and focusing on his heartbeat, he imagined it beating slowly, like a metronome–Tick-Tock-Tick-Tock. The game itself remains fast and intense, but connecting to a physical sensation in the middle of the excitement creates a calm center for focused, skillful play.

Like Agassi, you can create the experience of slowing down by connecting to a physical sensation. Sit quietly and mentally connect to your heartbeat or follow the rise and fall of your belly as you breathe. Do this for a few minutes several times per day. It connects your mind to your body, like the string of a kite, bringing you fully to the present moment, where your power base for action exists.

Step Four – Identify Internal Verses External Pressure

Pay attention to the source of your pressure. The reality of an impending deadline can be *externally* driven and not within your control unless you are able to re-negotiate it. What is within your control is the *internal* story you tell yourself about the deadline. Many executives bring extra pressure upon themselves by over-scheduling their day, working evenings and weekends, and saying "yes" to personal and professional activities they would prefer to have declined.

The internal story driving this experience is frequently anchored in unexamined assumptions. Some of these internal stories are: 1) if you work hard enough you will eventually get all the work done (you won't), 2) working long hours is how you demonstrate loyalty and effectiveness (there are better ways) and 3) saying "no" is a sign of weakness (often the opposite is true).

The next time you are at your wit's end with pressure, ask yourself "What is my part?" Write down all the beliefs and assumptions you've made about the situation. Examine their validity. Knowing your responsibility is particularly useful in identifying your boundaries of responsibility. Take special notice every time you hear yourself say "I should," and stop "shoulding" yourself.

One senior executive realized she had gradually eliminated her exercise routine by regularly working until 7 P.M. Her internal story was that working overtime was necessary to get all her work done and impress her new boss. At the suggestion of an executive coach, she experimented with leaving the office by 6 P.M., no exceptions. While leaving early generated a lot of anxiety within her, she came to see how activating her intention made her more efficient. No one noticed she was leaving work earlier. Her well-being was improving and her boss remained highly complimentary of her performance. She realized she had been responsible for choosing to work longer days, and she could chose differently. She now occasionally works late, but the choice is deliberate and not driven by fear.

Step Five – Eliminate Either/Or Thinking

Tall trees are a marvel in strength and flexibility. Their longevity depends upon give and take with the elements. If you see a tree that isn't swaying in the wind, but rigid and stiff, you know it is out of balance and will soon die. People are the same way; they need to respond well to the winds of change. Executives that become rigid in their point-of-view create a lot of pressure for themselves and those around them.

Yes, decisiveness is an important quality in a leader, and standing in a decision is vital to success. Either/Or thinking raises its ugly head during the heat of the decision-making process as you are weighing and evaluating the options. When you hear yourself talking in black and white terms, usually limiting decisions to only two very different consequences, you may be trapped in the inflexibility of Either/Or thinking. Inadvertently, you may be limiting your options, stifling creativity, and overlooking a great opportunity.

Like internal pressure, Either/Or Thinking is loaded with unexamined assumptions. The way out is to ask: "How do I know this to be true?" "Am I willing to be wrong about my assumptions?" and "What is the third right answer?" Curiosity and wonder are your allies during this inquiry.

Step Six – Reflect

From time to time, take a step back and review the importance of what you are working on in the context of bigger issues. This is not to suggest that you question the value of your work, but to reflect upon how it fits in the overall scheme of things. What were the promises and resolutions you made to yourself on 9/11? Most of us were jarred from our reverie and forced to reflect upon our lives. Don't wait for a tragic wake-up call to put your latest Very Important Project into perspective.

Start Now

Fifteen minutes of practice could revolutionize your day and transform the quality of your leadership. So begin each day by quieting your mind and activating your intentions. Throughout the day, slow things down by grounding in your breath. Become aware of all the ways you may be creating pressure unnecessarily and eliminate them. You may find it useful to establish a network of support when taking on something new, so tell a friend what you are up to, or consult with an executive coach who can hold you accountable to your goals.

Pressure is a constant component of life, and true leaders embrace the structural tension it generates. No doubt the pressure you experience is as real as a tennis ball flying towards you at ninety miles per hour. While it is unlikely that the speed of the game will change or the expectations of those watching it, but you can adjust your way of being with it. When you are able to rationally understand pressure and control your reaction to it, you will find you are a more productive leader than you ever imagined possible.

About the Author

Linda Brockbank-Curtis brings 18 years of corporate experience to her work as an executive coach. She has held officer and VP positions at U.S. Bancorp, and The Harris Bank. During her tenure at Visa USA, she led an award-winning business development team, managing relationships with several Fortune 500 companies. As the founder of On Purpose LLC, Linda coaches executives to emerge as powerful and inspired leaders.

To learn more about who Linda works with, visit her website at www.onpurpose-coach.com. Based in Mill Valley, CA, she can be reached at 1.415.381.2127 or via e-mail at linda@onpurpose-coach.com.

Harness the Power of "No" to Simplify Your Life

by Jon Busack, BS, NLP

The most powerful word in the English language is "No." It is a word of identity, possession, ownership, and control. "No" defines your boundaries and tells others who you are and what you stand for. "No" is your weapon against personal violation, misunderstandings, innuendos, and unnecessary expenditures of energy and money. In the business world, saying "no" is your power.

Unfortunately, many people, whether they're a self-employed professional or a Fortune 500 business executive, lose or give away their power by not using the word "no" enough. As a result, they're overburdened at work and at home, and they have little time for themselves. They take on a "superman" or "superwoman" role by being and doing all things for all people–*excluding* themselves. Why is it so difficult to say such a small word? Several reasons exist. Here are a few:

- Expectations and rules
- Fear of appearances
- No time to think

Below are solutions for each of these, plus a simple risk-free method of practicing "no."

When Expectations and Rules Interfere

Have you ever said "yes" because you felt saying "no" would be "breaking the rules"? Have you ever thought that you're not allowed to say "no" in certain instances because "that's not what 'good' or 'successful' people do"? Remember, you must live true to your heart. Sometimes people get so sidetracked by self-imposed rules and outside mandates that they don't say "no" when they should. The next time you feel that rules are interfering with your decisions, consider these guidelines.

Rules are Made to Benefit People

Some people will spend hundreds of dollars to redecorate a room so that it will match a twenty-dollar rug. Wouldn't it make more sense to spend twenty-dollars on a new rug that will match the room as it is? After all, the rug is there for the room, not the room for the rug.

A rule is like the twenty-dollar rug. Before you make huge changes to satisfy a rule, first make sure that rule is valid. Often it's the rule you need to change, not your decision.

221

Think about the rules you have within your business, home, and family. Are they beneficial to everyone? Are the rules still true to their original purpose? Does the original purpose of the rule even still exist? When you re-evaluate a given rule, you may find that it exploits innocent people and is not beneficial to the whole group. If you find this to be true, it is time to say "no" to that rule and either eliminate or change it to benefit everyone.

Define The Rule

What exactly *is* the rule and where did it come from? Is it written down anywhere? Did you imagine it? Does it even apply to you and your situation? Often, you will find that the eternal vigilance of small-minded people mandates rules inappropriately. Remember that rules imposed by peer pressure exist by illegitimate authority; therefore, they are not binding on you and you can indeed say "no."

Rules Can Be Broken

If you evaluate a rule for its purpose and justice, and it comes up wanting, it is time to break that rule by saying "no" for the sake of "sacred disobedience." This simply means that you must break some rules and disobey some policies to preserve the sanctity and intelligence of your life so that you can say "no" without fear of retribution. Regardless of whether you choose to follow or break the rule, you will face the consequences of your actions. The question to consider is which choice will yield the consequences you would rather face. Saying "yes" or saying "no"? Are you willing to take the necessary risks to manifest your choices?

Fear of Appearances

Sometimes people don't say "no" because they don't want to appear incompetent, inept, or uncaring to the other person. Should these feelings cross your mind, try the following technique.

Say No by Saying Yes, and Provide a Choice

Picture this: You are on schedule to ship the project to your best client on Friday. The client calls in with last minute changes, which will add at least a couple days' worth of work to the project. You know you can't comply with the client's request and still ship a quality project on time, but you still must make the client happy. After all, "The customer is always right." So what do you say? Instead of saying a complete "yes" to the client's request, say, "*Yes*, absolutely we can include the changes. *If* you allow delivery on Monday, then we can include these changes with this release. *If* Friday delivery is paramount, then we can ship these changes as a later revision. *If* the changes are required in Friday's release, then the overtime will increase the cost. *Which would you prefer?*" Now the client has a choice. You said "yes" by showing enthusiastic support for the client's cause while diplomatically saying "no" by giving the client a choice of reasonable options. This is also a way to ferret out the client's true priorities: schedule, budget, or thoroughness.

No Time to Think

Sometimes people don't say "no" because they feel they don't have the necessary time to think up alternate solutions. As such, they automatically say "yes" in order to save face, or because they are frazzled by the sudden urgency. They then regret it later. When this happens to you, try the following technique.

Say No by Saying Yes, and Upgrade Your Attention

When a client takes you by surprise with an important concern, say. "I am dedicated to you and your success, and I would like to give this matter the consideration it deserves. Rather than do you the discourtesy of off-the-cuff attention for something as important as this, may I call you tomorrow morning? I'll clear my desk and you will have my *complete, undivided attention*." In this case, you say "no" by directing the client's focus to your undivided attention at a better time and place. This also gives you time to ponder solutions and catch your breath.

It Takes Practice

For many people, learning to say "no" does not come easily. It takes practice. The trick is to start saying "no" to little things so that saying "no" to the big things becomes easier. People who never say "no" until they are in an extreme situation often severely overreact, thus not getting the results they want.

The following exercise will help give you the confidence to say "no" in any situation.

- **Step One** – During an off time, go through a fast food drive-thru. Order a burger, fries, and a soda. After the employee reads your order back to you and says, "Will that be all?" respond by saying, "No, wait a minute. I changed my mind." Then order a chicken sandwich, no fries, and a diet soda instead. Wait for the tally, say "thank you," and proceed as normal. Do this exercise every day until you feel comfortable saying "no." When you start to feel more confident, try it when there are a few cars in line behind you.

- **Step Two** – After you are proficient at saying no in a drive-thru, you can progress to a more personal situation. Try the same exercise while you're in line at a bank, a post office, a restaurant, or a grocery store. If you feel uncomfortable because other people are waiting in line behind you, remember how often you have waited for others, and take a turn for yourself. It's only fair.

- **Step Three** – When you feel at ease doing this exercise with strangers, try saying "no" to a low-risk person whom you already know. Slowly raise the stakes to the level at which you want to be proficient. It may take a lot of practice, but the day will come when you will be able to say "no" about an important issue to your spouse, employer, or important client.

Yes! Say No!

Those who can't say "no" are actually already very good at saying "no"– to themselves. Turn this around. Saying "no" in a healthy way is a great investment in yourself and brings great dividends.

Always remember that some people automatically assume your compliance if you don't explicitly say "no." If you want others to clearly understand you, then you must be able to say "no" with confidence. When you do, you'll greatly reduce those over commitments and you'll simplify your life. By saying this one little word, not only will you gain respect from others, but you will also have more respect for yourself, knowing that you are standing up for what you believe in.

If you need a little extra encouragement, a good counselor, trainer, or life coach can help you gain the confidence to say "no." The time and money spent will be well worth it in the end. Think of it as making an investment in yourself. Saying "no" is one of your greatest personal strengths. When you exercise it regularly, you will enjoy a much simpler, more peaceful life.

About the Author

Jon Busack, BS, NLP, is a Life Coach and NLP Master, offering fast, effective solutions for authentic living. With speed, compassion, and dignity, Jon helps people overcome their obstacles, communicate effectively, and enhance their relationships. Jon works one-on-one and with groups, face-to-face, and over the phone, helping people be true to themselves, yet survive and thrive in the real world. More information, including how to apply for Jon's free online personal empowerment newsletter, is available at www.SoulTherapist.com, or at 1.208.345.0660.

Increase Your Productivity in Three Simple Steps

The Simplicity System™ for Time Management

by Megan Warren-Dlugokinski

"Time is the coin of your life. It is the only coin you have, and only you can determine how it will be spent. Be careful lest you let other people spend it for you." —Carl Sandburg

Time is your most valuable asset, so be careful how you spend it. As a business owner or executive, you must leverage your time to your advantage so you attain success. This is often harder said than done, though, as information and choices bombard you daily at a mind-numbing pace. Without a good time management system, you will find it difficult to keep up. Unfortunately, most time management systems leave people frustrated. Sure, they sound great in theory, but they require too much effort to set up and maintain. The key is what you do with your time and information.

The fact is, you are busy. You are overwhelmed with the number of things on your "to do" lists, and you don't want a complicated system to manage your days. What you want is a system that is fast, flexible, and functional...and one that actually works. Fortunately, you can start using some tools today that will help you get more accomplished with less stress, leaving you with more time for guilt-free fun.

To understand how this works, think back to the much simpler days of your life, whether those days were when you were just starting in the business world or even when you were in college. Life back then was less complicated, and you had more time to play. Wouldn't you love to have that peace of mind once again? With the Simplicity System, you can.

Setting up your Simplicity System™ is as Easy as 1 2 3

1. Collect *all* the information and materials you need.

Before getting starting, you first need the proper tools to ensure a successful outcome. In order for any time management system to work you need a place to put all incomplete items. Anything you need to do, should do, or ought to do is an incomplete task that needs to be written down. The less you have to remember the better. Therefore, your planner will be your most important tool for managing your life.

225

Inside your planner, which can be either paper or electronic, you will keep your calendar, lists, contacts, and other frequently needed items. Consider your planner your portable or external brain for those days when it seems your memory has taken a mini vacation. Be sure you always have your planner available at all times or it won't be effective.

Keep only one calendar to enter all of your appointments, meetings, and recurring activities, both personal and business. With more than one calendar you run the risk of missing appointments and activities. Be careful that you do *not* fall into the trap of over-scheduling yourself and getting overwhelmed. Therefore, do not schedule more than 50% of your day to allow for unforeseen emergencies if necessary.

The biggest enemy of time is procrastination. A good way to notice important patterns in your life is to create a log of all of your activities and color code each activity according to activity type or theme with a different color. For example, you can use a blue highlighter to notate all tasks associated with billing, a yellow highlighter to notate all tasks associated with prospecting, a green highlighter to notate all tasks associated with family, etc. You can then see if you are spending too much or too little time on certain activities. You will also notice days or times that you are more productive. You can use all this information to restructure your time to fit your own needs and preferences.

On the flip side, focus is one of the greatest assets to time management. A good idea for business people is to schedule special days each week for specialized focused activities:

- The first are your money-making days where you focus on activities that grow your business and bring in income.
- The second is administrative activities that need to be done, such as bookkeeping, filing, and phone calls.
- The third, and arguably the most important of the three, are your days for rest and rejuvenation. Most business people rarely rest; however, you can't be productive if you are exhausted and stressed out. One rule of the rest day is that you do no business activities whatsoever.

As they structure their day, most people think "to do" lists are a good way to manage their time. However, daily "to do" lists are generally not a good idea, because people tend to put too many items on it and then feel like a failure on a daily basis. This is not a good way to reinforce a habit you want to keep! In order to consistently use a system you must set it up so that you are successful. If you feel you must use a daily "to do" list, then keep it very short, with no more than five items on it of things you *must* do that day. Avoid the temptation to add things you would *like* to get done that day, as it will dilute the list's importance.

Even better, instead of a "to do" list, create an "action list" with categories. By grouping similar tasks together you can accomplish things faster and easier. The traditional "to do" list is usually an incomplete listing of unclear tasks that never seem to get done. Another secret to the category list is to create work zones. For example, set up a call zone where you keep your contact list and call log, a mail zone where you keep shipping supplies, a computer zone where you keep your tech gadgets, etc. Then, create checklists for each zone for routine tasks that have multiple steps.

2. Organize all of your tasks.

One of the keys to being successful is organizing, both your things and your activities. Deciding how to organize your tasks and information related to a task is as easy as ABC. Follow these simple steps and you will be able to determine whether something is important, as well as how you should tackle it.

A = Action. If something you need to work on requires action now, put it in one of three places.

- **A-Z files within easy reach** – Use a fun color for these since you will be using them often. Here you will keep all of your action items that you need to do. When noting action items in your planner, write down what needs to be done, when it is due, and where the information is located. You can then complete the action item by the due date.

- **A current project file** – Anything with more than two steps is a project. List that item on a master project index and place it in a project file. If you have a deadline for a project, note it on the index.

- **Reading material** – Keep this in your reading work zone. Don't forget to take some with you when you leave the office. If you have to wait somewhere, you will still be able to use your time productively.

B = Background information. Keep general reference information in your filing zone. Also keep your list of projects you might want to do someday and your idea files in your filing zone.

C = Clutter. Clutter is trash, so get rid of it. The more you throw out, the better. Ask yourself, "What is the worst thing that would happen if this was gone?" If your answer is nothing, then toss it.

3. Plan and review your system and lists regularly.

Review all of your lists and calendar items on a daily basis so you stay on top of everything that needs your immediate attention. Also do a weekly review, where you go through your category lists, your calendar, and your planner. Make sure you schedule all the important items for the upcoming week, and confirm that you have completed all items from the past week.

Schedule these review sessions on your calendar. Once you have done the review, then you need to take action. The best way to decide what to do from your category list during your unstructured work time is to choose items according to four criteria:

- Your priorities.
- Your location.
- Your energy level.
- Your time available.

By taking these things into consideration, you will easily decide what you should be doing at any given moment.

Accomplish More in Less Time

The final three components of success are accountability, planning, and support. A mentor or coach can help you with all three. In fact, most successful business people have a mentor or a coach to help them achieve more, earn more money, and have more time for fun. Most coaches and mentors actually encourage you to have more fun and will help you find ways to add more play time into your life and increase your productivity.

The Simplicity System™ increases your chances of success by keeping it simple so you can maintain it. When you invest in yourself and structure your time wisely, your productivity will increase, and you'll have more opportunities for personal activities. So give the Simplicity System™ a try. You deserve it.

About the Author

Megan Warren-Dlugokinski is a work at home mom who artfully balances family and career. She helps entrepreneurial moms and dads who are time and organizationally challenged master systems and strategies that work with their unique strengths. In the process, she helps her clients create balance in their business and personal life, with a focus on fun, play, and humor. Using a combination of spiritual principles and outer strategies, Megan enables people to create extraordinary results.

For more information, please call 1.405.721.1791, email Megan@yourguidinglight.com, or for free articles, e-courses, audio classes, and other great resources, visit www.yourguidinglight.com.

Talk Yourself Into The Life You Want

Three Strategies for Permanent, Positive Self-Talk

by Bonnie Hall

"What do you want?"

This simple yet powerful question is both easy and difficult to answer. Think what would happen if you dedicated one week of your life to asking and answering that question. You would likely find answers that are extremely valuable for planning a direction and course for your life.

The only catch is that each time you ask yourself "What do I want," you must also do a "gut check" to unearth your true thoughts and feelings. As you tune in to the honest thoughts and feelings that emerge, you will get a powerful sense of what truth means for you on a given topic. As you answer, notice whether you feel a light, all-knowing confidence that leads to exhilaration and anticipation, or experience doubts and fears that cause a wave of heaviness to swallow you. In other words, does the voice inside you say, "You can do it!" or does your inner voice badger you about why you can't?

This internal dialog is your "self-talk." Along with your feelings and emotions, your self-talk is the most powerful engine driving you toward success, happiness, and the life of your dreams. You can have incredible talent, skills, and dedication, but if your self-talk is negative and self-defeating, then success and happiness will always be out of reach no matter how hard you work. Even if you have limited skills and talent, positive self-talk has the ability to propel you to the life you dream of and will sustain you as you strive for your goals.

You Are a Powerful Magnet!

Your self-talk, beliefs, and feelings are the forces that give you energy. They create the personal atmosphere you radiate to the world around you. You may have noticed that some people have a bad "aura," as though a dark cloud hangs over them, while others project great charisma. Both effects are the manifestations of energy that radiate from within. Your energy determines your own vibration and frequency, which in turn has the ability to attract or repel success and happiness. Think of your personal atmosphere as being the most powerful magnet in the world, for both positive and negative results.

229

You have the power to decide what kind of magnet you want to be. At this moment, do you believe you are a "vibrational" match to your dreams, or do you experience angst in your heart that makes you question whether you have what it takes? Whatever your answer, your feelings, beliefs, and self-talk must first become the mirror image of your dreams in order for you to achieve success. To accomplish what you want in life, nothing is more important than to align your inner dialog with your goals.

The following information will help small business owners and company executives reprogram their self-talk so they can find the tools to create permanent change and a meaningful and successful life.

Are You Listening to Your "Gut" Instinct?

To begin, you need to familiarize yourself with two aspects of your internal dialog so that you can learn to use both to guide you. The first part is your gut instinct, which acts as your internal guidance system. It speaks to you through your emotions or intuition. The second part of your internal dialog is your "self-talk," which is the constant conversation you have with yourself throughout the day. Think of your instinct as the part of you that is directly connected to your internal guidance system. When you learn to listen to it carefully, you instantly know what is best for you without having to think about it. Likewise, your "self-talk" is also a constant companion. It is never quiet and is with you every second to make sure that whatever you *want* and *believe in* becomes your reality. Your instinct and your self-talk may appear separate and distinct, but they each depend on the other, as they work together to make you who you are and who you want to become. This "YOU" has more potential than you could ever use, and this "YOU" has the power to move mountains.

But what if you are feeling disconnected from your gut feelings, from your internal guidance system? What if your self-talk is not very positive or even downright negative? What if your actions are based on fear, doubt, and insecurity? What if they are based on other people's paradigms, beliefs, or philosophies? If you judge your own goals and dreams by someone else's yardstick, what will the result of your life be?

If you could stand outside yourself, you would see that all your self-talk, beliefs, and feelings are compelling you to replicate all those internal beliefs through your actions. Your life is the mirror that doesn't lie. It reflects exactly what you have been thinking, feeling, and believing. So look at your present self and ask, "Is this where I want to be?" and "Is my self-talk a match to my dreams?" If you are aware that you've been talking yourself out of the life you want, you can just as easily talk your self into it.

Three Strategies for Talking Yourself into the Life You Want

Remember that every word you think or say is a powerful magnet that attracts or repels things and events into your life. To help make your self-talk positive and attract the results you want, you can consciously use three tools that will help you break through the invisible barriers that have been keeping you from your dreams.

The Three Strategies–

1) **Do a "gut check."** Negative self-talk can wreak havoc in your life. When you do a gut check, you'll realize what's going on inside you. To do so, think of a time when you knew you were going to get something you really wanted. At that point, you knew that nothing could stop you from reaching your goal. Remember every feeling and emotion you were having at the time, as this will cue you into how you want to be feeling whenever you state your goals and dreams.

   Next, recall a time when you had a very strong desire for something, but found yourself procrastinating, spinning your wheels and feeling stuck, unable to reach that goal. Again, remember every detail of that experience. These feelings will clue you into why it seems you are unable to reach your goals. The distinct feelings associated with these experiences will teach you how to pay attention and listen to your intuition. Your emotions and feelings do not lie, and they will always let you know if you are a "vibrational" match to want you want. With practice, you'll be able to instantly recognize what kind of magnet you are becoming. Armed with this awareness, you can discover any hidden blocks you may have not realized previously.

2) **Erase and replace.** This is a daily exercise you'll use to bring to light all the actions and attitudes that hinder you from achieving what you truly want. For instance, if you think, "I'll never make enough money," stop that thought immediately. Next, say to yourself, "Erase that thought," then replace the negative thought with a positive one, such as, "Money is fun to make and it is coming to me from many sources." The key here is to see yourself erase the old thought and say aloud your new replacement phrase. You can even visualize yourself using a chalkboard as you go through this process. Realize that this is not a quick fix, but an exercise that you need to repeat over and over until your new belief becomes a part of your "DNA."

3) **What you see is what you get!** You are always forming opinions and conclusions about what you observe in the world. Each one of these conclusions will attract whatever you're focused on and will continue to gain power in your life. Therefore, you need to control what you

focus on and make sure it is beneficial to you. Get in the habit of asking yourself two questions: "How do I want to see this thing that has my attention?" and "Do I really want this thing to grow and gain power?"

Success is a result of your attitudes and perspectives, and you always have the choice as to what your attitude will be. When you focus on something, whether you want it in your life or not, it will take over a part of your life. Your attention is like the oxygen that feeds a fire. Focus only on what will enhance your life. When you do, your energy will increase and will become a powerful force for success.

Live Your New Life!

When you master your self-talk and listen to your intuition, they become your greatest advocates and motivators. You will be happier, more fulfilled, and more successful than you can imagine. Do a gut check to clue you in to how you are really feeling. The more aware you become of your inner dialog, the sooner you will be able to replace negative aspects with positive ones. If you feel stuck, stop and ask yourself, "What do I need to believe and say to myself in order to become one with what I want?" As you incorporate positive self-talk and begin to live your new story, you will draw to yourself everything you need to make your dreams and goals come true.

About the Author

Bonnie Hall is the owner of "Inside & OUT – The Life Makeover Institute." She is a Life/Success Coach who works with entrepreneurs, service based businesses, and small businesses who are looking to take their life and business to the next level. Bonnie has developed innovative coaching programs and workshops in Self-Talk Mastery, Self-Discovery (lucrative life purpose), Self-Expression (secrets to manifesting your dreams), and Self-Image (how you want the world to see you). Her mission is to assist her clients in becoming a "vibrational" match to their dreams. For a free 40 minute, no obligation telephone coaching to assist you in having your self talk become a "vibrational" match to your dreams; or for more information about tele-classes, workshops, coaching programs, and speaking engagements, contact Bonnie Hall at: Inside & Out, The Life Makeover Institute, 6 Dale Avenue, Cherry Hill, NJ 08002; 1.856.428.2284; www.insideandoutcoaching.com.

Reclaim the Success of Your Youth

How to Keep Up When It's Time to Slow Down

by Katalin Halom

With each passing day our world gets a bit older. So do you. Yesterday you were in the prime of your life—respected, invincible and strong. But seemingly overnight, all that has changed. Suddenly, the birthday cake can't hold all the candles. Your success strategies of yesterday have lost their edge, much like you. Well-educated, bold, and reckless whiz kids are hard at your heels, vying for your position.

Angst-ridden, you jump into action and try to turn back the clock. You react by working harder and longer hours, but all you get are sleepless nights and rising blood pressure. Before you never had to worry about your health. Now the reserves are almost depleted and you still have the constant mind-boggling fear of growing old. Could early retirement be the solution? Nonsense!

Rather than panic, now is the time to recharge your batteries, re-evaluate, reassess, and reinvent yourself. Acknowledge the past, and then move on. Change direction or turn full circle if you wish. Regardless of the route you choose, take care of your body and your mind, and they will take care of you.

While changing directions can be difficult, the results are worth it. Whether you own a small business or a professional service firm, or even if you are a high-ranking corporate executive, the following eight steps will help you change fear into confidence and paralysis into energetic, well-planned action.

1) **Challenge your assumptions about age.** Get rid of your "inherited" ideas of what aging is supposed to be. You can remove this self-limiting emotional roadblock with the following exercise:

   - Schedule a visit to an art museum or picture gallery. (A good book on paintings will do as well.) Seek out a painting by an old master and reflect on its timeless beauty and radiance. (Be sure you choose an uplifting, bright and cheerful scene; portraits of suffering saints and martyrs won't do the job.) The canvas and the paint might be a bit cracked, but that doesn't depreciate its value. The same is true for you; you are a masterpiece of nature.

While the surface may not be quite as flawless as in your youth, you are still unique and precious.

2) **Greet the morning sun.** How you spend the very first hour of your day greatly affects the quality of the rest of your waking hours. Are you grumpy or energized? Depressed or full of vitality? Do the following exercise to set the stage for a good day.

- Each morning, after rising, open the window and stand up tall with you feet shoulder-width apart and your arms out to the sides at shoulder height, palms down. Take a deep breath. As you exhale, slowly bend forward from your hip joints, being sure to keep your back very flat. As you do, think: "Out with the old." Pull your abdomen in, pressing the air out of your lungs as much as possible. When you have released all the air from your lungs, inhale as you straighten up slowly. As you do, think: "In with the new." Repeat five times.

This deep, concentrated breathing along with the mental command energizes the body, clears the mind, and increases your brainpower.

3) **Take a stance.** A well aligned, upright body instantly elevates your mood, builds confidence, and increases your attractiveness, which ultimately impacts your professional options. Good posture is a powerful signal that shows to the world how vital and energetic you are. Practice the following exercise as often as you can.

- While standing or sitting, take a deep breath. As you exhale, tuck in your stomach (don't force it). Starting with your tailbone, vertebrae by vertebrae lengthen your spine upwards. Visualize a balloon attached to the top of your head holding it up. Breathe in and relax. Repeat five times.

Perform this exercise as often as possible, and soon you will see yourself in an increasingly positive light.

4) **Create a private wailing wall.** Every once in a while, despite your best efforts, melancholy will strike and you will feel sorry for yourself. No matter how unpleasant this state may be, it has great potential to cleanse your mind and soul (provided it doesn't last too long). The following exercise will help.

- Designate a part of your bedroom as your personal wailing wall. When the blues hit, stand facing that wall and bemoan the passage of time, the glorious past, your unappreciative boss or clients, etc. Exaggerate the emotions: gesticulate, make faces, lament. (Just make sure no one can see you!)

This seemingly silly exercise helps bring your fears and frustrations to consciousness and gets them out of your system before they can cause bodily and mental harm.

5) **Move your body.** The body and the mind are intimately connected. To be your best, physically and mentally, you need to develop an exercise routine. While a weekend game of tennis or golf is not enough physical activity for the week, don't go to extreme either. Accept that you do not need to perform as well as (or as much as) the twenty-somethings. Thirty minutes to an hour of moderate exercise most days of the week is all you need to improve your health, elevate your mood, and help preserve your mental functioning. The following suggestions will help get and keep you in shape.

- Schedule an appointment for a medical evaluation.
- Hire a personal trainer, take up walking, get a bike or a treadmill, go swimming, or lift weights. Do whatever you enjoy and is convenient.
- Give exercise high priority; schedule it into your day-planner like a business meeting.

You cannot afford to neglect your body. Your professional success depends largely on your physical and mental ability to keep up with the rapid changes in your chosen field.

6) **Search your soul.** Midlife is a challenging time when people tend to question whether the career path they have been following was really their choice. Maybe necessity or the wishes of their parents actually dictated their career decision. To get clear on your own dreams for the next stage of your life, carve out this week an hour or two for the following exercise.

- Take your phone off the hook and ask your family and friends not to interrupt you. Then, take a piece of paper and complete the sentence, "If I could start my life anew, I would be ... / I would do ...." Write down your wildest dreams, even if they seem impossible. Don't censor yourself or even consider what others might think. This is YOUR life, so write what you'd want to do.

This soul searching will help you find the most rewarding direction to take for the better half of your life.

7) **Enjoy your laurels, but don't rest on them too long.** Past glory is no guarantee for future success. Rather, use your rich experience of hard work and set out for new achievements. Reserve an hour of quiet time to take stock of your past and to plan your future.

- Whether you want to head in a new direction or just enhance your current one, define in writing those aspects you need to develop to be on a par with (or even above) your competition.

Analyze your strengths and weaknesses. Recall what you did to be successful the first time around—courage, learning, trying and failing and trying again. Didn't it take unwavering faith and the certainty that finally you'd reap the reward of all that effort? Did it also take good health and vitality? Why should that be any different now?

Use the inventory you create as a baseline from where to start your journey.

8) Ignore chronic complainers. Avoid those people who use age as an excuse for laziness. They rob your energy and destroy your vitality. They don't want you to change because then they would have to adjust to the new you.

- Identify the people who say such things as: "Well, at my/your age, I /you cannot/ should not ... anymore ...." Gradually faze those words (and those people) out of your life.

Note: Don't attempt to change your old routine all at once; the additional stress could sabotage your efforts. Let your body and mind easily integrate the changes. Get help if you need to. Remember, asking for help is a sign of wisdom, not weakness.

The Best is Yet to Come

The middle years are not a time of decline, but of maturity. It's not a time to mourn, but to bring in the harvest and then plant new seeds. Realize that the first half of your life was but a dress rehearsal for the better half yet to come.

You are never too old to be young if you only allow yourself to be. It's possible for humans to live up to 120 years. So you can either spend the next sixty or seventy years feeling sorry for yourself, full of regret for the time wasted, or you can get up and enjoy each wonderful day till the very end. The choice is yours. Choose wisely.

About the Author

Katalin Halom, a multilingual Business Mentor and Life Coach, uses a unique body-mind approach to help her international clientele overcome self-limiting assumptions in times of career and life transitions. She firmly believes that, regardless of age, each of us has an inexhaustible potential to go beyond the accepted limits of what is possible. For more information, please visit www.katalinhalom.com.

Supercharge Your Team's Expertise
Twelve Ways to Attain Lasting Knowledge
by Sue Lindgren, CMEC

You arrive at your office early, optimistic that you'll catch up on a few e-mails, only to find 129 new messages since the night before. You planned to respond to several old voicemails, but now you have eleven new messages. As you prepare for an 8 a.m. meeting, you check your calendar and realize you're scheduled to be in training for several of your priceless hours today. Exasperated, you think "Training? For what?" While the training's objective is to teach you to do more and be better, or at least different in some way, it rarely works as promised.

For a day, or maybe a week, the new training is the office "buzz." Sure, it's great in theory, but how practical is it? In reality, the improvement in performance from most training programs is rarely sustainable. People quickly forget much of the new information, until the next training program comes along.

What's Not Working?
Intelligent business owners, executives, and managers with sincere intentions invest in training sessions every day. In most cases, the participants want to learn, and the facilitators have useful information they enjoy teaching. Individuals and organizations spend large amounts of time, money, and energy implementing training programs, hoping for magic solutions to their problems. These same individuals and organizations are often disappointed with the results.

The problem is that we expect a brief training program to provide instant, "drive-through" solutions to situations that took years to create. As a society we are constantly exposed to the hype of the "easy fix." We've "sped up" the process for learning with virtual classrooms, webinars, and e-groups. The self-help section in your local bookstore is bursting at the seams with ideas for short cuts and easier ways.

Now, these methods are not all bad, but they are incomplete. People simply can't and don't learn from a one-time session. By its nature, learning is an ongoing process. What's more, most of us haven't learned how to learn. We can cram information for short-term use on a test or project, but we don't retain or master the information. For effective learning to take place, we need a new approach.

The following learning strategies will work for any business owner, executive, or manager committed to personal and organizational excellence.

How Do We Learn?

Sustained learning takes place over time. We achieve it through patience, repetition, coaching, and support. As a whole, we have developed lazy learning habits and expect instant results. This accounts in part for the incredible growth of the coaching profession. High performance organizations often rely on external consultants, trainers, and coaches for an outside "perspective" on their knowledge and abilities, or the lack thereof. But this reliance on consultants is often a sign of ineffective training within the organization.

Effective learning occurs the same way it always has. When you learned to walk, read, ride a bike, or drive a car, you had to practice and repeat the activity until it became natural. The same process applies to training programs within your organization. We have to implement systems that support true knowledge attainment, or learning won't be sustainable. That's why training alone falls short. You simply can't assimilate information and learn it without a shift in the total approach.

Ways to Enhance Your Learning Skills

Rather than attempt a quick fix, true leaders go for lasting results. Here are six learning strategies top performers use to maximize their learning potential.

1) **Make quiet time in your day–every day.** Use this time for reflection. Spend 10-20 minutes writing in a journal, going for a walk, meditating, drawing, or painting–anything that opens your mind to new ideas. As you do, remove yourself from any outside distractions so that you can hear your internal voice.

2) **Develop a beginner's mindset.** Give yourself permission to make mistakes, and be patient. Imagine you are a child learning a new skill. Keep an open and curious mind, and let go of your own personal expectations. Let new information enter your life and praise yourself for the new knowledge you retain.

3) **You don't have to make the right decision; you need to make a decision and then make that decision right.** Too often, we avoid making decisions because the fear of what could go wrong paralyzes us. The result of this inability to act is that everything stops and NOTHING gets done. While it is certainly important to give any decision sufficient consideration, it is even more important to make a deci-

sion and then act. You can then fine-tune your decision for increased effectiveness.

4) **Ask a question several ways to allow for a variety of possible answers. Then choose the answer that is best for you.** When you ask a question in a number of ways, you avail yourself of many possible alternatives. To solve problems, ask open-ended questions such as "What is possible?" "What actions can I take?" "How could this impact me/others?" and "What do I need to learn in order to be successful?" Listen to your answers.

5) **Focus on what you want.** Have you ever wondered why so many people seem to get stuck with what they say they don't want? That's what happens when you focus on what you don't want. The solution is to focus on what you do want! This shift will direct your thinking to positive solutions and help you to reach and sustain your goals.

6) **Create, nurture, and utilize your network of support.** You already have a network of support, composed of the people around you who are also facing the challenge that new training brings. Ask for help from your fellow participants. You can all learn from each other. You may also need to expand your network and add a coach or mentor to facilitate the learning process. Tend these new relationships well–together you can accomplish more!

Improve Learning Within Your Organization

To lead your entire company to sustainable learning, instill these six practices within your organization.

1) **Form "think tanks," mastermind groups, brainstorming sessions, and creative teams to foster ideas and input.** You can use these groups for specific projects as well as overall organizational improvement. You will find that the best ideas often come from unexpected people and places. Think outside the usual sphere of contact. For example, your clients could be a rich source of ideas and inspiration. When was the last time you asked them for feedback?

2) **Create a learning environment.** Train your managers to be coaches, and let them follow any training with individual and group coaching. This technique leads to sustainable progress, and it really works! Training combined with coaching reinforces the new concepts, drawing on repetition for increased retention. Challenge your employees to integrate new concepts into their daily activities, and then reward their achievements.

3) **It's better to have an outstanding team with a good plan than a good team with an outstanding plan.** When you support your team along with the learning process, you will experience positive results. Allow your employees to take ownership of their learning processes. Give them all the support they need to be top performers. When you set clear expectations and invite honest feedback, you are building a foundation for strong leadership, and strong leadership brings results!

4) **Act as if a goal is already successfully completed.** Most of us look at a goal and then immediately worry about the unknown obstacles. We may say to ourselves, "It's never been done before. I don't have the skills. The timeline is too short. The budget won't support it." But if you think and act as though you have already successfully completed the goal, you automatically shift your perspective to a positive approach. Obstacles will no longer make you hesitate. With this approach, you will feel prepared to take on any task.

5) **Keep improving your communication.** We can usually trace poor results to a failure of communication. Learn to listen carefully to others. Give people the freedom to be honest, to ask questions, and to give feedback. When you make communication a priority within your organization, you give your organization its best opportunity to excel.

6) **Make choices that reflect what is important.** To create an effective learning environment, decide beforehand what you want to accomplish. As you implement new practices for sustained learning and lasting retention, you'll gain an increased sense of competence and comfort with the new processes, especially once you see some results.

Lasting Rewards

As you learn to learn, you'll have greater success in all areas of your life. Personally, you'll feel a greater sense of peace as you think, talk, and complete tasks using a learning model. Professionally, you'll find that your return on investment will increase dramatically. You will retain your high performers, who will enjoy the benefits of a work environment that embraces effective continuing education, and your employees will show an increased enthusiasm for all aspects of their work. What better return could any leader ask for?

Realize that no drive-through solution to learning exists. However, if you're ready to effectively invest your time, money, and energy, you're on the way to sustainable learning, effectiveness, and fulfillment.

About the Author

Sue Lindgren, CMEC is a certified effectiveness coach and the founder of YESS! – Your Extraordinary Success Strategies, Inc. She specializes in corporate learning programs, with expertise in communication, leadership development, high performance teams and effectiveness coaching. She is also co-founder of Ideal Coaching, a company specializing in organizational and individual coaching programs and certification. Both companies are based in Minneapolis, MN. Sue is also available for executive retreats, group coaching, teleclasses, and speaking engagements. You can learn more about her work at www.sayYess.com or by calling 1.877.946.9377 (win-yess).

Even the Lone Ranger Had a Sidekick

How to Harness the Power of Collaboration

by Kelli Richards

Have you ever noticed how some people in business seem to prefer to work as "lone rangers"? We see this tendency in both small business owners who feel they must do it all, as well as in corporate executives who neglect to delegate tasks to their team. You may even have this tendency yourself. If you're unsure whether you're a lone ranger, answer these questions:

- Do you sometimes have trouble sharing ownership or delegating responsibility?
- Do you wish you could find a way to make more money without working harder?
- Do you wish you had more time to spend with your friends, family, or for hobbies and personal time for yourself?

If you answered "yes" to any of these questions, you may suffer from the Lone Ranger syndrome.

Doing it all yourself may seem heroic, but it can also make you feel isolated and uninspired, because you're limiting your thoughts and perspectives. Going solo, whether in your own business or by segregating yourself from the corporate team, is not the most effective way to achieve high impact results, as it can be draining, overwhelming, and stress provoking–all of which can leave you feeling flat and exhausted. If you're seeking to have a full, balanced life beyond your work, then the "lone ranger" approach can be a recipe for disaster.

Rely on Your Posse

When you exchange the solitary approach for collaboration with at least one other person, or even a team of like-minded colleagues, you open the doors to the exponential results that come from combined experiences, perspectives, and fresh ideas. You'll have more fun and be a lot more productive when you team up and share the workload around a set of common goals and agendas. Additional benefits are that you can make more money than you may be able to on your own, and you're likely to have more energy, which enables you to better serve your customers and tend to personal matters. When you're sharing the load your life will be more fun, balanced, and fulfilled, and you can focus on the things that matter most to you.

Some of the greatest successes of all time have been collaborative relationships. These include:

- Steve Jobs and Steve Wozniak (Apple Computer);
- William Hewlett and David Packard (Hewlett Packard);
- John Lennon, Paul McCartney, Ringo Starr, and George Harrison (The Beatles);
- Elton John and Bernie Taupin (songwriters);
- Andrew Lloyd Webber and Tim Rice (composers).

If you want to achieve a meaningful lifestyle and have greater life balance with reduced stress, then effective partnering and collaboration with other professionals is just what you need to reach your destination. Here's how to get started.

Define Your Strengths

Make a list of the areas of your business where you could use a partner or collaborator. For example, are you good at closing sales but lousy at collections or managing your finances? Do you enjoy spending more time with customers versus doing the administrative side of your work? Are you an expert in marketing but don't have a technical bone in your body? Find someone who can augment your strengths to tackle the facets of your business that you don't enjoy doing.

Creating a list of your strengths and weaknesses will help you identify specific areas where your business or corporate position could benefit by having complementary skills to augment your own. The right combination of collective assets offsets your individual liabilities, balances them, and makes you far more powerful and effective as team beyond what you could ever have achieved individually.

Search for the Right People

Identify potential collaborators who would be a good fit. You may already have individuals in your immediate circle who are obvious candidates. If not, networking and putting the word out may help you find potential prospects. Keep an open mind and allow the opportunities to present themselves, in addition to proactively seeking them out.

As you perform your search, don't limit yourself to your existing network. Seek referrals from past and current colleagues to make new connections. Expand your base by attending key trade conferences and events where prospective colleagues are likely to be. And don't overlook meeting potential partners online in chat rooms and special interest groups. Technology enables us to connect with people all over the world. Use this to your advantage.

Clarify Your Values

In order to collaborate effectively, you need to clarify your business and life vision and values. Outline what you value during business interactions and what you expect from others. As you evaluate your life and career, answer the following questions: Is your house in order in terms of a stable financial situation? Is your business/life in good physical condition and free of lawsuits? Do you have a good life/work balance (mix of work and rest and relaxation)? Are you focused on success and achieving your goals? If you answered no to any of the above, you may want to consider alternatives to doing it all yourself.

Share this information with any potential collaborators so you can determine whether your core values and goals are in synch with each other. Then, make a list of what's most important to you in your life: Is it more money? More time? A blend of meaningful work and time off? More quality time with friends and loved ones? Once you and your potential collaborator have this down on paper, you will see how your values and work style can agree.

Once you're informed about what is important to each of you and where you are on your individual paths, you can establish a much stronger foundation for how you want to shape and direct your work as a team in order to have a more fulfilled life. If you're generally in alignment, your chances of success together increase dramatically. And if you have a few areas of concern, you'll know about them early on and can readily address them as you progress.

Learn About Your Partners

Pay attention not just to the technical fit (i.e. complementary skills/talents) when collaborating, but also to the intangible style fit between you, as it will be a critical component to your success in working together. Do your work styles and personalities mesh well? Also, compare your individual values and goals. When you understand each other, you can respect and support one another's objectives, which is essential for each of you to achieve success.

To determine your fit with your potential collaborator, you can use work style assessment questionnaires, personality/behavioral profile tests, or call the person's past references as you would if you were hiring the person to be an employee. You can also take the direct approach and start by working on something small together. As you do, pay attention to the subtle nuances of how the other person operates in action. Be observant to pick up on key clues to the person's style. Compromise, sensitivity, and stellar communications between you and the other person are also paramount considerations. Finally, perform the due diligence and document your mutual intentions in writing.

Create a Winning Strategy

A winning strategy can be as simple as networking and offering referrals to each other's business, to doing cross-promotions to target clients, to forming consortiums between your businesses or departments. Beyond that, you can sub-contract one another on special projects, develop joint ventures between your companies, or create an outright partnership.

While the latter is probably the first thing most people think of when they hear the word "collaboration," a legal partnership is not without its challenges. Issues of fit, trust, and shared goals all need to be resolved, and you will need to reach an agreement as to how formal the partnership will be, again with written documentation in place between the parties. You need to be especially sure that you can trust and rely on this person, and that you communicate well. Perform any necessary due diligence upfront, which can include checking a person's previous track record, financial background, quality of their work, and references. Your future and your company's success depends on ensuring that all the critical components are in place.

Strive for the Finish Line

You've established your individual values and shared goals, your skills are highly complementary, your personalities mesh, and you communicate well; so far so good. Now you need to determine how you will document your partnership, what kind of legal and tax considerations play into how you formalize your alliance, and how you'll deal with income splits and liabilities, your responsibilities, and specific terms and considerations. What if one of you decides to move on at some point? All of this should be addressed and documented at the outset. As time passes, people tend to remember details differently, hence the need to write things down. Above all else, listen and respect each other. These are the hallmarks of success for any well-run collaboration.

Round Up Your Wagons and Form Your Own Winning Combination

Teaming up with others is the cornerstone of many successful self-employed professionals. When you do it right, collaboration makes your life much easier and more fun. You'll lead a richer, more fulfilling life and enjoy a successful career when you work smarter, not harder. Finding and working with great partners is the fastest way to achieve both goals.

About the Author

A veteran in the digital media arena, Kelli Richards partners major content brands, top artists, and dynamic companies by leveraging the convergence of entertainment and technology to create profitable new business channels for all. She also produces high profile events such as concerts, awards shows, fundraisers, and conferences. She offers life coaching for celebrities and other accomplished professionals who are seeking greater integration, balance, and fulfillment in their lives. Kelli works with clients all over the globe, but makes her home in the San Francisco Bay Area. You can find more details about Kelli and her company Brainstorm Marketing on her website at www.kelli.org, or by calling her office at 1.408.257.6155.

Creating a Life Far Beyond Success

by David Scarlett

"Merry Christmas, honey; we've just lost our business!"

Through convulsive sobs she asked, "How bad is it?"

"Oh, I'd say about $400,000 in debt."

And so, that dark Christmas started a journey for yet another failed entrepreneur. It was a journey that was to bless his family, teach him priceless lessons, and touch the lives of possibly thousands of business owners and leaders. What he learned could change your professional and personal life too, and help you attain a sense of purpose, depth, and joy.

If, like many business owners and corporate executives, you are consumed by business and your life has reached a point of dull pain, then it's time to make some changes. Do any of the following sound familiar?

- Your business calendar is full, but your relationships are hanging by a thread.
- Your push for profits leaves you little time for anything else.
- You're successfully climbing the corporate ladder, but still feel "empty."
- You're achieving precisely the financial success you planned, but you're wondering if accumulating the toys has been worth the sacrifice.

If you feel a void within and yearn for a place where you sense happiness, peace, and quality relationships, then review the principles and actions that can create for you a life that's far beyond success—an astonishing life!

A Miracle is Born

What a miracle you are! Throughout the ages, literature has praised your creation. "For thou hast made him a little lower than the angels, and hast crowned him with glory and great honor," says Psalms 8:5. Indeed, Psalms 139:14 goes on to say that you are "fearfully and wonderfully made."

Who can look upon a newborn child and not marvel at the wonder of his or her birth? The greater miracle, however, is the emotional/spiritual growth process—the one that takes you from helpless babe to powerful adult. It's a growth process you can repeat at *any* stage of your life!

Tragically, somewhere on the journey from birth to adulthood, your innocent vision becomes clouded. Events, experiences, and other people write ideas and conclusions onto the "window" through which you view the world. Those ideas are frequently incomplete, unfounded, and not aligned to true principles of happiness. They alter the way you see reality. But you adopt them. Now you assume that what you see on your window is the way that you and the world work.

What you assume plays out in your life. So is it any wonder that you operate in a way that is not inclined to bring you a sense of purpose, fulfilment, and lasting joy? It's time to reverse that trend—to clean the window through which you view the world. To start the process, do the following:

1. Listen to your still, small voice

History's pre-eminent thinkers and leaders have discovered that the source of man's deepest strength—the wonderful mystery of life—is almost entirely abstract. Yet, what might at first seem "soft" has very real and "hard" results.

For example, God (or the Universe) is consistently signalling answers intended for your spiritual growth. We often call that clear prompting the still, small voice. It's no wonder that the voice is foreign to most of us, as we are often caught up in the stress and busy-ness of life. So, to be inspired by the greatest Mentor in the Universe, reduce the noise in your life.

Noise can include the adrenaline of a hectic schedule, painful relationships, constant pleasure seeking, regular drugs and stimulants, hypocrisy, garbage entertainment, and immorality. All of these damage the delicate spiritual receptor within you.

To help reduce this "noise," today's leaders are rediscovering the power of meditation and prayer, as both help us to "clean our window." Research shows that people then think more clearly, function more calmly, and interact with others more effectively when their "windows" are cleaner. To rewrite what's on your "window," first reorganize your schedule. Create a weekly period of mental and spiritual renewal. This one hour will impact every facet of your life. Here's what to do:

- Find a place where you will not be interrupted.
- Be still and sit in a comfortable position.
- Practice deep breathing and other calming techniques.
- At the end of 15 minutes of quiet, record what you *feel*.
- Spend the next 30 minutes reading some wisdom literature. Listen to the greatest thinkers of all time.
- Continue this process for four weeks; then you're ready for the next step.

2. Take stock of your situation

Having now achieved some absence of "noise," you need to examine your life. First, recognize that life is not something that happens while you're focusing on the next quarter's profit goal. Life's battles are often won during the inspired planning. So plan to live a life on purpose, not by accident.

To take this step towards a happier future, invest in a full day's vacation and go somewhere uplifting and peaceful. In this relaxing setting, take stock of your life. What are you tolerating that irritates or hurts? Examine your business life (maximum stress), family (relationships unravelling), other relationships (few genuine friends), finances (constantly in debt), physical health (lethargic and overweight), and home environment (poorly decorated). Recognize that recording this is part of the process of change and healing. Think and write.

After taking stock, perform the following creative exercise, which will help free you from your present existence. Close your eyes and imagine your ideal life as it would be precisely three years from today. Be there. Describe all of the areas where you're currently tolerating discomfort. Be beautifully detailed. Smell it. Hear it. No limitations. It should leave you breathless.

This scene represents all that you truly value and need. Record this wonderful vision. Try to think beyond just accumulating things or cramming pleasures. When you're finished, take yourself to a time two years from today. What would you need to do in two years to make the three-year vision possible?

Next, see the picture you'd be living exactly twelve months from today. Describe your preferred life at this point. With those visions in front of you, pick three areas from your "taking stock" exercise that you are tolerating. Just three. Then, keeping your 3-2-1 vision in mind, address the first toleration, and plan small changes. Do this in the sequence of exercising faith, considering your plan, preparing for the change, taking action, maintaining progress, and rebounding from lapses. The process works something like this:

- Exercising Faith – (Together with Love, there is no greater power!) "I know that the process of change can work for me. And that I have the power to change."
- Considering – "I have the following burning reasons to desire change." "I'm considering the following options…."
- Preparing – "I'm carefully developing an action plan." "I have openly expressed my plan to others."

- Taking Action – "I'm boldly taking baby steps daily, as promised." "I meditate daily on the three-year vision."
- Maintaining – "I keep a journal and review the changes weekly." "I reward myself when I reach minor goals."
- Lapsing – "I'm learning good lessons from temporary failure." "I know that lapses are part of change."

Repeat this process with each of the three tolerations and you're on your way!

3. Focus on the greatest home run

The world cries out for honorable leadership. In its most perfect form, the business leaders' role is a mighty stewardship. But which of your stewardships is designed to give the greatest long-term happiness and personal growth? Your business leadership or your family leadership?

Don't swallow the lie that devoting your best effort to the corporate bottom-line holds greater sway than nurturing a human life to emotionally healthy maturity. Don't sell your soul for power or money and short-change your family in the process.

The price of getting this balance wrong is high. A dysfunctional home life will invariably impact your capacity in business. But, with the pressures on you to achieve, how do you get it right? The answer is simple (yet tough): make a decision.

Schedule two hours every week for your family. Hold that time sacred. With your family, play, draw, sing, dance, laugh, walk, bike, swim, read stories, cook brownies, or do anything else you like to do as a family. The activity doesn't matter; simply be with them and devote your full attention to them. These people *are* your business! Do the same with your spouse. Schedule time together. This is an investment in your happiness. Don't let your account go overdrawn, or bankrupt.

Then, do the same, one-on-one, with your direct reports at work. Don't use the time to manipulate. Instead, talk about them and their concerns. Ask them how you, and the business, could be better. Promise to give their thoughts serious consideration. Then report back to them to show you mean what you say.

Become a Servant/Leader. When you invest in relationships and don't cheat your family, you will be richer than you can possibly imagine!

Your Extraordinary Legacy

Making the changes of habits and character described here requires discipline and courage. But they are the very things that will enable you to become an extraordinary person. You will be happier and honored, not for the accolades or wealth that you amass, but for the attractive and inspiring Being that you become. Like stars, we were placed in human orbit to illuminate this world. May your changing life be a light to give courage to others!

About the Author

David J. Scarlett is a business/life coach, speaker, and creator of The Soul Millionaire programs and products. As CEO of The Inspired Coaching Co., Ltd., his practice serves small business owners, senior professionals, and corporate executives, helping them to build lives of purpose, fulfilment, and joy, supported by streams of passive income. His background includes 20 years at senior levels in Financial Services and Christian Ministry. A father of four, David and his wife/mentor Wendy currently live in West Sussex, England.

For more information please call +44 (0) 1342 317650 or email: david@theinspiredcoachingco.com or visit www.soulmillionaire.com.

Snap Out of It
Do Something About Your Dreams!
by Pamela Slim

All of us get stuck when trying to take action on our long-term life goals, which can include changing careers, breaking old habits, starting a new business, taking a radical sabbatical, or redefining interpersonal relationships. Fortunately, there are hundreds of ways—many of which are in this book—to define your life goals, mission, and purpose. While *identifying* your life's mission is indeed an important and tough process, more people actually get stuck trying to *implement* their dreams.

The good news is that a few simple actions will alleviate the pressure and fear that hold you back. The following steps will nudge you in a positive direction, toward the life you are meant to live.

Step One – Change Your Attitude and Expectations

To shake yourself out of your stupor and gain some momentum, you must first alter your preconceived notions. Common myths about great achievers often stifle our own success:

> **Myth**: Successful people are naturally gifted, strong, and courageous.
>
> **Fact**: Most successful people feel terrified—just like you do—when they try something new. Many have average intellect, and most had to struggle to get to their current positions. What separates them from the rest of us is that, despite feeling afraid and insecure, they take action.
>
> **Myth**: Successful people rarely fail.
>
> **Fact**: Successful people fail all the time. They simply don't allow the fear and disappointment of failure prevent them from trying again.

Keep these facts in mind and create a realistic expectation of what it will take to implement your dreams. Before you begin the remaining steps, help yourself by adjusting your attitude:

- **View your journey as a spiritual adventure**. French philosopher Pierre Teilhard de Chardin once said: "We are not human beings having a spiritual experience. We are spiritual beings having a human experience." In these terms, your human struggles are vital to your growth as a spiritual being. In fact, they may be the only paths to major life breakthroughs.

252

- **Fail often—and enjoy it!** High standards and a track record of accomplishment are wonderful additions to a resume. Unfortunately, if you apply these standards to a radically new life goal, they will absolutely paralyze you. In order to avoid paralysis, you must expect that you will struggle and fail.

Action: Reflect on your own spiritual path, whatever that may be. What is important to you? What do you hope to contribute to the world during your time on earth? Why do you think you were brought here? How does your life goal fit into this plan?

Keep these answers in mind if you get frustrated or discouraged as you follow the next steps. Your ability to persevere will depend to a great extent on the way you perceive your journey.

Step Two – Work Backwards

It is often difficult to imagine how you will get from where you are today to where you want to be in the next three to five years. The types of jobs that interest you may require experience that you lack. Perhaps you need more cash or credit than is currently available to open your own business. Or maybe your current employer does not offer the six-month sabbatical required for you to produce an independent film.

Many people freeze in this phase and throw their hands up in resignation. To overcome these barriers, you must *get extremely concrete with what it will take to realize your life goals*. Identify the specific skills, information, resources, and contacts you will need to for future success, and then work backwards to your present position. Now you can create a specific action plan.

Action: Create a profile that describes exactly what it will take to bring your vision to a reality. Consider the following needs:
- **Skills** – knowledge, experience, information;
- **Equipment** – infrastructure, software, supplies, raw materials;
- **Money** – start-up and maintenance costs;
- **People** – influential mentors, partners, suppliers.

Which of these skills can you develop in your current job or life situation? (Remember, volunteer activities are an excellent—and free—way to develop skills!) How can you begin to obtain the equipment, money, contacts, or information that you need? If you are not very clear on exactly what you need to succeed, you will never get there.

Step Three – Create Positive Consequences for Your Actions

Once you identify a task you need to complete to reach your life goal, you may realize that your actions lack immediate positive results. Often, doing something you deem necessary to achieving your greatness can be *painful, excruciating, frightening, and generally unpleasant*!

Whenever you try something new or difficult, huge waves of fear and self-doubt often surface. This "Death Spiral of Doom" announces its approach with a loud, sucking noise. As it pulls you down a dark, spinning hole, every negative comment you have ever heard rushes through your head:

"Who do you think you are?"

"No one from your background has ever made it in this business!"

"Why would anyone ever pay to listen to you?"

This force is so strong that at the slightest sign of discomfort, you sprint back to safe ground—which usually means stopping dead in your tracks. In order to overcome this extremely powerful emotion, you must create positive consequences, reinforcements, and rewards for accomplishing tasks.

The results of accomplishing your goal are your positive consequences. For instance, if you open a successful restaurant, what will happen?

1) You will work with fresh, fragrant food all day.

2) You will use your imagination to create interesting dishes.

3) You will never again wear nylons to work in a gray cubicle!

For reinforcements, seek out trainers, coaches, support groups, therapists, family, and friends who provide ideas, encouragement, and feedback as you undertake your adventure. They should be available as soon as you hear the sucking sound of the Death Spiral of Doom. Also, make sure to provide yourself with rewards. For instance, if you write the first draft of your business plan, take yourself snowboarding for the weekend. Rewards need not be big; they must simply be timely and meaningful to you.

Action: Draw three columns on a piece of paper. In the first column, write your long-term goal. In the second column, describe the positive and negative consequences of accomplishing your goal. If you succeed, what will be the results? What if you do not succeed? In the third column, identify **specific rewards** to ensure positive consequences. This step is crucial! If you fail to incorporate these reinforcements into your plan, you greatly increase your chances of returning to paralysis.

Step Four – Surround Yourself with People You Admire

Whom do you admire? Whose life looks like the one you want to have? In order to accomplish your dreams, surround yourself with people who do the kinds of things to which you aspire.

Do not talk yourself out contacting someone you admire by saying, "He's too busy," or "She's too important." People love to talk about themselves! They appreciate acknowledgement of their expertise or positive lifestyle. Many people will gladly spend fifteen minutes speaking with you or answering an e-mail. If all goes well, you may even find future opportunities to correspond. By identifying and surrounding yourself with people you admire, you are much more likely to accomplish your life goals.

Action: Brainstorm a list of people you know—and don't know—who are outstanding in your field of interest. What do you hope to learn from them? If they were sitting in front of you, what would you ask?

Next, identify where these people hang out. Do they attend conferences or speak publicly? If you have the opportunity to meet them, request a few minutes of their time and ask the questions that you prepared. Otherwise, track down an e-mail address and send a note.

You will be amazed at how willing people are to spend time with you. And if they aren't ... they may not be the best people to connect with anyway! Over time, you will develop a strong circle of positive, accomplished friends and mentors who will help you achieve your goals.

Step Five – Do Something . . . *Anything* . . . Right Now!

Enough of the analyzing, prioritizing, making lists, and gathering your reinforcements! Spending more time in the planning phase will actually decrease your energy and momentum. Now is the time to take a step towards your dream!

Action: Pick up your notes. Choose one item on the list—even a very small task—and **DO IT**. Make a phone call, create a spreadsheet, or look up something on the web. The key here is action, not perfection. Once you begin accomplishing tasks related to your life goals, you will feel a power surge of energy!

Go For It!

Everyone struggles with fear when trying something new. You are not alone. By following these simple steps, you can knock yourself out of the paralysis and actually see your dreams become reality. Enjoy your adventure!

About the Author

Pamela Slim works with individuals—both inside and outside the corporate world—who are unsatisfied in their current careers, struggling to implement lifelong dreams, or looking for more satisfaction out of life. A highly-sought speaker, Pam conducts individual coaching sessions and group workshops. Corporate clients include Cisco Systems, Hewlett Packard, and Charles Schwab. She has also spent fifteen years studying and instructing martial arts. Work and travels have brought her to many parts of the world where she learned French, Spanish, and Portuguese. Her company, Ganas Consulting, is based in Phoenix, Arizona. For more information, go to www.ganas.com or call 1.480.663.3252.

Ten Easy Organizing Steps for More Focus, Time, and Success

by Pam N. Woods

With a shrinking workforce, an expanding workload, and change coming at warp speed, you need an edge—some kind of advantage to keep up with the demands of your career and to stay ahead of the competition. You may have looked for a solution that would permit you to be more productive and profitable with less time and effort, and without sacrificing the enjoyment of your friends and family, recreation, and life itself, only to decide it is an impossible dream.

Well guess what? It's not a dream…and the solution is so simple that most people overlook it. Fortunately, a ten-step solution exists that every business leader, manager, and professional can master for greater personal and professional effectiveness.

Order is our society's foundation and the underpinning from which all else emanates. In fact, order is so basic to our way of life that we often take it for granted. Just as countries in chaos strive to restore order so as to build their nations, individuals must instill order and organization in their lives to thrive and prosper.

The question is, how do you do that? The answer: You organize your work, your play, your thinking, and your being. Organization is essential for building and sustaining a great life. It is a fundamental survival skill and, when maintained, it is a distinct competitive advantage.

Test Your Level of Organization

Running your life effortlessly requires organizing proficiency. No substitute for this skill exists. While you may have an administrative assistant to help you from 9-5, he or she cannot be with you 24/7. If you're uncertain of your own level of organization, ask yourself the following questions:

- Do you often misplace keys, files, important documents, or other items?
- Do you have piles of paper scattered on your desk?
- Do you consistently miss deadlines without someone reminding you of them?
- Do you run late for meetings or miss appointments?
- Do you let opportunities pass you by?
- Do you regularly feel overwhelmed and overworked?

If you answered "yes" to any of the previous questions, then an organizing makeover will substantially improve your life.

A Lack of Organization Comes with a High Price

Clutter is chaos. And if you have physical clutter, then you likely have mental clutter as well. Such clutter and chaos cost you more than you may think. Clutter zaps your time, drains your energy, prevents you from being your best, and causes stress. In fact, opportunities may be parading in front of you right now, and you may not recognize or pursue them because mental and physical clutter blocks your view or consumes your time. Eventually, this clutter results in strained relationships and diminished work capacity.

But hold on…you needn't feel embarrassed if you are organizationally challenged. Organizing competence is not a matter of instinct, but of education. Unfortunately, few schools include organizational skills as part of their curriculum. Therefore, you must take the initiative to learn it yourself.

The Benefits of Organization

Good organizing skills can transform your life in a short period of time because you can apply them to all parts of your daily routine. For example, you can organize your work area, your files and other important documents, your computer, your briefcase, your calendar, as well as projects, telephone calls, meetings, your home, and your car. You can improve virtually anything in your life by organizing it.

The benefits of organization are well worth the effort because you will be more focused, have more time and energy, be more productive and profitable, have more control over your life, and be happier. In fact, no downside to organizing exists!

How to Get Started

The easiest way to organize your life is to start with something tangible and then move on to organizing the intangibles. Your office is a good place to start because it is tangible; it is where you spend the majority of your waking hours and where productivity and profits are at stake. Use the following ten steps to begin:

1) Identify eight major categories of items you keep in your office/work space. Be sure to select no more than eight categories, otherwise you will find it difficult to remember what category an item belongs in. Designate each category with a name that has meaning for you and that represents a broad grouping of similar things. The following is an example of an effective grouping strategy:
   - **Operational** – company strategy and action plans, policies and procedures, passwords, and phone numbers.

- **Financial and legal** – budget reports, purchase orders, coupons, receipts, and contracts.
- **Supplies** – writing instruments, paper clips, stapler, ruler, scissors, paper, forms, and business cards.
- **Records** – client, employee and vendor files.
- **Product materials** – brochures, product guides, and portfolios.
- **Resources** – tapes, articles, magazines and books.
- **Projects** – past, current, and future ideas.
- **Tools of the trade** – things unique to your profession.

2) Physically sort every item in your workspace into the eight categories identified in step one. Collect eight large boxes and mark each with the name of a category. Then, sort the most visible clutter first. Pick up each piece of paper, each file, and each item in your workspace one at a time, and put it in the appropriate box. Next, sort the items concealed in your desk drawers, file cabinets, and/or overhead bins. Again, sort one item at a time until EVERYTHING in your office is in one of the eight boxes.

3) Eliminate unnecessary items. This is the most important and often difficult step. Challenge yourself to keep only the essentials and get rid of the rest. Define the criteria you will use to cull each category. For example, you may want to dispose of anything you have not accessed for a year or more, discard all broken items, and return all extra supplies. Most of the unnecessary papers will probably go into the shredder. However, if there are some things you want to give to others in your office, donate to charity, or send to storage, make a separate pile for each one. Then, when you're finished sorting, move 'em out!

4) Arrange the items in each category. Go through the materials in each category one by one and put them in order. You can put each category in alphabetical order, date order, subject matter order, or number order, or use any system that corresponds to the way you work. Just be consistent.

5) Make a rough sketch of your workspace and appoint a place to store each category of item. Ask yourself three questions before deciding where to store each item:
- Where is the most convenient place to store this category? For example, if you need access to this material while on the phone, the ideal arrangement is to put it in a container you can reach while talking on the phone.
- How frequently will I need access to this category? The less you access the material the farther away from your desk you can store it.

- Will the volume of material in this category easily fit into the container I have available? If not, consider another storage option.

6) Purchase storage units for any leftover categories of materials. To best utilize your space, think vertical. A wide variety of vertical storage systems are available at organizing and office supply stores.

7) Create an outline or table of contents for each storage area. List the major categories, as well as any subcategories. Once you're in the habit of putting everything back into its assigned space you won't need to refer to the outline.

8) Place each category of item into its new space in your office. Once you have completed this step, stand back and admire your work. You will feel energized by a new sense of control and accomplishment.

9) Spend five to ten minutes at the end of each day putting all materials away into their assigned space. When you do, you won't dread walking into your workspace each morning, and you won't waste time looking for materials. Another benefit is that people who visit your office won't wonder if the material they leave with you will end up lost in a heap somewhere.

10) Repeat this entire process bi-annually, annually or whenever you take on new assignments. Remember, organizing is not a one-time project. It is a lifelong process and habit, requiring a few minutes of your time every day.

Endless Possibilities

You can use the described organizing technique to organize any space within your workplace or home. Simply change the names of the eight major categories to apply to the specific materials you will be organizing. If you prefer collaborative projects, you can always seek the services of an Organizing Coach, who has the expertise to guide and support you through your organizational makeover.

Organize Today!

Effective organization enhances your sense of control and competence, and it increases your energy and productivity levels—all of which are prerequisites for greater career success and profitability. Now that you have mastered the process of organizing your workspace, you can move on to other areas of your life. Consider all of your daily activities as potential targets for increased organization and simplicity, and start improving your life today with the organizing skills you have learned. You'll quickly find that the effort is well worth the reward.

About the Author

Pam N. Woods is the founder of Smart WorkLife Solutions, an Iowa-based coaching company serving business leaders and professionals. With more than 20 years of outstanding results as an insurance executive and Vice President of Human Resources, Pam leverages her corporate experience, resourcefulness, and wisdom to co-create customized solutions to fit her clients business, career, work-life balance, and organizing needs. More information about organizing is available on Pam's website, www.worklifecoach.com, or by calling 1.515.225.2479.

Section Five –
Wealth Building

The Three Steps of Genuine Wealth Building

by Robert G. Allen

Imagine doing a task once and getting paid for it for the rest of your life. Imagine waking up in the morning, going to your mailbox, and retrieving numerous checks all paying you for work you did years ago. Imagine checking your bank account online and seeing various direct deposits for information you created and now sell to people on a regular basis. Now, imagine all this happening every single day, even though you no longer go into an office or produce new work. That's what happens when you have a system for wealth-building.

Everyone wants a foolproof system for generating true wealth —one that requires little to no hands-on work and enables them to earn money forever, whether they're at the office or relaxing on a sunny beach. Unfortunately, few people ever develop a wealth-building system that truly works. Whether they own their own business or work for a large corporation, most people are so focused on their present business, career, or job that they neglect to look into the future to devise a system that will enable them to completely walk away from their present work and still earn money.

Why does this happen? Frankly, because nobody teaches us how to create a wealth-building system. We receive no formal education in the most critical of all life skills—how to develop an income stream that lasts a lifetime. Think about it. Did you ever attend a class in all of your public education entitled Wealth Building 101? Probably not.

Instead, you likely learned that you should go to school, get a good job, and retire with a modest pension and whatever retirement accounts you happened to accumulate. But this is not true wealth. True wealth comes when you're *always* making money, even while you sleep. True wealth is not when you're simply drawing off past savings. When you have a wealth-building system in place, your relationships, your happiness, and your future are brighter.

Fortunately, creating and sustaining wealth is not as complicated as most people think. If you follow the three steps of wealth-building (the Dream, Team, Theme process), you will be able to create the level of long-term income you and your family deserve.

Step One – Have a clear vision or dream of what you're trying to accomplish

What kind of lifestyle do you really want? Compare what you're living now with what you really want, and then go out and create it. When you picture what you want, over time you will achieve it.

Keep a clear vision of your financial goals. Maybe you want a successful business with a hundred employees or five offices worldwide. Visualize the details of your aspirations. Cut out a picture of your dream house with the white picket fence and big tree with a tire swing in front, then hang it somewhere where you'll always see it. Tape a picture of that red Corvette you've always wanted in a visible place and look at it every day. You naturally progress to what you see, and by focusing on visual images of what you want, you'll achieve your dream of financial success.

Unfortunately, most people never reach their goals because they have fears that are more real than their dreams. The key is to make your dreams more real than your fears. Once you are successful at doing that, then you will be moving toward what you really want. The only time you want to have a fear is if that fear is a motivating factor moving you toward what you want. And frankly, if you want to be technical about it, you need both—fear and a dream. You need a dream that's very clear, motivating, and attractive, and you need a fear that moves you towards it—something that drives you to move away from what you don't want and toward what you do want. Combine both of these together and you have a force that's both motivating and powerful.

Building a millionaire mindset, displaying self-confidence, and having a burning desire are what make an entrepreneur and high-level executive different from an ordinary person. Entrepreneurs and high-level executives see into the future; they see what they want and they strive forward towards it. This is really the foundational part of success. Sure, you can launch toward success without it, but you're probably not going to be able to go through the pain or the ups and downs if you don't have something that drives you.

Step Two – Assemble your team

Next, you need a team of people to help you. These can be mentors or money partners who help you make your dream a reality. This is the one aspect many people have a difficult time grasping, as by nature business owners like to be free. They like to do things on their own and often don't like talking their plans over with anyone else. So they end up trying to do everything themselves. However, if you want to achieve any kind of major success, you must realize that no self-made millionaires exist.

To be successful, you must involve a team of people. These people may not be part of your organization, they may not be part of your hired staff, but they are the people who are adept at seeing the things you are not good at seeing. They can help you identify your strengths, weaknesses, and blind spots that may be holding you back. Plus, you can often learn from the past mistakes of your team, which will save you both time and money in the long run.

Step Three – Define the theme that guides you

With your dream firmly in place and your team assembled, you're ready for the final stage—determining the direction you're going to pursue and the vehicle to take you there. What system are you going to use to create long-term wealth? At this point, you must evaluate two critical factors.

First, you need multiple streams of income (multiple themes, if you will), because you never can tell which one is going to be the one that gets you to your goal faster. Just like a fisherman, you need to have many lines in the water so you'll have a better chance of making a catch. You can also learn things from one activity that may help you in another. Additionally, when you have several streams of income, it isn't a disaster if one runs dry.

Most people would disagree with this concept, thinking they need to be focused and put all their efforts into one thing. That is simply not true. In fact, the most successful people in the world have many business endeavors going on all at once. They operate many businesses and reap the benefits of all of them. The challenge is that most people are focused on only one thing; they are married to their career or their job or their business because they don't understand the concept of residual income, which is the second critical factor of phase three.

What exactly is residual income, and how do you know if you're earning it? First, with residual income, you work hard once, and it unleashes a steady flow of income for months or even years. You get paid over and over again for the same effort. Here's the question that tells you if you're earning residual income: "How many times do you get paid for every hour you work?" If you answered "only once," then your income is linear, not residual. Linear income streams from a salary or a one-time hourly wage. With linear income, when you don't work, you don't get paid. Wouldn't you prefer to be compensated hundreds of times for every hour you work? Of course you would!

Many business experts say that you have to work *on* your business, not *in* your business. While that's a theoretical way of saying it, a more accurate statement is that you should only want to work on businesses that don't require you to work in them. They must be businesses that generate residual income. In fact, don't even get involved in a business unless you can walk away from it and still earn money. Your goal should be to create a stream of income that enables you to earn money even if you're not actually there doing the work.

For example, real estate can create residual income, as can some forms of network marketing, and info-preneuring (where you're marketing information using a system that creates several streams of income). These are businesses you can build, walk away from, and still collect checks. The business works even when you don't. That's when you'll have achieved one of the great dreams of most people—the ability to earn money while you're asleep.

Wealth is When Small Efforts Yield Great Results

Creating wealth for yourself and your family is not a difficult process. It's simply a matter of taking specific small steps, which accumulate into great results. So get clear on what you really want in life, gather support from your team, and then develop systems that generate multiple streams of residual income to keep your prosperity flowing. When you do, you will have mastered the keys to genuine wealth building and can live the lifestyle of your dreams.

About the Author

Robert G. Allen is one of America's most influential financial advisors. He has shared his successful wealth-building techniques in popular seminars and information products for the past 20+ years throughout the U.S. and Canada. Thousands of millionaires—representing billions in wealth–attribute their success to his teachings. Robert G. Allen is the author of numerous books. His most recent book, *The One Minute Millionaire*, (co-authored with Mark Victor Hansen) is an innovation of style in both fact and fiction. As co-founder of Enlightened Millionaire Institute, Robert G. Allen's goal is to teach people how to be millionaires in Real Estate, Internet Market, Investing, and Info-preneuring. For more information, please visit www.robertallen.com.

Fearful of Outliving Your Money?

Rest Easy with Three Proven Investment Strategies

by Jonathan Cylka

W ill you have enough money to maintain your current standard of living during the "golden" years of your retirement? No matter how hard you try to stop the passage of time, you can't. And your retirement years are approaching.

If you're like most business owners or executives, you may not be sure you can answer this question. But it's a question that's vital for your future. All executives know they want some way to attain long-term gains, but they don't know the best strategies to use to achieve their financial goals. Unfortunately, time and energy constraints, fear of losing money, and issues of trust between them and their investment advisor keep many people from making the right investment decisions.

Realize, though, that as the world around us continues to change, the need for a sound investment strategy that produces long-term results is more important than ever. With human life spans continuing to grow, people need more money later in life to sustain their standard of living. Consider this: according to the Census Bureau, a man used to retire at age sixty-five and die when he reached seventy-two. That meant he would need, on average, enough money to support himself for seven years. Now, however, the average man retires at age sixty and lives to age eighty-four. That translates to a life span of twenty-four years in retirement, and it's growing longer every day. Naturally, women continue to outlive men, so they have even more years to plan for. So it's easy to see why a common concern among business owners and executives like you is whether they will outlive their money and have to rely on others to support them during their golden years.

Compounding this problem is the fact that inflation continues to rise and takes a larger and larger toll on an individual's buying power. In other words, in the future, it will cost more for your dream vacation, gifts for the family, and the rounds of golf than it did in the past. For example, compare the price of a new automobile just ten years ago to a new car today. The price has risen substantially.

Knowing these facts, you need an investment strategy that will produce higher income in the years ahead. Remember, when you live in an economy of rising prices, you must have a rising income stream in order to maintain your current standard of living. Whether you understand investing and manage your own accounts or simply don't have the time to know the ins and outs of investing, the following strategies will give you insights into simple yet important ways to reach your financial goals.

Investment Strategy One – Create your exit strategy

All investors should develop a sell strategy before they buy anything. For example, if you work within a corporation, you need a strategy for utilizing your pension, 401K plan, or whatever retirement assets you have set aside.

If you are a business owner, you have a slightly different focus, as one of your main goals is developing a business with the goal to one day sell it to an outsider or transfer it to a succeeding family member, thus allowing you to retire and pursue your personal dreams. Another goal is that proceeds from the business can support your family should you die prematurely. The irony is that while many business owners understand the importance of planning the business's day-to-day activities, they fail to plan for the ultimate long-term goal—exiting the business.

In fact, the majority of executives continuously invest money and time into their business or into their retirement vehicles, but they don't have any idea how to get it out. The answer is for executives to start planning an exit strategy today, even though it may be many years until they plan to retire.

To devise your exit strategy, talk with your investment professional or advisor about your business and personal goals. Also, with your advisor, answer the following questions: What age do you want to retire? If you own a business, to what kind of person, company, or investor would you want to sell your business and for how much? What kind of lifestyle do you want your family to enjoy should you die? How will your assets continue to support you and your family in the event you become disabled? Should option strategies that could help you reduce risk and improve return be a part of your portfolio? Would you like to use "Green" investments? If you buy and sell stocks, should you use trailing stops?

These are delicate matters to discuss, and many people prefer to avoid such topics, but you must address these issues if you want to create an investment strategy and a lasting income that will support you and your family for the long-term. With your advisor, create a "contingency plan" for each scenario. At this point, you may need to get other professionals involved, such as your attorney, insurance agent, or tax advisor, as legal, tax, and insurance issues will likely arise. Once you and your team create an action plan, be sure to review it yearly to ensure you're on track.

Investment Strategy Two – Define your short-term investment goals

Knowing what you want financially in the long-term is one thing; knowing what you want your money to do for you right now—in the short-term—is another. Do you want enough money to take a European vacation this summer? Do you need funds to send the twins to college next year? Would you like to buy your dream home within the next five years? Whatever your short-term goals, you must define them with your investment advisor so he or she can direct you to the appropriate short-term investment options.

Whether your particular goal qualifies as short-term or long-term is up to you. No magic number exists to define a short-term goal. Realize that no matter how secure you feel with your long-term investments, you always need some type of short-term investment strategy for those unforeseen emergencies and opportunities that arise. Smart investing is always a matter of balancing your future financial needs with your current ones.

Using a laddered, fixed-income strategy that provides liquidity gives you dependable short-term dollars that will be there in the future and could increase your overall yield. This means that you purchase variable maturities and variable interest rate instruments to make sure you have money coming available at specific times in the future. For example, you can purchase four certificates of deposits with a three, six, nine, and twelve month maturity. Every three months you now have dollars available to use. This will give you a higher yield than cash without jeopardizing your total liquidity of short-term income on a yearly basis. When the CD matures, you can then decide if you need to use the money or reinvest it in another short-term vehicle, or in a longer-term vehicle, which may offer a higher yield.

Investment Strategy Three – Follow a proven asset allocation formula

One of the most fundamental tools of investing is asset allocation. You likely already have some type of allocation within your portfolio. The most easily recognized asset allocation model is the circle that is cut up into growth, growth and income, and income. This is a very general form of diversification for investments. For the layman it might even do okay; however, you likely want to do better than just okay.

Unfortunately, most investment advisors do not plan nor implement a complete asset allocation formula, thereby putting their clients at risk.

These investment professionals weigh the portfolio too heavily in favor of the growth category and do not include asset classes that negatively correlate to stocks (such as commodities, real estate, etc.). These negatively correlated investments can provide a better return when the market goes down.

A true asset allocation model should have your assets separated into a multiple of twenty plus asset classes. Which asset classes you use is dependant on your investment horizon, your goal timeline, and your risk tolerance. Realize that this portfolio is also not static. It is changing just like the market and the economy. The most astute investors have used this strategy for years.

When you allocate your assets, always ensure that some your money is readily available (easy to liquidate if necessary) for emergencies or opportunities. Also, when making an investment, always have some type of time horizon, goal, or exit strategy in the back of your mind. Write it down on your statement or a ledger that you keep. Invest those dollars with that time frame, goal, or strategy in mind.

Forming a pyramid structure with your money will aid in lowering your market risk and increasing your overall return. Short-term investments should fill the bottom of the pyramid while longer-term investments are at the top. Be sure that you and your financial planner rebalance your asset allocation model at least every eighteen months or when the market in telling you to change.

Retire Without Worry

Whether your retirement means traveling the world to exotic locations or lounging in your backyard in your favorite chair, you'll need money to make your dreams come true. People who fail to plan for their golden years rarely attain what they want; therefore, work with your investment professional to devise an intelligent strategy to help you to meet your financial needs today and in the future. With a genuine financial plan that uses these three investment strategies and that is specifically designed for you and your goals, you have a clear target of what you're aiming for and you greatly increase your chances of success.

About the Author

Jonathan Cylka is an investment professional for NEXT Financial Group, Inc., Member NASD/SIPC, located at 6631 Main Street in Williamsville, New York 14221. For business owners and executives who want to plan the retirement of their dreams, Jonathan specializes in using a distinctive, multi-step approach to money management. To receive a copy of his free report entitled *The 7 Biggest Mistakes Business Owners and Executives Planning for Retirement Make with Their Money and How to Avoid Them* send an e-mail to jonathan@jonathancylka.com, or feel free to call 1.716.633.1515.

Want a Healthy Bottom Line?

Focus on Your Own Health First

by George C. Huang, M.D.

W ith the rise of technology and sedentary, office-based jobs, many people have become physically out of shape. As a result, chronic conditions such as obesity and high blood pressure are on the rise. But the more out of shape you and your employees are, the more the company's bottom line suffers.

Consider this: If you're an employer, current research shows that unscheduled absenteeism can cost the company up to $602 per employee per year, not including direct costs such as overtime pay for other employees, hiring temps, missed deadlines, lost sales, sinking morale, and lower productivity. For a company with one hundred employees, that equals over $60,000 in lost profits. If you're an out-of-shape business owner, the costs to your profits can be much greater, as chronic fatigue and reduced stamina and vitality can cause you to miss or not optimize numerous opportunities.

The fact is that your health is the core foundation of every other important aspect in your life, including your business or career. If you're not physically fit, then you are less likely to develop a thriving business that's going to last. However, when you optimize your health, you'll be more productive and have increased vitality and well-being, which translates to greater creativity. You'll also have the stamina needed to handle any business challenge.

The Psychology of Healthy Profits

Just as successful people adhere to a "psychology of success," physically fit people follow a "psychology of fitness." And guess what? The principles are the same. In fact, when you master the following ten principles, you'll have the means to enhance not only your health and your business profits, but also all other areas of your life, including your spiritual, mental, and emotional health.

1) **Gain clarity.** When it comes to their health, most people don't know what they really want. More important, they may not even know why they want what they say they want. In order to gain clarity, pinpoint specifically what your health goals are. Do you want to reach a certain weight or body composition? Do you want to run a marathon? Do you want the stamina to work a ten-hour day and be able to play with your kids at night and on the weekends? Just as business goals have a

271

specific and measurable target, so too should your health goals. So get a clear picture in your mind of what optimized health looks like. Once you're able to picture what you want, your body will work to make that vision reality.

2) **Reprogram your "fitness blueprint" that's holding you back.** Your "fitness blueprint" is your mind's thermostat of how fit you should be, your body image, your drive to do something about it, your initiative to take care of yourself. With the wrong "fitness blueprint," no matter what you do, you can't seem to make any health progress. To reprogram your internal blueprint, first identify the hidden hurdles that have held you back. What keeps you from being your healthy best? Next, identify your top ten values. How can these values help you overcome your hurdles? Finally, make sure your business's purpose is consistent with your ten values. If it's not, then your business is out of alignment with your inner desires, and attaining lasting success will not be feasible.

3) **Set realistic expectations.** Realize that getting physically fit is the result of focusing on consistent, high-impact habits, not miracle quick fixes. So simply thinking that you can reach your target weight and have increased stamina by tomorrow afternoon is not possible. You wouldn't set a business goal with such unrealistic expectations, so neither should you do so for your fitness goals. The more realistic you make your fitness goals, the more likely you are to reach them. And the more physically fit you are, the more fiscally fit your business will be.

4) **Focus on progress, not results.** Many people beat themselves up because they are so focused on the end result, that if it doesn't happen soon enough, they resign. As a result, they give up when success is right around the corner. So rather than focus *solely* on your ultimate health goal, acknowledge the progress you make along the way and celebrate all wins, no matter how big or small. Even losing one pound or lowering your cholesterol by several points is definitely an accomplishment towards your vision. Be proud of the small victories, as each successful step brings you closer to your goal.

5) **Gain balance in your life.** All aspects of your life contribute to your health. That means you can't focus exclusively on business activities and expect to have a healthy personal life or physical fitness level. You need to give all aspects of your life equal attention. One suggestion is to schedule physical activity into your day-planner, just as you would schedule a business meeting, your volunteer activities, or your child's school play. Only then will you consciously make the time to tend to your health needs.

6) **Manage the little voice in your head.** It's easy to listen to that little voice in your mind that tells you to give up. But listening to that little voice robs you of so much potential, both personally and professionally. When that voice tells you to give up on your health goals because "it's just too hard," picture the image of a healthy you and healthy business in your mind. Because the mind cannot distinguish between what is real and what is vividly imagined, positive mental imagery changes the physiology of your mind and body, effectively silencing that little voice.

7) **Focus on your strengths, natural abilities, and talents.** Such a mentality enhances your self-confidence and increases your effectiveness in reaching your health and fitness goals. To uncover your strengths, natural abilities, and talents, ask five people who know you to identify these items for you. What they say may surprise you, but you will gain new insight into the image you portray to the world. You may be surprised how focusing on these very same characteristics in your business leads to greater efficiency and effectiveness.

8) **Surround yourself with a committed success team.** Neil Armstrong couldn't have stepped onto the moon without a committed team behind him. The same concept goes for you. Making the lifestyle changes that result in optimal health and vitality requires committed teamwork, guidance, and coaching. At home, share your health and fitness objectives with your family so they can help you stay focused. At the office, initiate a company-wide health goal. By developing a support network for on-going education, guidance, accountability, and inspiration, you boost your confidence, productivity, and longevity, and you accelerate your ability to getting the results you want.

9) **Eliminate your "I know that already" mentality.** Most people think they already know what to do to be healthy, but the problem is that their current knowledge is likely based on myths and fallacies, passed down through the ages and perpetuated in the popular media. As a result, many people are acting based on antiquated or misinformation and they don't even know it. The fact is that most people don't realize how much their health impacts their success. And when they ignore new findings or act on old information, they shut their mind to new teachings. Think about it…if all the information you have been acting on to date were correct, you would be healthy and successful without even trying. So be open to new possibilities. Become a lifelong student of health, nutrition, physical activity, and habits of success. Your expanding knowledge and wisdom are keys to transforming the quality of your life and your business.

10) Make the commitment to succeed in achieving your health and fitness goals. Realize that your truest power and greatest success comes from making the choice to take responsibility for and control of your health. A commitment to health and fitness is really a commitment to your vision and your mission. And when your mission and vision are larger than yourself, you will have the resolve and commitment to change your mindset and approach your new healthy lifestyle with confidence and power. As Abraham Lincoln once said, "Always bear in mind that your own resolution to succeed is more important than any one thing."

Protect Your Number One Asset

Even though "health" does not appear on any business's balance sheet, your health and the health of your employees is the biggest asset any company has. Without it, you're slow to respond to market shifts and miss upcoming opportunities. With health, you have the stamina and agility to outwit your competition and capitalize on every opportunity that comes your way.

When you understand that your health affects your success, you'll experience a shift in the way you view life. You will unleash your unlimited potential and follow through on what it takes to realize your optimal health, well-being, and productivity with longevity. Obstacles you were never able to overcome will now seem surmountable because you'll have the needed energy and confidence to tackle any challenge. And in the long-term, the healthier you become, the more you'll attract other healthy people to your business, which will give you the competitive edge that leads to lasting success.

About the Author

George C. Huang, M.D. developed Fitness Is Forever Training to help people live healthier, wealthier, and more productive lives. Dr. Huang is a board-certified plastic surgeon who left his successful practice when he realized how he could make a deeper, more lasting impact on people's lives through coaching and mentoring than he could with the scalpel. Along with being a former national-caliber tennis player and his extensive training in transformational education, he is uniquely qualified to help you to eliminate time, money, and motivation as obstacles to being fit for the rest of your life.

For more information, please visit the Fitness Is Forever website at www.FitnessIsForever.com, email us at info@FitnessIsForever.com, or call 1.425.338.7877.

What 80% of Businesses Don't Know

Tips for Improving Your Working Capital Management

by Anindya Kar

W hat is the number one way to prevent failure in business? Take a minute to really think about your answer. What comes to mind? Increasing patients or customers served? ... Effective marketing? ... Location, location, location? ... Improving patient or customer care? ... Being the best in your industry?

Although these are all essential aspects of business, the answer isn't any of the above. The number one way to prevent business failure is to properly manage your working capital.

To ensure that we're all on the same page, working capital is simply defined as the difference between your current assets and current liabilities. If this figure is positive, you have working capital available. This working capital may exist as inventory, accounts receivable, or cash on hand.

Working capital management is a critical management issue for growing businesses or medical practices. Take the example of a growing doctor's office: As expenses rise with patient-load increases, you accrue more outstanding cash, particularly before receiving reimbursement from the health insurance payors. At this point, your incoming cash does not nearly offset your costs going out. This may be manageable while you work with payments for past services; however, eventually the time lag may become a significant stress-point for your business.

By adopting a few working capital management strategies, you can make your assets work for you, without becoming beholden to banks.

Strategy One – Get Paid Now

Let's take a look at the most obvious area: accounts receivable. What do your receivables do for you when they are not being paid? While your profit margins may look stellar if you have a lot of orders, you have essentially loaned all of your clients the amounts of your invoices—until they decide to pay you. Doctors, in particular, know the pain of this situation. Insurance payors are particularly adept at prolonging the time for payment; they realize that the longer they take to pay, the greater their profit margins.

Is this just another cost of doing business? Well, not necessarily. Eighty percent of small business owners, medical practitioners, and small hospitals are completely unaware of a resource Fortune 500 companies have used for decades: accounts receivable funding.

Banks often measure accounts receivable at as low as 50% of their overall value as collateral for a traditional loan. In accounts receivable funding, however, accounts receivable are calculated at full value. Plus, you accrue no debt for this financing, as you essentially sell your accounts receivable for payment against the full value.

Perhaps the idea of selling your revenue stream makes you nervous. But consider this: You usually receive 80% of the entire amount of the invoice within one or two days—at least 28 to 118 days sooner than usual. This cash injection allows you to make capital improvements for your business to generate more revenue, leverage the cash for discounts on your inventory, cover operating costs, or provide bonuses to your employees, for instance.

As your invoices are paid, your funder will repay the other 20%, minus the negotiated fee (average four to five percent of the invoiced amount). Don't get hung up on the "cost" of the funding. With proper management of those funds, you will more than make up for fees by the investments made in your business. Your day-to-day business costs may stay the same, but the tremendous increase in incoming cash will enable you to rest easy.

Homework–

Review your accounts receivable aging report. Note the average payment time from one of your best clients or insurance payors. Assuming payment of 80% of the invoice value in fourty-eight hours, make a list of ways to use that money for your business:
- Cash discounts on inventory (estimate in dollar amounts).
- Buying or leasing new equipment (anticipated return in additional sales).
- New marketing campaign (anticipated additional revenue).

After you total the increased income generated by implementing this strategy, you can easily see the real benefit.

Strategy Two – Shorten Your Operating Cycle

Your operating cycle starts when you take cash out of your account to begin work for a client, and ends the day the client pays you. If you complete a project on Tuesday, for instance, but do not invoice until the following Friday—or even the end of the month—you lose days of income. Since you need the cash in your account—not just in your profit margins—you must minimize the time between service rendered and service invoiced.

Homework–

Review how long you usually take to invoice a client. If that period of time exceeds a week, have your staff shorten that time. This adjustment will decrease the payment time by as much as 25%.

Strategy Three – Collect Past Due Accounts

Do you have a significant number of invoices out more than sixty days? If so, is your staff doing anything to shorten this timeframe? Call the clients whose invoices have been out thirty days and inquire about the invoice. Devoting a few hours a week to completing this task is money well spent if it ensures that even half of your outstanding invoices are paid a couple of weeks earlier.

Some delays in the healthcare industry, for example, are intentional. Prolonging the turnaround for payment controls costs. In these cases, you don't have any recourse. As any doctor can tell you, calling the insurance company to inquire about a claim can be a fruitless task.

Homework–

Review your collections procedures and tighten up your ship, if needed. Assign one person to follow up on invoices outstanding for more than thirty days. Realize, though, that collections results fluctuate with your clients' priorities. Don't count on this as your only means of improving your cash flow.

Strategy Four – Turn Existing Equipment Into Cash

As we know, keeping current with technology improvements are constant and necessary to remain competitive. Leasing is a way to stay up-to-date without incurring the charges of frequently buying new equipment.

But have you ever considered leasing equipment that you already own? One option is selling your equipment to a leasing company, and leasing it back from them. This way, you generate some cash for your business. You will, of course, incur the lease payments.

Homework–

Take stock of what you own. If you need capital, contact a few leasing companies and gauge their interest in purchasing equipment for you to lease back. Alternatively, a Certified Cash Flow Consultant will shop for you. Since they are independent consultants paid by the leasing companies, you will avoid any additional charges.

Strategy Five – When In Doubt, Outsource

Outsourcing certain support areas of your business, in which you are not an expert, is an excellent way to reduce payroll and insurance costs. You will spend a higher dollar per hour for importing experts, but the reduced costs (no health or workers' compensation insurance) usually compensate for the cost variance.

Be sure to hire these experts with as much diligence as you would any in-house employee. As you'll typically retain this type of assistance through specialty staffing houses, interview the individuals to be assigned. As integral members of your team, they must be as reliable as any employee on your payroll.

Homework–

Contact area firms that provide the kind of staffing you need. Compare the cost of those contracts against the cost of keeping these staff on payroll. Be careful: Consultants can get expensive, so be sure to build cost controls (i.e., fixed fee for a weekly basis or hourly with a "not to exceed" clause) into your contract. Be clear on their scope of work, to whom they report, and how you define satisfactory performance. In addition, you must directly approve any staff changes.

Strategy Six – Inventory When You Need It

Inventory that sits in the warehouse, not being sold for income, eats away at your available cash flow. It is an asset, sure, but it should not become a liability because it is not quickly converted to cash. Over-ordering of inventory gets many businesses into trouble.

Review your inventory forecast all the time, and be aggressive. Know your options in times when you have shortfalls. Fulfilling customer orders on time is a number one priority, so don't take unnecessary risks. If you simply hoard inventory to offset any chance of being caught off-guard, you lose the potential profits made by managing it more aggressively.

Homework–

Review your current and projected inventory for the coming months. Do you need to make changes, or is it all under control? Make any necessary calls to your suppliers to negotiate better terms or better understand their supply controls.

Make Your Working Capital Work for You

Working capital management is a key element to business success and the number one way to prevent business failure. By implementing strategies such as accounts receivable funding, outsourcing, or inventory manage-ment, your business can optimize the return on assets it already possesses. Your company will then be well positioned to handle future growth or economic downturns.

About the Author

Ms. Anindya Kar is a Certified Cash Flow Consultant who specializes in helping her clients create predictable cash flow through conversion of business assets to on-going cash. Her company, AKSF Funding Group, based in Oakland, California, works with medical practitioners, commu-nity hospitals, and businesses. A portion of her company's revenue is donated to programs dedicated to nurturing and educating children in a structured and supportive environment, as well as the development of a foundation committed to this mission. You may contact her for more information at 1.800.406.1399 or akar@aksffunding.com.

Five Keys to Your Success
From Business Start-Up to Exit Strategy
by Jeffrey L. Knapp, Esq.

W hether you are a new entrepreneur or are ready to retire, business ownership is filled with a range of successes and snafus. Business planning and estate attorneys who build life-long relationships with clients gain a perspective that uniquely qualifies them to provide sound business advice. The crux of this advice is simple: Begin with the end in mind.

Proper planning is essential. Predictability of profit is necessary to plan for expansion and retirement, as well as disability and untimely death. For example, in the two weeks preceding this writing, two clear instances of the consequences of failing to plan were:

1) An estate planning attorney whose death forced the retirement of his long-time trusted secretary and turned his practice from an asset that might have been sold as an ongoing entity to a potential liability that likely requires the purchase of additional malpractice insurance, and

2) The owner of a successful advertising agency whose death caused the firm to lose all of its employees and accounts, and his widow to lose her equity in the office building to foreclosure.

These are two unfortunate examples that could have been readily prevented with a bit of foresight and action.

Where are you in terms of your business? Are you:

- An individual in career transition?
- A professional in a solo or small practice?
- An owner/manager of an established enterprise?
- An entrepreneur mulling a new venture?

Regardless of your circumstances, five essential keys will help you focus your vision, create and sustain value, achieve your definition of success, and leave your legacy in business.

Key One – Find an Experienced "Thinking Partner"
To clarify your thoughts, spend time with a qualified "thinking partner." An alternative to a business coach or consultant, a thinking partner may save you tens of thousands of dollars in consulting fees and other unnecessary business commitments. This partner will not tell you how to run your business; rather, he or she will help you remove the filters, blinders, and assumptions that may otherwise limit your thoughts and thus limit

your success. Your thinking partner may pose insightful questions such as, "How certain are you that the ladder you seek to climb is leaning against the right wall?" Your partner will listen intently before asking additional insightful questions—questions that only you can answer.

In addition to propelling you towards business success, an experienced thinking partner will also enrich your personal relationships by teaching you how to identify other thinking partners. For example, as of this writing, a select group of thirty-six committed individuals have read and discussed a powerful book not yet available in the United States, and each one is qualified and available to serve you as a thinking partner. Believe it or not, but over 80% of these individuals are attorneys, and none of them are psychologists. So potential thinking partners are everywhere and can offer insights you may not notice on your own due to their varied experiences. The key is being open and finding such people. Working with one or two of these professionals will also serve as a springboard to the second, third, fourth, and fifth keys to success.

Key Two – Develop Your Strategic Vision™

Surely you have some type of vision for your enterprise. But that vision may be the equivalent of those old Polaroid photographs—fuzzy, slow to develop, and eventually fading—in a world where crisp, digital images can be at your fingertips. And guess what? You actually have all the makings of your crisp, clear vision for business success locked within you. The key to capturing what lies within you and putting a readily achievable plan for success at your fingertips is a powerful tool called Strategic Vision.

In a time when the business world suffers from an excess of consultants and an overload of information, Strategic Vision is uniquely suited for achieving measurable success. Before you spend your valuable time and money, develop a clear picture of where you are going and precisely how to get there. With the guidance of an experienced advisor, you can choose the areas, concerns, and building blocks of your business that you need to address.

Strategic Vision can also be adapted in part or in whole to your personal, family or civic activities. Even if you prefer to keep the focus of your Strategic Vision "strictly business," trained facilitators understand the inherent tensions and sometimes fluid priorities among such things as your lifestyle objectives (including cash flow, security, freedom of choice), your business objectives (including control, perpetuation, retaining and/or transferring value), and your estate planning objectives (including tax reduction, family harmony, and perhaps philanthropy).

Key Three – Form an Appropriate Business Entity

People often overlook the legal elements of planning, whether in personal life—where at least seven out of ten Americans die without a will—or in business—where at least seven out of ten family businesses will not survive from this generation to the next. Estate planning clients understand that a quality legal vehicle, such as a living trust, prevents the "personal fuel" of investments, insurance, real estate, and personal effects from spilling out in the driveway. Likewise, a quality legal vehicle will contain your "business fuel"—your investment of capital, time, ideas, and skills. A corporation or limited liability company (LLC) will keep that fuel far from your driveway and out of the parking lot, Main Street, and the Internet.

If you have any assets worth protecting, do not operate as a sole proprietorship or general partnership. Build a firewall between your existing assets and whatever risks, great or small, you take on in your business venture. Your choice of protection will depend upon your Strategic Vision and your specific income tax circumstances.

A knowledgeable counseling-oriented attorney will help you decide between the traditional "C" corporation and the newer LLC, which has essentially rendered the "S" corporation obsolete. For instance, an expert will advise a single-owner business to opt for the single-member LLC, which combines asset protection and streamlined income tax filing. The ownership structure of any business entity should dovetail with your estate planning in order to eliminate the spilling of any "business fuel" in the event of unforeseen circumstances.

Key Four – Plan Now for Continuity and Succession

The definition of "success" is followed by "succession." (It's true—check your dictionary!) We all hope for a healthy and lengthy retirement; however, you should plan *now* for all causes of business succession. The term "business succession" often refers to a certain type of "buy-sell" agreement between or among the principals of your business entity. Many small entities are not in a position to engage in such specific planning that is funded with the purchase of life insurance policies on the individuals involved.

Continuity planning is a viable alternative. Any individual business owner can immediately take steps to ensure that their customers, employees, and loved ones are protected. Continuity planning gives peace of mind to all the stakeholders, including you, your loved ones, your referral sources, your employees, and your customers or clients by utilizing existing disability and life insurance funds under specific circumstances. Also, rather than simply concluding that if you are gone tomorrow your clients will end up elsewhere, you can determine *and achieve* the true value of your business through proper planning.

Unfortunately, the majority of professionals who seek to counsel you on business succession issues have not done their own continuity or succession planning. Here's a sensible tip: Work with an attorney (and perhaps an insurance professional) who *"walks the talk."* Qualified professionals in this area should be able to demonstrate what they have done in their own practices and explain the reasons for their decisions. You *will* learn more about the specifics of business continuity by contacting a professional who is well versed in integrating continuity plans into businesses.

Key Five – Regularly Update Your Strategic Vision™

With regard to the *principle of "begin with the end in mind,"* you may consider business succession to be the "end" of your business timeline. Perhaps you believe that success is a journey rather than a destination, and your definition of success is the "end" you are seeking. Whether you define success as a comfortable retirement, or as the series of accomplishments along the way, the path is paved with regular updates to your Strategic Vision. Update your Strategic Vision, and use it as a tool for ongoing focus and accountability, perhaps even in weekly meetings with your support staff or team. In order to ensure that you achieve all of your goals, your facilitator should be available at regular intervals to assist you.

Strive for the Long Haul

You likely have heard statistics about businesses that fail within five years or don't make it to the next generation. Be smart. Avoid becoming such a statistic by planning wisely with the help of a qualified advisor. *Review the five keys, d*evelop your Strategic Vision, and if you truly begin with the end in mind, you will experience success in business… and beyond.

About the Author
A national pioneer in business continuity, Jeffrey L. Knapp, Esq., focuses on estate, business and charitable planning at The Knapp Law Firm LLC. Based in Basking Ridge, New Jersey, the firm has additional conference facilities in New Jersey, New York and Florida, and has an unparalleled network of planning professionals throughout North America. Mr. Knapp has completed a three-year post-doctorate in multidisciplinary wealth strategies planning, is a nationally-recognized speaker, and has now co-authored one book each on estate planning, business planning, and charitable planning. He can be contacted at The Knapp Law Firm LLC, at The Wealth Strategies Center, 11 S. Finley Ave., Basking Ridge NJ 07920, telephone 1.888.KNAPP.LAW or 1.908.696.0011, fax 1.908.696.0030, e-mail knapplaw@eclipse.net, website www.knapplaw.net.

The Four Timeless Principles of Intelligent Investing

by Kaushal B. Majmudar

You may or may not consider yourself an investor, but each month you make countless choices between competing alternatives for your time and money. You decide on a daily basis to either spend your money, which is an investment in consumption, or to save it. If you save, you have to decide where to put your savings and for what purpose.

The choices you make have a major impact on your quality of life. Properly invested, your savings can give you the freedom to use your time in ways that make your life meaningful. Your decisions also affect many other people; the sum of millions of such "investment" decisions drives our entire economy, effecting your community and country. Therefore, each financial decision you make is a responsibility and has consequences far beyond what you may have realized.

You can make more informed investment decisions by learning and applying four timeless rules of intelligent investing. Some people discover these principles through trial and error, while others were lucky enough to learn them at a young age. These principles work for all types of investments, including stocks, bonds, real estate, precious objects and private businesses. Use these principles and you will improve your investment results and reduce risks compared to those who are ignorant of or fail to apply them.

Knowing the four principles of successful investing can give you confidence and a sense of direction when you invest. Instead of acting impulsively, you can make better investment decisions using an approach that has worked for many successful investors who created or are creating fortunes through investing. Warren Buffett, currently the second richest man in America, has espoused and advocated these principles for decades.

Some other benefits of learning and applying these principles include:
- Avoiding most of the common mistakes investors make;
- Understanding how to assess the quality of your investments;
- Having peace of mind because you are positioned for long-term success;
- Creating the freedom to live the life you want.

Of course, how you apply the principles and your own skill will certainly have an impact on your results. Nevertheless, anyone properly applying these principles over time can expect to get better results than they would have without them.

The Four Timeless Principles of Intelligent Investing

1. Be Businesslike When Investing

The first principle states that you need to think about and approach investment decisions rationally, not emotionally or based on fear and greed. Think of investing as an extension of your business activities. Every successful businessperson does homework and gathers facts prior to making an investment commitment. Moreover, you should be actively involved in your investment decisions, knowing they were made for the right reasons. Don't passively accept investments others sell you just because the person recommending them appears to be an expert.

Each investment you make should provide for safety of principal along with an adequate return. Investments not meeting this definition are speculations masquerading as investments. When studying an investment, think of it as though you were buying the entire company or asset. For example, you should invest in a company only if you would be happy owning the whole business at its current value, based on the price per share you are paying for a piece of it. If not, you may be speculating instead of investing.

A businesslike approach to investing also means that both the quality of the investment and the price you pay are equally important. Businesspeople love to get quality bargains, and they try not to overpay. An investor who overpays is violating this principle and may soon be in trouble.

During the 1998 to 2001 investment bubble, many people did not make businesslike investment decisions. They speculated and paid heavily inflated prices for overvalued shares. Many of those "investment" decisions were made for the wrong reasons, including greed. Later, when the bubble burst, fear prevented people from investing in potential bargains that might have helped recoup losses. The poor results recently suffered by investors violating this principle illustrate the importance of applying this rule.

2. Stick To Your Own Circle of Competence

The second principle instructs you to stick to what you know. If you don't understand what a company does and how they make their profits, don't make the investment. If you follow this rule, it may mean that you will have to pass on seemingly great opportunities that you do not really understand. However, adopting this approach will also keep you out of trouble. It will help you focus on those opportunities where you have an edge while decreasing your risk of permanent losses.

The recent bubble is again instructive. Motivated by the seemingly easy riches available to all, many people invested in companies they didn't understand. During the period when stock prices were rising indiscriminately, this approach seemed to work for everyone except those who refused to participate. However, the correction, when it came, occurred so swiftly that most investors suffered major losses—losses that might have been avoided had they limited their commitments to more familiar opportunities.

3. Insist Upon a Margin of Safety

Many investors believe that this third principle is the most important. In essence, this principle states that you should seek to protect yourself against investment downside by asking yourself: "What is the **worst** that could go wrong if I make this investment?" Then, you make the investment only if you can live with the worst-case scenario, or if the resulting loss would not be too severe in the aggregate. Otherwise, you should pass. One of the most dependable ways to obtain this margin of safety is to require a discount between the price you pay and the value that you get. One way to assess value is to determine what a smart buyer would pay to purchase 100% of the business. In essence, you need to look at a number of qualitative and quantitative factors to determine how much distributable cash flow the business will generate in the future. When you can make this assessment dependably, and when the price you pay is less than this value, you have a margin of safety.

Many investments made during the bubble had no margin of safety. As the market plunged, the resulting losses devastated investors who had not planned for the possibility of loss.

4. Pursue a Reasonable Rate of Compounding

Albert Einstein called compound interest "the most powerful force in the Universe." Even relatively small sums eventually grow very large through consistent compounding. Therefore, the fourth principle says that your goal in investing should be to compound your resources at a reasonable rate over time, rather than to seek instant riches or to keep up with the short-term investment performance of others. By adopting this rule you will not only take advantage of the extraordinary power of compounding, but you will also make decisions with a longer investment horizon and thereby be more likely to identify promising opportunities in both the long- and short-term.

During the bubble, investment horizons continued to shrink until the only information that seemed relevant was where prices were expected to go in the next few hours or days. This focus missed the significant risks involved, resulting in losses when market psychology inevitably changed.

Invest in Your Future

Now that you know the rules, it's time to apply them. First, look at your past investment decisions and ask yourself if you would have made different choices using these principles. As with any concept or process that is new to you, you initially have much to learn. The above rules are simple, but their proper application is not always easy.

Resolve to re-read and apply these ideas until they become second nature. You may also want to seek the guidance of someone who can mentor you in their proper application. To obtain the best results from these rules, you will need to devote the time and effort necessary to consistently apply them, or else hire an advisor who understands and will implement the above guidelines on your behalf.

By applying these principles, you have the potential to become an intelligent investor. You can also use these guidelines to evaluate potential advisors by probing whether they know and apply these principles for their clients. Those who had the luck or smarts to invest with Warren Buffett over the past forty-five years enjoyed the opportunity to turn each $10,000 they invested into over $250 million after taxes, fees, and expenses. While you may not achieve results this outstanding, by following these timeless principles you can be confident that you are on the right path to preserve and grow your wealth in a way that can meaningfully increase your personal freedom.

About the Author

Kaushal B. Majmudar is President and Managing Partner of The Ridgewood Group, a New Jersey based investment management firm that works with individual and institutional clients to help them put intelligent investing into practice. He is an expert on explaining and implementing the philosophies of intelligent investors like Warren Buffett. Mr. Majmudar is an honors graduate of the Harvard Law School and Columbia University. He can be reached by phone at 1.973.409.9764 or by email at info@ridgewoodgrp.com. You can also visit The Ridgewood Group website at www.ridgewoodgrp.com for more information on Mr. Majmudar and on intelligent investing.

How to Dramatically Increase Your Income

The Amazingly Simple Secret to a More Profitable Business

by J.D. Miller

If someone asked you to name the single most important factor for great business performance, what would your answer be? Net Income, right? You know that no number is more important when measuring the performance of a small business or professional practice. But like many business owners, you may not know exactly which numbers to manage to dramatically increase your business net income.

Although operating your own business can be a very gratifying experience, one day you are probably going to want more time to do the things you enjoy outside of your business. You may want to pursue other interests, spend time with your family and friends, or work as a volunteer to make the world a better place for your children and your grandchildren. These are all worthy objectives that don't involve your business.

Whatever you want to do down the road, you will accomplish it quicker and easier if you can eventually sell your business at a nice profit. To turn that possibility into reality, you must start improving your income statement now, not just as a good management habit but also as an investment in your future. The value of your business depends on it.

Your income statement determines the value of your business. The more net income your business generates, the more your business is worth. When your Net Income grows, it:

- Increases the value of your business;
- Increases what you can pay yourself;
- Makes your business easier to manage;
- Makes your business more fun.

If you doubled your Net Income in the next year, what would that do to the value of your business? It would probably double its value, wouldn't it? The key to increasing the value of your business is to increase your Net Income without working harder.

No one wants to pay a lot of money for a business if the Net Income only increases when you, the owner, does more work or when you work more hours. The value of a business is determined by how much Net Income it can generate without the owner working more hours. For example, suppose you have the opportunity to buy one of two businesses: Business A or Business B. Both of these businesses generate a quarter of a million dollars a year in Net Income. You have the money to buy either business, so the price is not a problem. Which one would you buy?

- Business A generates a quarter of a million dollars of Net Income each year but you have to work 50 hours a week, 50 weeks a year. You get two weeks vacation.
- Business B generates a quarter of a million dollars of Net Income each year, but you only work 30 hours a week and you take a vacation every other month. You get six months vacation each year, and the six months that you work, you only have to work 30 hours a week.

You'd buy Business B, wouldn't you? It has much more value. You work less to get the same amount of income as Business A. And because you have to work fewer hours in your business, you have more time to grow Business B.

How do you get your business to generate more income like Business B without you working harder? You use a simple three-step process that will help you dramatically grow your business net income.

Making the Numbers Work for You

Before we go any further, let's define some terms you'll need to know to make the three-step process work.

- **Net Income** is what is left over after you subtract your Cost of Sales and your Operating Expenses from your Total Sales. If you own a service business, such as a law office, a consulting firm, or a landscaping service, Net Income is what's left over after subtracting your Operating Expenses from your Total Sales.
- **Total Sales** is what you are paid for what you sell. Generally this is a mix of products and services.
- **Cost of Sales** is what you pay for what you sell. For example, it could be the cost of your inventory, or your manufacturing costs.
- **Margin on Sales** is how much your Total Sales is greater than your Cost of Sales.
- **Operating Expenses** are what you pay to run your business (even if you don't sell anything) and include expenses like insurance, rent, telephone, employee salaries, and your own salary.

With those definitions in mind, you can use the following process to increase your income:

- **Step One – Evaluate your income statement**. Your Total Sales and Cost of Sales are key to your business's profitability. They are the numbers that increase your net income every year.

- **Step Two – Set up systems** to make each of these numbers work better in your business.

- **Step Three – Measure the results** over a meaningful period of time for your business. This could be yearly, monthly, weekly or daily.

Exhibit 1

Income statement, year ending December 31, 200X
(Amounts in thousands of dollars)

	Amount	**Percent**
Total sales	$100	100%
Cost of sales	67	67%
Margin on sales	33	**33%**
Operating expenses	33	
Net income	**$0**	

Exhibit 2

Projected income statement, year ending December 31, 200X+1
(Amounts in thousands of dollars)

	Amount	**Percent**
Total sales	$400	100%
Cost of sales	267	67%
Margin on sales	133	**33%**
Operating expenses	33	
Net income	**$100**	

Exhibit 3

How much must Total Sales increase to increase **Net Income** by $100?
(Amounts in thousands of dollars)

Total Sales, Exhibit 2	$400
Less, Total Sales, Exhibit 1	$100
Increase in Total Sales	**$300**

Step One

Your income statement should look similar to the income statement in Exhibit 1. Yours will have a lot more detail, listing all of your income and expense accounts, but it will follow the same general format.

Your income statement likely has much larger numbers than in these exhibits. While the number in Exhibit 1 may appear to be small numbers, they are actually rounded to the nearest $1,000. The zeros representing the thousands are dropped to make the exhibits easier to read.

Many people get caught up in complexity when they see large numbers. You may find it easier to learn these concepts and apply them to your business if you round your numbers to the nearest thousand dollars as the exhibit illustrates.

The numbers in Exhibits 1 and 2 illustrate how Total Sales and Cost of Sales work. Once you understand how these key numbers increase net income, you can use them to dramatically increase your net income.

Step Two

Exhibit 1 shows Total Sales of $100 and Net Income of zero. Total Sales is just enough to pay the Cost of Sales and the Operating Expenses. Net Income is zero.

If Total Sales increased to $400, then Net Income increases to $100. (Exhibit 2)

When developing your own system, ask questions about your *Projected Income Statement* numbers like:

1) How much additional net income do you want next year? In Exhibit 2, that increase in net income is $100.

2) How much must your Total Sales increase to give you this net income increase next year? Total Sales increase by $300. (Exhibit 3)

3) Is the amount of your increased Total Sales a reasonable goal? In Exhibit 2, is Total Sales of $400 this year a reasonable goal?

Obviously, the amount of the increased sales, to $400, must be a reasonable goal. To make the number more manageable, try breaking the Total Sales number down into smaller amounts. For example, the $400 in Total Sales in Exhibit 2 is $33.33 per month, or $7.69 per week. Ask yourself, "Can I see my business sales increasing by $7.69 per week?" If this increase isn't reasonable, if you can't see your business sales increasing to this amount, go back and set a new Total Sales target. But remember, when you reduce the Total Sales target, you may also reduce the amount of your Net Income increase.

Once you've set your Total Sales goal, determine how you and your employees will generate these sales. Keep in mind that there are only three ways to increase your sales:
- Increase the number of your customers.
- Increase the number of times each customer buys from you.
- Increase the amount that each customer buys from you.

Develop programs with your employees to increase sales. You and your employees can come up with a lot of great ideas.

Step Three

Once you've set up your systems, you must decide how to measure what happens to these numbers over a meaningful period of time. This could be monthly, weekly, or daily. What's the most effective measurement period for your business?

Your measurement system should be simple, easy, and frequent so that you'll do it. It could be as simple as comparing your Total Sales each week to your Total Sales Target for the week. If you beat your Total Sales target for the week, celebrate! If you don't, have a brainstorming session. Get ideas as to how to beat your target the next week.

Measure your Cost of Sales in the same way. You should be as serious about measuring this number as you are about measuring your Total Sales. Compare your Cost of Sales to your Cost of Sales target each week. Then watch what happens to your Margin of Sales. Once it grows large enough to pay all of your Operating Expenses, you'll discover that every additional dollar of sales *sends money directly to your bottom line*, to your Net Income.

When your income statement shows dramatically increasing net income, year after year, your income statement shows what your business can really do. That's where the real value of your business is.

About the Author

J. D. Miller is a leading CPA financial planner. For the past 30 years he has helped owners of closely held businesses focus their efforts on the parts of their businesses that make them the most money. As an instructor and conference speaker for the California Society of CPAs and as the chair of new national conferences, J.D. has helped hundreds of other CPAs develop and improve their skills. He is one of the first 300 CPAs in the country to earn the prestigious specialization designation, Personal Financial Specialist. J.D. received his BS in Accounting from the University of California, Berkeley, and his MBA-Tax from Golden Gate University, San Francisco. Contact him at: 1350 Tennessee Street, Vallejo, CA 94590; 1.707.642.8987; 1.800.675.4272; www.jdmillercpa.com; email: trustedadvisor@compuserve.com. CA insurance license 0C57792.

Tap the Ultimate Source of Abundance

How to Put More of You into Your Business

by Amanda Murphy

Corporations that ignore consumers' real needs…Company leaders who engage in questionable business practices…Business owners and employees who do work they don't enjoy simply to pay the bills…such is the state of today's business world. We feel forced to pursue profit at the cost of our health, our well-being, and our planet. Our souls are dying.

The key to bringing the world back to life will also bring you abundance in your business. The world needs people who are vibrantly alive and ready to build a new kind of business. We need businesses that express our missions as human beings and make a contribution to the planet——and thrive in the process.

Think of yourself as a piece of steel. If that steel is not magnetized, its particles are randomly arranged, all facing different directions. However, the same particles in a magnetized piece of steel have one basic difference: they are arranged all facing the same direction. Because of this alignment, they produce an irresistible magnetic pull. This force is so strong that other pieces of steel will begin to magnetize simply by being in the presence of the magnet.

You will create the same magnetic attraction when your vision, your values, and your vocation are perfectly aligned. When planning a business, very few people take the time to look inside, to align their unique natural gifts, talents, and desires with the product or service their business provides. Yet it is this very combination of your unique abilities and the clients who will benefit from them that will bring your business to life. When you have accomplished this, you become irresistibly attractive to all you desire with far less effort. The question is, how do you do this?

Answering the following questions will help you attract abundance through your business. When you have done this, you will thrive in ways you cannot imagine.

1. Why do you do the work you do?

Most owners are in businesses because they saw an opportunity or because they have some professional experience they can conveniently sell. Their business is simply what they do and does not necessarily reflect their greatest talents or passions.

However, if you take the time to examine your gifts, your talents, and the particular message you have for the world, you will discover inspiring ways to earn money by sharing those talents. When your business expresses who you are, clients instinctively recognize that you are sincerely and personally committed to their happiness and success. No one can fake true concern.

To determine your own special abilities, make some notes about yourself.

- List your natural talents, skills, gifts, and characteristics.
- What have you loved to do or been fascinated by since you were a kid?
- What is your secret dream that you have never told anyone?
- In what situations would people benefit from your special talents?
- Most important, what is one of your beliefs that would improve our world if you were able to share it with everyone?

2. With whom do you want to work?

Most business owners have customers or clients they dread dealing with, yet they continue to do business with them month after month. Whether you realize it or not, your customers know what you're thinking about them.

Therefore, it is in everyone's best interest for you to be proactive and "fire" clients who are not a good fit for your business. This will free you to focus on the people you care about. When you do business with people you like, they will naturally bring out your best work and inspire you to become better at what you do. Your better efforts will attract more perfect customers who will inspire you further. From there, your ability to thrive is unstoppable.

- Think about the kinds of people you really care about. *Why* do you care?
- As you look for the perfect group to serve, reflect on your personal experiences. Your target market will almost certainly be people who are in situations that you yourself have experienced or have knowledge of.
- Look back over your records and make some notes about your favorite clients. What are they like? What do they do? What is so enjoyable about doing business with them?
- Examine your least favorite customers. What makes them so difficult?

- When you have identified a target market of people who inspire you, become an expert in their particular problems or concerns. What are they experiencing? What pain are they feeling as a result?
- How can you immediately improve their lives?

When the right prospective customer crosses your path and you can clearly and simply describe exactly what they are feeling, they are captivated. They feel understood and validated, and they will trust you to take care of their concerns.

3. What do you do for your clients?
Generally speaking, a customer's primary concern is to find someone who can solve their problem and make their pain stop. Therefore, you need to see your business from your customer's perspective.

- Tell your customers how *they* will benefit from working with you or buying your product.
- Tell them exactly how you, your product, or your service will solve their problem.
- Explain what their new and improved situation will look and feel like.

For example, instead of saying, "We provide accurate, professional bookkeeping services," say, "We make sure you have the precise financial information you need, when you need it." Rather than making a statement of fact, such as, "We are attorneys who specialize in small businesses," present your service through their eyes, as in, "We take the mystery out of protecting what you've worked so hard to build." Make a list of the benefits your customers will receive as a result of working with you or buying your products. Make sure each one is stated in specific terms a client can identify with, and then market this to your customers.

4. How do you set yourself apart?
Becoming an expert in your field is the best long-term way to attract abundance. The path to becoming an expert is paved with passion.

- Think about which aspects of your profession keep you up at night, analyzing possible solutions.
- Where does your imagination go when you are musing about the issues in your field?
- Are there topics you read about voraciously?
- Do you sometimes read others' opinions and instantly know your information is better?

Your answers to these questions will help you recognize your areas of greatest interest in your field. Your expertise lies in these specific knowledge areas. You don't need to have all the answers to be an expert; in fact most experts rely on many other professionals in and out of their field. What makes you an expert is your will, your drive, your passion, your confidence, and your ability to create solutions for your customers' needs.

Remember, people draw conclusions about things and about each other within a matter of seconds. You may have twenty seconds to convince a potential client or customer that you are the solution to his or her problem. After that, you become lost in a current of information overload. So set yourself apart from the crowd, and watch your business soar.

5. The Final Key To Building an Abundant Life – What Permission Do You Need To Give Yourself?

You already know deep down what you want to do. You have an idea what changes you need to make in your business. You know what's not working.

You may be holding yourself back from taking the actions you know you need to take. Somewhere in your subconscious you may be following harmful "rules" you've made for yourself. You may believe you don't deserve wild success. You may believe that work can't be fun. You may believe that you owe it to those around you to maintain the status quo.

When you identify your restrictive beliefs, you can decide to let go of them. Be truthful with yourself. What permission do you need to give yourself to make all of your dreams a reality? Some examples may be: "Fire (or hire) those three people," "Take only the jobs/assignments that I would enjoy," or "Make more money than anyone I know." Be specific.

Write the permissions you will give yourself here, and then allow yourself to actually grant them.

"I give myself permission to…":

The Sky is the Limit

You now have the tools to develop a business strategy that capitalizes on your unique abilities and interests. Since many people are unable to objectively observe themselves, if you have difficulty answering any of these questions, brainstorm ideas with a business partner or a business coach. This is important, because the sooner you incorporate these abilities into your business presentation, the more prosperity you are able to attract. You will know what you have to share with the world, and this knowledge is your single most powerful wealth-attraction tool.

Any of your competitors can read the same business books and articles you do, but none of them can duplicate your heart and soul. Find the right answers to these five questions and you can be certain your prospects will say, "I have GOT to work with you!"

About the Author

Amanda K. Murphy is a professional small business coach based in Seattle, WA. She wrote her own pink slip in 2000 and specializes in helping people make a great living doing what they love. Amanda has completed a BA in education, an MBA, and professional coach training. She is an active member of the International Association of Coaches, the International Coach Federation, and Coachville's schools of coaching. Amanda also provides business coaching and training for www.BrandingGym.com. Amanda K. Murphy can be found at www.WriteYourOwnPinkSlip.com; or at 1.206.937.5452.

Five Small Business Tax Strategies The IRS Doesn't Want You to Know

by Mark A. Stempel, EA, CFP

Wealth building is not dependent on how much you earn, but on how much you keep. Unfortunately, taxes often take a huge bite out of people's wealth.

As a small business owner, income taxes are your largest single expense. For example, if you are like most small business owners who files a Schedule C and are in the 25% federal, 5% state, and 15% self-employment tax brackets, then 45¢ of every dollar you earn goes to taxes. Ouch!

Taxes are, in essence, "the elephant in the kitchen." We can pretend it isn't there, but it will still eat us out of house and home. With 45¢ of your income going to the government, it is no wonder that many struggle to run a business, support a family, save for retirement and put away money for their children's college education.

Fortunately, you can legally give the government less and keep more of what you earn. If your business structure is a sole proprietor or a single member LLC, and you file a Schedule C, you can take advantage of some little-known tax strategies that will enable you to build and accumulate wealth. The key is to become educated about these tax strategies, and put them into practice. Here are five tax strategies you can begin using immediately to help you build and accumulate wealth.

Strategy One – Let the IRS Help Pay Your Mortgage

Second to taxes, your next biggest expense is housing. Whether you rent or own your home, your monthly payment can be substantial. However, by taking advantage of the home office deduction, you can have the IRS help you make your monthly housing payment. In order to be eligible to claim a home office deduction, you must use part of your home *regularly* and *exclusively* for business purposes. This means that your home office must be the principal place where you conduct business or where you meet with clients in the normal course of business.

Here's how quickly that home office deduction can add up. Let's say the total square footage of your home is 1,500 square feet, and your office and storage space is 500 square feet. This means that the business use percentage of your home is 33%. Now you can take a tax write off of

33% of your mortgage interest, real estate taxes or rent, home repairs/ maintenance, utilities, homeowner's insurance, security system, water, sewer, garbage removal, snow plowing, lawn care, and maintenance. If your housing costs are $18,000 per year, you can write off $6,000. In the combined 45% tax bracket, you will receive a tax break of $2,700. So, in essence, the IRS has just contributed 15% to your housing costs.

Strategy Two – Let the IRS Help Fund Your Children's College Education

If you are a small business owner with children between the ages of eight and eighteen, you can employ those children in the business. By having your children work for you, you can take advantage of tax benefits as you jump-start your children's college fund. You can pay your children wages of up to $7,750 per year tax-free.

To understand the benefit of this arrangement, consider this scenario: You pay your child $7,750 in wages for one year. At tax time, your child claims a standard deduction of $4,750 and funds a deductible IRA for $3,000. Your child does not need to pay taxes on this. You claim the $7,750 in wages as a deduction on your Schedule C. Since you are in the combined 45% tax bracket, this saves you approximately $3,500.

You can do this for as many children as you have. As long as they are under age eighteen, their wages are exempt from Social Security, Medicare, and Federal Unemployment Tax. The money in the IRA continues to grow, and it is not taken into account for financial aid purposes. When your children pull the money out to pay for college, they can use the hope and lifetime learning credits to offset any potential taxes. You have now used the $3,500 that you would have paid to the IRS in taxes to help fund your child's college education.

Strategy Three – Let the IRS Help Buy Your New Car

If you think you can't afford a new car for your business, think again. You can get the IRS to pay for almost half of the cost of your new car. Normally when you purchase a car for your business, you are subject to limits of what you can write off. Over six years, the maximum write off for an automobile is $20,835. However, you may be able to write off the full cost of your car in the first year.

Because of a little known clause in the Internal Revenue Code, SUVs with loaded gross vehicle weight greater than 6,000 pounds are not considered "passenger automobiles;" therefore, yearly depreciation limits for autos do not apply. So let's say you purchase an SUV for $40,000 with loaded gross vehicle weight of 6,005 pounds. You use the SUV 100% for business, so you can take a deduction for the full cost of $40,000. Since you are in the combined tax bracket of 45%, you receive a tax refund in the amount of $18,000. In effect, the government has contributed $18,000 toward the purchase of your new car. How's that for tax savings?

Strategy Four – Let The IRS Help Pay Your Medical Bills

You can claim all of your medical expenses as a small business expense. Usually a person's medical expenses are deductible as a personal itemized deduction on Schedule A as long as they exceed 7.5% of the income. However, with a Section 105 Medical Reimbursement Plan, your business can deduct 100% of your family's health insurance premiums, out-of pocket medical, and vision and dental expenses not covered by insurance. This includes alternative health care such as massage, acupuncture, and counseling.

To qualify for this strategy, you must legitimately employ your spouse in your business, pay your spouse a reasonable wage, and file certain Internal Revenue Service forms to establish the Section 105 Medical Reimbursement Plan. This plan allows you to reimburse your spouse for all of his/her and his/her family's medical expenses (including yours since you are also part of the family). These expenses then become an employee benefit deduction on your Schedule C.

For example, let's say that you have $7,500 in medical expenses for the year with income of $100,000. Under normal circumstances you would not be able to write these expenses off. Now, with a Medical Reimbursement Plan, you can write off the full $7,500. Since you are in the combined 45% tax bracket, this strategy saves you $3,375 on your taxes.

Strategy Five – Let the IRS Help Fund Your Retirement

Most people would love to save $40,000 per year for their retirement. As a small business owner, you can. Most small business owners use a SEP-IRA or Simple IRA as their retirement plan. So if you are the sole owner of a small business and your income is $135,000 in 2004, according to the law you can only contribute $27,000 to a SEP-IRA or $13,050 to a Simple IRA.

However, why settle for $27,000 at most? With a Solo 401K, you can contribute $40,000 (a $27,000 employer contribution plus a $13,000 employee deferral). If you are over age 50, you can also make a "catch-up" contribution of $3,000 in 2004, increasing your Solo 401K contribution to $43,000. Using a Solo 401K allows you to contribute an additional $16,000 per year into your retirement. At a 25% federal and 5% state tax rate, using a Solo 401K saves you an additional $4,800 on your taxes. The IRS has just paid for almost one third of the additional $16,000 investment into your retirement plan. To take full advantage of this strategy, employ your spouse in your business and use this strategy for him/her as well.

Take Action Now

Remember, the key to wealth building is not how much you earn, but how much you keep. When you implement the tax strategies above, you can keep approximately $30,000 of your hard-earned money. This "extra" money can go towards realizing your dreams and goals rather than lining the pockets of the IRS. Continue to educate yourself regarding these and other small business tax and financial strategies. Then take full advantage of this information by implementing the tax strategies in your business now.

If you need help, work with a tax and financial advisor who specializes in working with small business owners. This person should be able to save you at least his/her fee; otherwise, he or she is not worth the expense. Be sure to find someone who knows that he/she works for *you,* not for the IRS.

Now is the time to kick "the elephant" out of your kitchen and stop him from eating you out of house and home. The longer you wait, the less you will have. You owe it to yourself. Your financial future depends on it.

About the Author

While working for the IRS in the 1980s, Mark Stempel became increasingly aware that the needs of self-employed professionals for unbiased tax and financial advice were not being met. In 1989, Mark left his job to form his own tax and financial planning firm. Today, Mark provides fee-only comprehensive tax and financial advice to help self-employed professionals build and accumulate wealth. He is a certified financial planner, an enrolled agent, and a professional coach. Mark is located in Tucson, Arizona and works with clients nationally. Find out more about Mark by visiting his website at www.markstempel.com or call 1.866.531.9977.

"Inherently, each one of us has the substance within to achieve whatever our goals and dreams define. What is missing from each of us is the training, education, knowledge and insight to utilize what we already have."

—Mark Twain

A Note of Thanks from the Publisher

by John Robert Eggen

I have spent more than twenty years in the publishing field, working with numerous teams in the creation or marketing of sixty-seven books and count-less information products, and I assure you that the collaborative "dance" that takes place during this process is awesome. As with any project of this magnitude, the end result is only as good as the people who contributed to the process.

The team behind this book is the reason it is so outstanding. As its publisher, I am humbled and gratified to have worked with such a diverse and talented group whose gifts have made an indelible contribution to the book's value and success.

This project would never have become more than an idea if it weren't for the support and guidance of the experts and professionals associated with Mission Publishing, each bringing his or her own talent to the table at just the right moment. My thanks to these friends and colleagues:

- Jill Clair—my wonderful executive assistant whose constant friendship, support, skills, and willingness to go the extra mile were pivotal to making this book and The World's Greatest Mentors™ publishing program a success.
- Nathan Clair—whose behind-the-scenes support and friendship are greatly appreciated.
- Joyce Edelbrock—a friend and publishing and marketing pro whose creativity and intuition provided insights and solutions throughout the entire project.
- George Foster—a brilliant cover designer whose willingness to help brainstorm a book title on Christmas Eve will never be forgotten.
- Dawn Josephson—an excellent editor whose expert guidance and never-ending patience in working with all the authors and myself made this book a reality.
- David Josephson—whose design assistance was helpful in creating this book.
- John Kremer—the book publishing expert whose recommendations on many projects over the past seventeen years have been instrumental.

- Pete Masterson—the publishing production genius whose expertise took this book's interior design to a higher level of excellence.
- Dan Poynter—the sage publishing specialist whose consultations over the past twenty years have been a priceless resource.
- Lori Prokop—a savvy publisher and marketer whose recommendations at key stages were pivotal to the project's success.
- Joyce M. Steel—a "grammar guru" whose keen eye helped to finesse the promotional writing for this project.
- Dottie Walters—the leading public speaking mentor whose consultations on this project were a definite contribution to the book's success.
- Ernie Weckbaugh—a graphics and publishing veteran whose advice and willingness to help during the early stages of this project were important.

And thank you to all the contributing authors who are a part of The World's Greatest Mentors™ publishing program. The insights you've shared in this book will inspire countless readers to reach for new heights in their businesses and in their lives.

A special thanks goes to the celebrity business mentors in the book. Their expertise and first-hand experiences are a cornerstone of this project. Their staffs' tactical support, friendliness, and generosity paved a smoother path to the book's completion. To this end, I'd like to extend an extra thanks to:

- Brian Tracy—the world-class business strategist whose mentoring over the past fifteen years and interest in participating in this book launched the project.
- Shirley Tillinghast—Brian Tracy's executive assistant who was always willing to help whenever I called.
- Victor Risling—Brian Tracy's vice president whose advice at a critical stage made a huge difference.
- Mark Victor Hansen—the leading expert on human potential whose leadership, friendship, and active assistance throughout the project were central to the project's success.
- Patty Hansen—whose continuous help, generosity, and friendship are always appreciated and will always be remembered.
- Debby Le Fever and Trudy Marshall—Mark Victor Hansen's executive assistants who were willing to lend a hand whenever I contacted them.
- Robert G. Allen—America's most influential financial guru whose friendship, mentoring, encouragement, and never-ending help were crucial in making this project successful.

- Denise Michaels—whose feedback and support at the beginning of the project made a difference.
- Bob Proctor—whose mentoring and help contributed to the project's success in more ways than I can express.
- Alejandra Cespedes—a public relations expert whose interest in the project at an early stage contributed so much.
- Robert Middleton—an outstanding marketing mentor for self-employed professionals and a friend whose initial interest in the book and whose generous advocacy of the project were a cornerstone of its success.

Many other people, both knowingly or unknowingly, have shaped me into the person I am and planted in me the seeds of this project, as well as those of numerous other publishing endeavors I've done in the past…and of the many more I hope to accomplish in the future. My deepest, heartfelt thanks to:

- Paul Twitchell—who became my first mentor in 1970 and whose leadership development program and personal consultations have, more than any other single influence, made me the person I am today.
- Tom Flamma—my second mentor who posed a question to me one day in Philadelphia that has shaped my entire approach to life.
- Harold Klemp—a mentor whose guidance that "God is in the details" has increased the quality of all I have done for more than two decades.
- Dr. Carol Parrish—my friend and teacher.
- Jay Abraham—the genius information publisher and the world's most successful marketing consultant whose 1988 invitation to become his protégé took my work to a new level of effectiveness; untold numbers of my clients have benefited from my association with Jay, and they will continue to benefit from his influence in my life in the future.
- Michael Gerber—the small business systems guru I first met in 1979 whose liberating viewpoint has benefited my business and all my clients' businesses since he and I started working together.
- Dan Sullivan—whose enlightened approach to business and living has made a major contribution to my life.

To all my friends, too numerous to mention, but especially to Harold Ware—my successful friend whose wise and discerning input on this and other projects is always deeply appreciated, and to Barbara Rawles—whose clear understanding of my mission has been a source of reassurance during less-than-optimum times.

Finally, I must acknowledge the thousands of publishing and marketing clients I have been fortunate enough to serve for more than twenty years. I wish I could name all of you, but it would fill up an entire book. Thank you for the privilege to know and serve you.

About the Publisher

Mission Publishing contributes to society by publishing material from authorities whose knowledge is transforming their industries, their professions, and the world. Ten percent of Mission Publishing's profits are donated to charitable causes that reflect the company's values.

The company's founder, John Robert Eggen, has more than twenty years of experience as a leading publishing and marketing mentor for thousands of innovative and socially-conscious experts, professionals, and entrepreneurs. Clients range from professionals who are unfamiliar to those outside of their own specialized niches, to world-renowned experts including Brian Tracy, Mark Victor Hansen, Robert G. Allen, and Bob Proctor.

Mission Publishing is the multimedia publishing division of John's highly successful firm, The Mission Marketing Mentors, Inc. Before starting Mission Publishing in 2003, John helped his clients to successfully develop and/or market sixty-seven books, including last year's #1 *New York Times* best-seller *The One Minute Millionaire*. In addition, he has helped his clients create and market countless other information products.

John has both written and been interviewed for articles in local, regional, national, and international media, including features for leading industry publications like *Publishers Weekly*. He has been a popular guest on radio and television shows across the United States and Canada. In addition, John frequently shares his expertise with audiences across the United States, Canada, and Europe through his featured speaking engagements.

Before founding his publishing and marketing mentoring firm in 1983, John built and sold a successful nationwide business while he was in his twenties. Subsequently, he joined a privately-owned investment banking firm and served as a financial advisor to high net worth owners of closely-held businesses and professional firms.

John graduated with a B.A. magna cum laude from the State University of New York at Buffalo in Buffalo, NY, where he studied the 5,000-year history of Western Civilization. Struck by the role that innovations play as catalysts for all human progress, he devoted his M.A. program at the same institution to researching the development and marketing of innovations. To research and predict future trends, he engaged in Ph.D. work at the California Institute of Integral Studies and Sancta Sophia Seminary.

For more information on Mission Publishing, go to www.missionpublishing.net. For more information on The Mission Marketing Mentors, go to www.missionmarketingmentors.com.

How You Can Become a Published Author

Mission Publishing is conducting a search for individuals of high integrity who meet the following criteria:

- Are professionals or experts in a particular field. We are considering professionals and experts in various niches of business consulting and coaching, financial services, law, holistic health, self-improvement, spirituality, and in other fields.
- Possess distinctive knowledge or expertise that qualify you to become a recognized leader in your field.
- Are passionate about getting your message out to help the marketplace you serve, as well as the world.
- Want all the benefits that becoming a published author with a high-credibility book can give you.

If you qualify, you may be eligible to join the ranks of Mission Publishing's published authors. We publish books and a variety of other highly sought-after information products and programs.

Contact us by email at AuthorInquiry@MissionPublishing.Net.

Special Announcement

Here is the Fastest and Easiest Way to Get the Business Breakthrough You Want

If you want to overcome your business or financial challenges and take a quantum leap forward in success, here is the shortcut you've been searching for.

Discover the incredible advantages of working with one of the world's greatest business mentors. Experience the definite difference these wise and trusted experts can make in your business or financial life.

Do you want to overcome challenges in business strategy, leadership, marketing and sales, personal growth, or wealth building? The mentors in this book can help you.

Most of the mentors offer free information as well as books, audio learning products, and personal mentoring sessions (remember, they areas close as your telephone). Many of them also offer workshops, seminars, and a variety of other services and programs.

Take advantage of the access to each mentor that you get as a special bonus with this book. Start right now. Simply go to the end of each mentor's chapter and locate the contact information listed there. Contact him or her and ask about a free initial session in which you can get to know more about the expert's work and how it can help you.

Keep in mind that the mentors in this book have helped millions of business owners, professionals, and corporate executives create the breakthroughs they want. Now it's your turn to benefit!

Take advantage of this opportunity. Turn to the contact information at the end of a mentor's chapter and contact him or her right now.